NTC's
Dictionary
of
FAUX
AMIS

C.W.E. Kirk-Greene

National Textbook Company
a division of *NTC Publishing Group* • Lincolnwood, Illinois USA

• PREFACE •

Call them *faux amis, mots-pièges,* treacherous twins or what you will, they are an inherent part of the language. A knowledge of them is indispensable to users of the language at all levels in order to avoid misunderstanding or worse. Such misunderstandings can be slight and amusing but they can also be serious. There are many stories told about such instances—that a government was offended because it understood *La France demande que...* as "France *demands,*" for example. Among recently culled examples is the well-known store that displayed a notice telling shoppers, in the event of the elevator breaking down, to wear out (*user*) the telephone.

It would be interesting to have some sort of frequency count of false friends, for even in the early stages of learning French one is likely to be confronted by such deceptive words as *le car, le curé,* and *la monnaie.* By the intermediate level, students can expect to have to recognize such additional examples as *la cave, la prune, le store,* and *sympathique.* At an advanced level, more refined words are likely to be met; for example *éventuel, fastidieux, truculent,* and *versatile.* Outside the academic world, in diplomatic, business, and social circles, in everyday language, there are numerous traps. One should not misunderstand the reference to the *armement* of a ship or the offer of *chips,* or the reference to *délai* where no delay is meant. It is also important to understand the modern sense of *un omnibus,* the subtle sense of *regretter,* and the meaning of *le service civil.*

There are two main types of false friend. The "standard" one looks like an English word but its meaning is different. Sometimes the meaning is quite different (*le ballot:* bundle, *le verger:* orchard); sometimes it is close to the English (*une étable:* cowshed rather than stable), or a question of nuance, as in *troubler.* The other type is where the word does mean what it looks like, but it has another meaning (or meanings). A good example is *la serviette* with its three common meanings, or *une expérience* (experience but also experiment). Some words need particular care, as the false translation may make excellent sense—for example by understanding *le car* as car or *la monnaie* as money.

In addition, this book gives a number of semi–false friends. Among others, these include words which, while not being exactly like English words, may still suggest one. Examples of this are *attachant* (as in *une jeune fille attachante*) and *la scolarité* (not scholarship). Such words as *confortable, la collection, la dévotion,* and *les minutes* mean what they look like they mean and should give no trouble in translation, but they are dangerous in the sense that they do not have the full meaning of the English word. Thus, *collection* will not do for church.

In a number of cases the deceptive resemblance between the French and the English words is purely fortuitous—for example, *la chair*/chair, *le chat*/chat, and *une haltère*/halter. It may be that some instances are more amusing than useful, but it is a rash person (as any experienced teacher will testify) who declares that such words can never mislead. In many cases, however, the English words are deceptively similar because of a common origin (usually Latin), or French influence; whence the confusion, for example, between *la cave* and cave, *coi* and coy, *fou* and fool, *le lard* and lard. The correct meanings may be quite different (in the above list: cellar, quiet, mad and bacon), but it is usually not difficult to see some connection. In a number of examples French has kept the original meaning or sense while in English this has become obsolete, specialized, or rare, and a second meaning has taken over. For example, *inférieur* has the literal sense of lower as well as the figurative sense of inferior, *intoxiquer* means "to poison," which is an obsolete meaning in English, and *versatile* means changeable, while in English it now normally means changeable in a particular way, i.e. with regard to talents.

Franglais (and *anglomanie*) has brought its own false friends. *Le building* is not an exact equivalent of "building" and *le footing* does not mean "footing." In addition, there is the French fondness for abbreviation, particularly by omitting the second part of the word (English tends to omit the first part). Thus we get such examples as *le cherry* (for *le cherry brandy*) and *le pull* (for *le pullover*). Indeed, one can play an intriguing game guessing what the missing word may be. Does *le dry* stand, one may well wonder, for dry cleaning, a dry shampoo, or what?

This book does not claim to be complete. Indeed it does not set out to be so, as this would be virtually impossible. But it is hoped that it will seem reasonably full, expecially as regards the most famous examples. With reference to the translation of the English words, such translations do not necessarily preclude other possibilities. Meanwhile, the two languages are alive, and one may expect to see new false friends, while some may disappear.

Les Mots-Amis et les Faux-Amis (Methuen) has been a *point de départ,* and particularly useful books on the subject are still Koessler and Derocquigny's erudite *Les Faux Amis* (Librairie

Vuibert), Felix Boillot's amusing *Le Second Vrai Ami du Traducteur*
(Editions J. Oliven), and J.B. Anderson's very informative *Le Mot
Juste,* revised by L.C. Harmer (Cambridge University Press). As a
guide for my original draft I used mostly Harrap's French
dictionaries. I would like to express my sincere thanks to
Monsieur Michel Charlot (sometime *Lecteur* at Christ Church,
Oxford) for very generously giving of his time to read through
the bulk of my manuscript and for making some invaluable
comments. I would also like to thank Monsieur Henry Bouillier,
Directeur of the Maison Française, Oxford, and his staff for their
kind welcome and for the pleasant ambiance which was so
conducive to work.

abbé (m) Abbot, priest, 'Father'.
Abbey = *abbaye* (f).

abrutir May mean to brutalize (to turn into a brute), but also just to exhaust or render mindless. *ça m'a abruti*: it left me exhausted, dazed, knocked out.

abus (m) Not abuse in the sense of insult, but in the sense of misuse. *un abus de son pouvoir*: misuse of his power.
Can also mean a mistaken conception. *C'est un abus de croire que le gouvernement s'y intéresse*: it is an error to think the government is interested in it.
Abuse, insults = *insultes* (f).

abuser Not to abuse or insult, but to misuse. *Il abuse de ma générosité*: he takes my generosity too much for granted. *Il ne faut pas abuser du vin*: you must not over-indulge in wine.
In addition to this idea of going too far with someone or something, there is the idea of deception, of leading astray. *Ils nous abusent avec leurs grandes phrases*: they delude us with their fine language.
S'abuser: to deceive oneself.
To abuse, insult = *insulter*.

abusif Wrongly used, misconceived, improper, overdone. *Grèves abusives*: unjustified, or prolonged strikes.
Un père abusif (une mère abusive) is not a father who uses insulting language, but a too possessive father (mother).
Abusive, insulting = *injurieux, grossier*.

abusivement Wrongly used, improperly. *Il a employé ce mot abusivement* does not mean that he used this word as a term of insult, but in the wrong sense.
Abusively, insultingly = *injurieusement*.

accent (m) Accent, and the strains of music, as in *en entendant les accents de la musique*: on hearing the strains of the band.

acceptation (f) Acceptance. *L'acceptation de tout le monde ici est essentiel*: everybody here must agree.
Acceptation (meaning, sense) = *acception* (f)

accès (m) Access, but also attack, outburst (fever, anger, etc.). '*Encore un accès de paludisme. Le troisième*' (Paul Pilotaz, *Combat avec l'homme*, Mercure de France).

accident (m) Accident, but also means the undulation of the ground. *Il s'est blessé à cause de l'accident du terrain*: he hurt himself because of the undulating ground.

accidenté May refer to accidents (*un pétrolier accidenté*: a damaged tanker), but often means rough, uneven, undulating. *Un paysage accidenté*: a hilly countryside.

accommodation (f) Adaptation.
Accommodation (for example in 'to look for accommodation') = *logement* (m), *chambres* (f).

accommoder To accommodate is sometimes a possible translation, but it usually means to suit, adapt, or prepare (of food).
But it cannot mean accommodate in the sense of 'having room', which is *avoir de la place, loger, tenir*.

accompli Accomplished, but also means thorough, complete. *Un gentleman accompli*: a perfect gentleman.

accoster To accost (often pejorative), greet someone, but also (of ships) to berth or come alongside. To accost in a pejorative sense is also *raccrocher*.
(It is not surprising to find in both languages many words originally connected with the sea and ships.)

accusé Accused, or prominent. *Des traits accusés*: prominent features.

accuser Not only to accuse, but also to accentuate, reveal, emphasize. *Son visage accusait la détresse*: his face was marked by distress. *Cette robe accuse sa jeunesse*: this dress brings out her youthfulness.
It can also mean to acknowledge, as of a letter (*accuser réception d'une lettre*).
It is also sometimes the equivalent of 'to blame'.
And it can mean to take, feel a blow = *il accuse un uppercut*: he takes an uppercut.
S'accuser: to accuse oneself, or to stand out, be prominent.

achever Means to finish, complete. *Il a achevé son livre*: he has finished his book.
Also means to finish off, in the sense of 'to kill'. *Il respirait à peine et on l'a achevé peu après*: he was scarcely breathing, and they finished him off shortly afterwards.
To achieve = *accomplir*.

acompte (m) Instalment, deposit, advance.
Account = *compte* (m). *Mettez cela sur mon compte*: put that down to my account.
Account (version, description) = *récit* (m).

acquitter To acquit, discharge (someone). Also to discharge someone from a debt.
To fulfil an obligation, pay what one owes (*d'abord il a acquitté ses impôts*: first he settled his taxes).
To receipt a bill. *Demandez qu'on acquitte la facture*: ask for the bill to be receipted.

acte (m) Act, in various senses.
Also certificate (*acte de naissance*: birth certificate), deed. *Signature des actes*: signing of the deeds.
Note the idiom *faire acte de présence*: to put in an appearance. But Act of Parliament is *loi* (f).

action (f) Action. *Une bonne action* is a good deed.

Action can also mean share, in the financial sense. *Les actions baissent*: shares are going down.

actuel Occasionally actual, but normally it is present (day), current, topical. *Un problème actuel*: a topical problem. *Le gouvernement actuel*: the present government. *Les prix actuels*: present-day prices.
(*Les actualités* (f) means current events, or newsreel.)
Actual = *véritable*, *même*, etc.

actuellement Not actually, but at the present time, at the moment, nowadays. *Actuellement il fait de plus en plus froid*: at the moment it is getting colder and colder. *Qu'est-ce qui se passe en France actuellement?*: what is happening in France now? *Actuellement j'ai beaucoup à faire et je ne peux pas accepter*: at the moment I have a lot to do and I can't accept.
Actually = *effectivement*.

addition (f) Addition, but also – for obvious reasons – the bill, as in a restaurant. *Demandez l'addition*: ask for the bill.

adepte (m/f) Sometimes has the sense of adept but usually means 'follower', so that *les adeptes de ce genre de poésie moderne* refers to their interest and not to any skill. *Les adeptes des sports d'hiver*: winter sports enthusiasts.
Adept = *habile*.

adéquat Has the sense of appropriate, suitable.
The English 'adequate' often = *suffisant*, or, of (school) work, *passable*.

adhésion (f) Adhesion, but also just means 'belonging', for example to a party, association. *Beaucoup d'adhésions depuis Noël*: a large rise in membership since Christmas.

adjudant (m) (Note the difference in spelling.) Warrant officer or sometimes sergeant-major.
Adjutant = *adjudant-major* (m).

adjudicateur (m) Is either someone who allots a contract or (at an auction) someone whose job is to offer items.
Adjudicator = *juge* (m).

adjudication (f) Adjudication, award, tender, awarding of contract. *'Une deuxième tournée de pastis et il reprit: "J'avais obtenu du gouvernement une adjudication pour le sauvetage du Michel-Say"'* (Jacques-Yves Cousteau et Frédéric Dumas, *Le Monde du silence*, Hachette, Bibliothèque Verte).
Can also mean an auction.
Adjudication (often) = *jugement* (m).

adjuger To adjudge or allocate. In an auction: *Une fois! deux fois! adjugé!*: Going, going, gone!
To adjudge (a matter) = *juger*.
              (someone guilty) = *déclarer quelqu'un (coupable)*.

admissible Admittable, and admissible, what can be permitted, and it often means 'eligible' (as of candidate for a post). In exams, it is used to refer to those who have qualified to take the oral exam.

admission (f) Admission (to a school, club, etc.), entrance or entry, but not used for admission, acknowledgment (of facts), although it comes from *admettre*. In this sense the noun is *aveu* (m). *De son propre aveu*: by his own admission.
Admission free (in shops, etc.) = *entrée* (f) *libre*.

adresse (f) Address (note the difference in spelling), and also skill. *Il ne manque pas d'adresse*: he is not lacking in skill.
Cela fut dit à votre adresse: that remark was meant for you.

affaire (f) Affair, business. *Un homme d'affaires*: businessman. *Une bonne affaire*: a good deal, a bargain. *La belle affaire!*: Is that all, then? So what?
An 'affair' = *liaison* (f) *(avec quelqu'un(e))*.

affectation (f) Affectation, but also posting to a job. *Il a une nouvelle affectation*: he has a new posting.

affecter To affect, in both senses. *Ceci affecte tout le monde*: this affects everyone.
To pretend, to adopt (an attitude). *Il affecte de paraître paresseux*: he puts on the impression of being lazy.
But also has the meaning of to allocate or post (to a job). *Il a été affecté chez nous*: he has been posted to us.

affluence (f) Affluence, but nowadays nearly always used in the sense of 'rush'. *Les heures d'affluence*: rush hour. *L'affluence des gens dans les magasins*: the crowds of people in the shops. *L'affluence touristique*: the tourist rush.
Affluence = *richesse* (f).

affluent (m) Tributary. *Les affluents de la région*: the tributaries in the region (not the affluent people, who would be *les riches*).

affronter To affront, face (a danger).
To affront (someone) = *offenser*, or indeed the noun can be used – *faire un affront à quelqu'un*.

agenda (m) Notebook, diary. *Avez-vous vu mon agenda?*: Have you seen my diary?
Agenda = *l'ordre* (m) *du jour*. *A l'ordre du jour*: on the agenda.

agent (m) Means 'agent' in a wide sense, as well as policeman (*agent de police*).

agglomération (f) Agglomeration, cluster. Also built-up area. *Il y a beaucoup d'accidents dans les agglomérations*: there are a lot of accidents in the built-up areas.

aggravant Aggravating, that is to say 'making worse' (the literal meaning).
Aggravating (in the sense of annoying) = *agaçant*.

aggravation (f) Making worse, worsening. *L'aggravation de la crise pétrolière*: the worsening of the oil crisis.
Aggravation (in the sense of annoyance) = *agacement* (m).

aggraver To make worse, i.e. *rendre plus grave*. *Le tout est aggravé par le mauvais temps*: the whole thing is made worse by the bad weather. *Cela*

aggravera la tension dans la capitale: that will increase the tension in the capital.
In English to aggravate can also mean to annoy or upset = *ennuyer, agacer*.

agioteur (m) Not an agitator, but a speculator on the Stock Exchange. Agitator = *agitateur* (m).

agiter To agitate, but also to wave, shake. *Le chien agite la queue*: the dog wags its tail. *Agitez-le deux fois avant de le boire*: shake it twice before drinking.

agonie (f) Death agony, death throes. *Il est à l'agonie*: he is at death's door. *'Enfin arrivèrent les jours d'agonie pendant lesquels la forte charpente du bonhomme fut aux prises avec la destruction'* (Honoré de Balzac, *Eugénie Grandet*).
Agony = *douleur* (f) *affreuse, supplice* (m).

agonisant Dying, at the point of death. *Un ami agonisant*: a friend who is dying.
Can also be used figuratively. *Une habitude agonisante*: a custom that is dying out.
Agonizing = *navrant, angoissant*.

agréer To accept or approve, hence (in a letter), *Veuillez agréer l'assurance de mes salutations distinguées*: yours truly. *Ceci n'est pas encore agréé. en Angleterre*: this is not yet approved (accepted) in England.
Also means to suit. *Si cela vous agrée*: if that suits you.
To agree = *être d'accord*.

agrément (m) Can be consent, approval, but often means pleasure or amenities. *Vous y trouverez sûrement de l'agrément*: you will surely find pleasure in it.
Agreement = *accord* (m).

aile (f) Means wing. It should not be confused with aisle (*nef* (f) (*centrale*)).

aimer To like or love, but it has been known for it to be mistranslated as 'to aim' = *mettre quelqu'un en joue, viser*.

aisé Easy, but also well off (compare 'in easy circumstances').

aisément Easily (without difficulty) or comfortably.
Il vit aisément: he lives comfortably.

Aix-la-Chapelle Note that it is the same place as Aachen (its German name).

ajuster To adjust, but also to take aim. *Ajuster quelqu'un*: to aim at someone.

alcoolique Can mean alcoholic (of people or things, including drinks), but alcoholic drinks are usually *boissons* (f) *alcoolisées*, as opposed to soft drinks, *boissons non-alcoolisées*.

aliénation (f) A reminder that, in addition to the normal sense of alienation, it has the technical sense of the word, which in everyday English is insanity. (Hence *un aliéniste*, who looks after mental patients, a word replaced by *psychiatre* m/f.)

allée (f) Drive, avenue, path. *Il suit la belle courbe de l'allée avant d'arriver à la maison*: he follows the fine sweep of the drive before arriving at the house.
Alley = *ruelle* (f), *passage* (m).

alléger To lighten, mitigate (*léger*: light).
To allege = *alléguer*.

alliance (f) Alliance, also marriage. *Une alliance entre deux pays*: an alliance between two countries. *Une nièce par alliance*: a niece by marriage.
Also a wedding-ring. *Il a trouvé l'alliance par terre*: he found the wedding-ring on the ground.

allier To ally, unite by marriage, blend. *S'allier à une famille*: to marry into a family.

alliés (m) **alliées** (f) Allies, but also relations by marriage. Camus in *La Chute* comments pungently on the word – '*Quant à ceux dont c'est la fonction de nous aimer, je veux dire les parents, les alliés (quelle expression!), c'est une autre chanson.*' *Parents et alliés*: family and relations (as used in obituary notices).

allô Hello (telephone). As a normal greeting, 'Hello' is *salut* or, if said in surprise, *tiens!*

allure (f) Can mean walk, gait, also speed. *Il roule à bonne allure*: he goes along at a good speed.
It also means appearance, behaviour. *Avoir de l'allure*: to have a certain distinction.
Allure = *charme* (m), *attrait* (m).

altérable Which is liable to deteriorate or become spoilt.
Alterable = *changeable*.

altération (f) Change for the worse in some form or other, faltering of voice. *Dès ce moment on a remarqué une certaine altération*: since that moment a certain deterioration was noticed.
Alteration = *changement* (m).

altéré Faded of colours, drawn of features, faltering, broken (with emotion) of voice; it can also mean thirsting. *Un homme aux traits altérés que je n'ai pas reconnu*: a man with drawn features whom I did not recognize. '*Tu as sûrement aussi connu beaucoup de jeunes filles, dit-elle d'une voix un peu altérée*' (Alphonse Narcisse, *L'Ombre de la morte*, Plon).
Altered = *changé*.

altérer Not 'to alter', but to alter for the worse, tamper with, spoil, falsify. *Le mauvais temps a altéré ces produits*: the bad weather has spoiled these products. *Rien ne va altérer son bonheur*: nothing will mar her happiness. *On a altéré le texte*: they have produced a garbled text.
Altérer can also mean to give a thirst. *Cela vous altère*: that gives you a thirst.
S'altérer: to change for the worse or to break (with emotion), falter (of a voice).
To alter = *changer*.

alto (m) Means a viola (stringed instrument). An alto voice is *alto* (f), or *haute-contre* (m) (i.e. counter-tenor).

amateur (m) May mean amateur as opposed to professional. But the idea of doing something for pleasure rather than profit has been extended. *Un amateur de beaux livres*: a book-lover. *C'est un grand amateur de pâtisseries*: he is a great one for cream cakes.

amazone (f) Now normally means a female horse-rider. *Chaque matin on voit passer des amazones élégantes*: each morning you see elegant women riding past.
Note also *monter en amazone*: to ride side-saddle.
Amazon = *femme* (f) *athlétique*, *'gendarme'* (m).

amender Usually has the sense of to improve (or to amend a Bill (politics)). Amend also = *corriger*, *rectifier*.

aménité (f) Charm, grace, pleasantness. *'Car il usait sans aucune aménité de sa nouvelle autorité de chef du service'* (Marcel Aymé, *Aller retour*, Gallimard). Amenities = *commodités* (f), *agréments* (m) (sometimes *civilités* (f)).

ampoule (f) Ampoule, phial (medical), also light-bulb, also blister.

ancien Old, ancient or senior or former. *Meubles anciens*: antique furniture. *Un élève ancien*: a senior pupil. *Un ancien élève*: an Old Boy. *Un ancien ministre*: a former minister. *Un ancien champion*: an ex-champion.

angine (f) Angina in everyday English usually suggests heart trouble. This = *angine de poitrine*; otherwise *angine* is likely to mean angina in the sense of tonsillitis or some throat trouble.

Les Îles Anglo-Normandes The Channel Islands.

Anglo-Saxon (m) **Anglo-Saxonne** (f) Anglo-Saxon, but is also used to mean English-speakers. *La pause-café que les Anglo-Saxons appellent quelquefois 'elevenses'*: the coffee-break that English-speakers sometimes call 'elevenses'.

Anglo-Saxon Anglo-Saxon, often used to mean simply 'English-speaking'.

animation (f) Animation, liveliness, but may also be used as an abbreviation of *le cinéma d'animation*: cartoon films (animation). Thus *Oxford, capitale de l'animation cette année*: Oxford, the centre for the cartoon film festival this year.

annonce (f) Announcement, but also advertisement. *Les petites annonces*: the small ads.

annuité (f) Usually means an annual repayment against money borrowed. Life annuity is usually *rente* (f) *viagère* or *viager* (m).

anonyme Anonymous, but *société* (f) *anonyme*: limited company (business).

antenne (f) Antenna. Aerial (TV, etc.), channel (TV).
But has also a very different meaning – a first-aid post, field dressing station (*antenne chirurgicale*).

anticipation (f) Anticipation, but *un film d'anticipation* is a science fiction film. Whether this term will oust *science fiction* is doubtful.

antiquité (f) Antiquity. Also (in the plural) antiques. *Un marchand d'antiquités*: antique-dealer. *Antiquités anglaises*: English antiques.

anxieux Anxious, but in English the word also means wanting, concerned (I am anxious to . . .). In this case some such phrase as *je veux bien, je suis impatient de* . . . is required.

apologie (f) Apology, in the sense of vindication, justification.
Apology (in the sense of being sorry) = *excuses* (f).

apparent Can mean apparent (not real), but often means apparent in the sense of visible, distinct. *A-t-il acheté la chaumière à cause de ses poutres apparentes?*: did he buy the cottage because of its visible beams? *Leur difficulté est apparente*: their difficulty is clear.

apparition (f) Can be an apparition (ghost) but frequently means appearance (on the scene).

appel (m) Appeal, but is also just a call (wireless, telephone). Or it can refer to a roll-call. *Faire un appel de phares*: to flash one's headlights.

s'appliquer To apply oneself. *Je vous conseille de vous appliquer à avoir ce poste*: I advise you to make an effort to get this job.
To apply (for a job) = *solliciter un poste*.
(*S'appliquer* also means to apply, be applicable.)

appointements (m) Salary. *Je m'occupe de vos appointements*: I will see to your salary.
Appointment = *rendez-vous* (m).
(to a job) = *nomination* (f).

appointer To pay a salary (to). *De plus en plus d'employés appointés*: more and more salaried clerks.
To appoint = *nommer*.

appréciation (f) Appreciation, but often judgment, estimation, valuation. *Je le laisse à ton appréciation*: I leave it to you to judge. *Le service est à l'appréciation de la clientèle*: the service charge is as customers deem fit.

apprécier To appreciate, also to value, estimate, judge.

appréhender To apprehend, arrest or dread.
To apprehend in the sense of to understand, realize = *comprendre*.

apte Means fit, fitted, suitable. *Il est particulièrement apte à ce travail*: he is particularly suited to this work. *Apte au service*: fit for military service.
He is apt to = *il a tendance à*.
Apt (expression) = *juste, qui convient*.

arc (m) Arc, arch. Also bow. *Il a plus d'une corde à son arc*: he has more than one string to his bow.
(Noah's) ark = *arche* (f) (*de Noé*).

arche (f) Arch or ark. *Les arches d'un grand pont*: the arches of a big bridge. *L'arche de Noé*: Noah's ark.

archiviste (m/f) Archivist, but also filing clerk.

ardent Can mean ardent, passionate, keen, but is also used (of things) to mean burning, hot. *'Avant une heure, même les jours les plus ardents, je partais par le grand soleil . . .'* (Jean-Jacques Rousseau, *Lettre à M. de Malesherbes*). *'au pied des falaises ardentes qui réverbéraient le soleil . . .'* (André Gide, *Si le Grain ne meurt*).

ardeur (f) Ardour, but also burning heat. *Les aoûtiens se moquent de l'ardeur du soleil*: the August holiday-makers make light of the burning sun.

arguer To argue (that . . .), deduce, assert, put forward a pretext. To argue (quarrel) = *se disputer*.

argument (m) Argument for or against something. In English, argument often means little more than a quarrel – *une dispute*.

aria (m) Familiarly it is used for bother, worry. *Quel aria!*: what a 'to-do'! (rare). Aria = *aria* (f) – a difference of gender.

armement (m) Armament, but can also just mean (of a ship) the fitting out. It is also a general word for shipping, as in an article lamenting the lack of French cruise ships: *'mais le drapeau tricolore est à peu près totalement absent révélant la grande misère de l'armement de croisière français* (*Le Figaro*, 10 January 1979).

armer To arm, but also fit out (a ship). *Ce navire arme maintenant à Cherbourg* – means nothing more sinister than that this ship is now being fitted out at Cherbourg. Also to cock (a weapon). *Armer quelqu'un chevalier*: to dub someone a knight Also to wind on (camera film).

armurerie (f) Barracks, armoury, but also arms factory, gunsmith's shop or the making of arms.

arrêt (m) Stop, stopping (also stop as in *arrêt d'autobus*: bus stop). Also decree. Sometimes means arrest. *Maison d'arrêt*: jail. Arrest (usually) = *arrestation* (f).

arrêter To stop or arrest. Also means to fix, settle. *Sa résolution est bien arrêtée*: his mind is firmly made up. *Il a arrêté ses plans*: he drew up his plans.

arrière-pensée (f) Mental reservation or ulterior motive. Afterthought = *réflexion* (f) *après coup*.

arriver Has three useful meanings. To arrive, to happen and to succeed. *Je n'arrive pas à le faire*: I can't manage it.

ouvrage d'art (m) Not a work of art, but a technical term for the building of bridges, tunnels, etc. Work of art = *oeuvre* (f) *d'art*.

artère (f) Artery or main road.

artiste (m/f) Artist, also actor, actress, theatrical performer, artiste. *L'entrée des artistes*: stage-door.

as (m) Ace (cards), also ace, champion, first-rate performer. *C'est un as*: he is top class!
(The s is pronounced, but one must not be misled into thinking of 'ass'.) Ass = *âne* (m).

asile (m) Asylum (the two words have the same origin). *Asile d'aliénés*: lunatic asylum, mental hospital. It can also mean asylum in the political sense.
It is also a general word for home, shelter (as for old people – *asile de vieillards*).

asparagus (m) Is not recommended for eating. It means asparagus-fern. Asparagus = *asperge* (f).

aspersion (f) Sprinkling, but not aspersion in the sense of 'to cast aspersions'. *Une petite aspersion comme ça ne fait pas de mal*: being sprinkled with a little water like that does no harm.
Aspersions (to cast aspersions) = *calomnies* (f).

aspirant (m) Aspirant, candidate, suitor, but also midshipman.

aspirer To aspire (to).
Also to aspirate (*il faut aspirer l'h*: the h is aspirated), and to breathe in – hence *un aspirateur*: a vacuum-cleaner.

assassin (m) Assassin, but it is often just the equivalent of murderer. *La police est aux trousses de l'assassin*: the police are on the heels of the murderer.

assassinat (m) Assassination or murder.

assassiner To assassinate, but also to murder. *C'est dans la forêt, paraît-il, qu'il a assassiné ses victimes*: it is in the forest, it seems, that he murdered his victims. *Le roi a été assassiné*: the king has been assassinated.

assignation (f) The word is used in two technical senses – assignment of money or shares (financial), and a summons to appear (legal), served with a writ or subpoena.
Assignation in the sense of meeting = *rendez-vous* (m).

assigner To assign, fix, also in legal language to summon or cite someone. *Assigner quelqu'un en référé*: to apply for an injunction against someone.

assises (f) Assizes, also (regular) meeting, conference. *Tenir ses assises*: to hold one's meeting.
It can also mean foundations, layers.

assistance (f) Assistance, but also congregation, audience. *Toute l'assistance a ri*: all the spectators laughed.

assistant (m) **assistante** (f) Can mean assistant, but often means bystander, somebody who is present. *Il descendit de sa voiture, la jambe blessée, et il* *demanda à quelques assistants de téléphoner à l'hôpital*: he got out of his car with an injured leg and asked some bystanders to telephone the hospital.

assister Means to assist, but *assister à* means to be present, to witness. *Ce jeune homme a assisté à l'accident*: this young man was at the accident. *J'ai assisté à son mariage*: I attended her wedding.

assomption (f) Assumption (of the Blessed Virgin).
Assumption also often = *supposition* (f).

assorti The word has the same two conflicting meanings as it has in English – assorted, matching or assorted, mixed. But 'assorted' is probably more used in the second sense, so that *il porte un pullover jaune et des chaussettes assorties*: he wears a yellow pullover and matching socks. *Des bonbons assortis*: assorted, mixed sweets.

assortiment (m) Although assortment has the two meanings of the French word, it usually suggests in English a mixture rather than a matching. Thus *un assortiment de boissons*: an assortment of drinks, but *tous ces fauteuils en rouge, c'est un assortiment que je trouve parfait*: I find all these armchairs in red to be a perfect matching.

assumer In the sense of to assume a responsibility.
To assume (suppose) = *supposer*.

assurance (f) Assurance, confidence, also insurance (assurance).

attachant Fascinating, interesting (e.g. book) and (of people) likeable, prepossessing. *Une jeune fille attachante*: an attractive girl.
It does not have any idea of someone who clings unduly to you (= *collant*).

attendre To wait (for). *Je vous attendrai avec plaisir*: I shall wait for you with pleasure.
To attend = *faire attention, s'occuper de, servir (quelqu'un)*.

attention (f) Attention. *Attention!* Look out!
But, as a military command, attention = *garde-à-vous!*

attirer To attract. (To pull, draw – *tirer* – towards.)
To attire = *vêtir, s'affubler*.

attractif Attractive – really in a literal sense as a magnet that attracts.
Perhaps under the influence of *franglais*, it seems that it is being used more widely as in *rémunération attractive*: attractive salary.
Attractive = *attrayant*.
          (woman) = *séduisant(e)*.

attribuer To attribute, also to assign, allot. *Les boissons attribuées aux campeurs*: the drinks allotted to the campers.

aubergine (f) Aubergine (egg-plant), but if this does not seem to make sense it is probably being used in its familiar sense of a (woman) traffic warden. The following reference is to Dominique Lavanant (and her new film) and her experience of being a traffic warden – '*Péripétie supplémentaire dans la vie de cet ancien professeur de français en Angleterre, puisque, auparavant, elle avait effectué un passage rapide au couvent. "Les femmes en uniforme me fascinent véritablement. Sa tenue pour une aubergine, c'est son voile.*

Et le carnet à contraventions, son livre de prières''' (Michel Delain, *L'Express*, 29 December 1979). They are called *aubergines* because of the colour of the uniform, and the word is still used even though the colour may have changed.

audience (f) Audience, in the sense of hearing, or a royal audience. Often refers to a (legal) court hearing, and a newspaper may have *un compte rendu d'audience*: a court report.
Audience (theatre, etc.) = *assistance* (f), *auditoire* (m).

audition (f) Audition, but also hearing (e.g. of witnesses in court).
Also sometimes recital or concert.

auditoire (m) Audience. *Il ne peut pas se plaindre de son auditoire*: he cannot complain about his audience.
Auditorium: *salle* (f).

auditorium (m) Studio (for auditions, recording) for wireless or television.
Auditorium is *salle* (f).

auréole (f) Aureola, glory, halo. Also, more down to earth, circular stain, ring (*aucune auréole!*: not a mark!, as an advertisement might say).

autonome Autonomous, but *un plongeur autonome* is a skin-diver and *un scaphandre autonome* is an aqualung.

autonomie (f) Autonomy, but also means cruising range. *Ce sous-marin a une autonomie impressionnante*: this submarine has an impressive cruising range.

avancement (m) Advancement, progress but often promotion. *Je suppose que la possibilité d'avancement te tente?*: I suppose you are tempted by the possibility of promotion?

s'avancer To advance, but familiarly it can mean to stick one's neck out. *Sans m'avancer trop, je dirais qu'il est dans le pétrin*: without sticking my neck out too far, I would say he is in the soup.

avantageux Advantageous, but also conceited. *Est-ce que c'est parce qu'il a gagné plusieurs fois qu'il a cet air avantageux?*: Does he have this conceited air because he has won several times?

aventure (f) Adventure, but also chance (as in 'peradventure'). *Il se promène à l'aventure*: he walks aimlessly, as chance takes him.
Can also mean an (amorous) affair, but *la bonne aventure* is fortune-telling.

avertir Not to avert, but to warn. *Il faut l'avertir*: we must warn him.
To avert = *détourner*, *éviter*.

avertissement (m) Warning, notice. *Sur le mur il remarqua un grand avertissement*: on the wall he saw a large notice.
Also Foreword to a book.
Advertisement = *affiche* (f), *réclame* (f).

avis (m) Opinion. *C'est mon avis*: it is my opinion.
Also means notice. *Avis important*: important announcement.
Sometimes advice.
Advice (often) = *conseil(s)* (m).

aviser To glimpse. *Il avise une table libre*: he spots an empty table. Also to take steps about doing something, to see to it.
To advise = *conseiller*.

axe (m) Axis, axle. But *les grands axes* refers to the main roads. *Pas mal de neige mais les grands axes sont dégagés*: quite a bit of snow, but the main roads are clear.
Note *l'Axe*: Axis (powers).
Axe = *hache* (f).

axer To centre (on a theme), to direct towards. *La conférence sera axée sur le thème 'loisirs-vieillesse'*: the lecture will have as its theme 'leisure and old age'.
To axe (personnel) = *débaucher*.

B

babyfoot (m) Table football. *On joue au babyfoot?*: shall we play table football?
Baby foot = *petit pied de bébé, peton* (m).

bachelier (m) Bachelor in an academic sense.
Bachelor (unmarried) = *vieux garçon* (m), *célibataire* (m).

badge (m) Strictly speaking a scout's badge. Doubtless under the influence of *franglais* its use has been extended; for example it tends to be the badge of (political) demonstrators, often with some slogan on it.
Badge (usually) = *insigne* (m).

bagage (m) *Bagages* (in the plural) is the usual word for luggage (although note *avec armes et bagage*: with all one's belongings, and the familiar *plier bagage*: to pack up and go).
The singular use is normally figurative (but *un bagage à main*: a piece of hand luggage), meaning academic knowledge. *Ce jeune professeur est arrivé avec un mince bagage*: this young teacher arrived knowing very little (about his subject).

bague (f) A ring. *Des bagues de diamants*: diamond rings (not bags of diamonds!).
Bag = *sac* (m).

baie (f) Bay (geographical or window), also berry.
To be at bay = *être aux abois*.

bail (m) Lease. Note the familiar expression *ça fait un bail (que je les ai vus)*: it's ages (since I saw them), and *renouveler son bail (de vie)*: to take on a new lease of life. In the latter example both languages use the same image.
Bail = *liberté provisoire* (f), *caution* (f).

balance (f) Pair of scales. *Rester en balance*: to be in the balance.
Balance (as in to lose one's balance) = *équilibre* (m).

balancé Well built. *Un garçon bien balancé*: a well-built lad.
Well balanced (mind) = (*l'esprit*) *bien équilibré*.

balancer To balance one thing against another, weigh up, also to swing (*une balançoire*: swing, or seesaw), *se balancer*: to rock. To balance something (so it does not fall) = *tenir en équilibre*.

ball-trap (m) Note that this refers to clay-pigeon shooting.

ballade (f) Ballad (poetical), ballade (musical, as in the ballades of Chopin). But ballad in the sense of a sentimental song = *romance* (f).
(Do not confuse with the familiar *balade* (f) = walk, drive, trip.)

balle (f) Ball (as for tennis). Also bullet. *Balle perdue*: stray bullet.
Also bale (of cotton).
Ball (as for rugby) = *ballon* (m).
      (dance) = *bal* (m).
Snowball = *boule* (f) *de neige*.

ballon (m) Balloon, also (foot)ball. It is also a brandy or wine glass (owing to its 'balloon' shape). *Un ballon de rouge, s'il vous plaît!*: A glass of red, please!
Note *un ballon d'essai* for a feeler, a testing of opinion.

ballot (m) Bundle. Also kit-bag, as here – '*Le chauffeur et un jeune soldat mince, blond et souriant, en extirpèrent deux caisses, et un gros ballot entouré de toile grise*' (Vercors, *Le Silence de la mer*, Editions de Minuit).
Also (slang) means idiot.
Ballot = *tour* (m) *de scrutin*.

ballotter To shake, toss (waves).
To ballot: *voter au scrutin*.

ban (m) Banns in church, as well as banishment, ban.
Also roll of drums before an announcement, round of rhythmic applause.
Un ban pour le roi!: Three cheers for the King!
Le ban et l'arrière ban: all one's supporters, the whole lot.

banc (m) Bench, seat. *Banc de jardin*: garden seat.
Not 'bank' except in *banc de sable*: sandbank and *banc de nuages*: bank of clouds, and similar expressions. Can mean workbench. *Banc d'essai*: testing-bench, an expression now common in a figurative sense of trying something out.
Also means shoal (fish).
Bank (grass) = *talus* (m).
      (river) = *rive* (f).
      (money) = *banque* (f).

bande (f) Band, strip. (Recording) tape.
Bande dessinée: comic strip.
Also band, gang.
But band (musical) = *orchestre* (m), *musique* (f).

bar (m) Bar (where one drinks).
Also a fish – bass, sea perch. *Une auberge où le bar est une spécialité*: an inn where the bass is a speciality.
Bar (iron) = *barre* (f).
The Bar (legal) = *barreau* (m).

baraque (f) A building in a rather poor state, hut, also booth at a fair. *Les soldats ont dû passer la nuit dans une baraque où il faisait très froid*: the soldiers had to spend the night in a shoddy building where it was very cold.
Barracks = *caserne* (f).

barbarisme (m) Barbarism (a grammatical term for misuse of words with regard to sense or their form).
In the other English sense of barbarism (from barbaric) = *barbarie* (f).

barbe (f) Beard.
Rire dans sa barbe: to laugh up one's sleeve.
Faire quelque chose à la barbe de quelqu'un: to do something to his face, under his very nose.
Barb (wit) = *trait* (m).

barge (f) Barge, also a bird – godwit. *Du côté des marais on voyait quelques jolies barges*: over towards the marshes some pretty godwits were to be seen.
Barge also = *péniche* (f).

baril (m) (Small) barrel, cask, keg.
Barrel = *tonneau* (m).
Gun-barrel = *canon* (m).

barrage (m) Barrage. Also weir, dam and road-block. *Devant nous un barrage et un groupe de gendarmes*: in front of us a road-block and a group of policemen.

barrer To bar, but note the popular *se barrer*: to run off, beat it. *Je me suis barré dans le corridor*: I made off into the corridor.
Barrer also means to cross out something, cross (a cheque).
Also to bar (the way), cox, steer (sailing boat).

barrière (f) Barrier, also gate.
Sound barrier: *mur* (m) *du son*.

basket (m) Basket-ball. This is a typical familiar abbreviation where the first part of the word is retained, *le basket-ball* being more correct, but more bother to say!
Also used for basket-ball training shoes. *Michel comme d'habitude portait ses baskets bleus*: Michael as usual wore his blue training shoes.
Basket = *panier* (m), *corbeille* (f).

basse (f) Distinguish between *une voix de basse*: a bass voice and *à voix basse*: in a low voice. *Ils parlaient à voix basse*: they were whispering.

bassin (m) Basin, also bedpan. Also dock, basin.
It means too an ornamental pond. *Le gosse est tombé dans le bassin*: the kid has fallen into the pond.

Another meaning is pelvis.
(Hand) basin = *cuvette* (f).
Basin (e.g. food) = *bol* (m).

bassine (f) Pan, bowl, large basin.
(Hand) basin = *cuvette* (f).

bât (m) Pack-saddle. *C'est là que le bât blesse*: that's where the shoe pinches.
Bat (sport) = *batte* (f), *raquette* (f).
    (mammal) = *chauve-souris* (f).
Off one's own bat = *de son propre chef*.

battement (m) Beating, but also has the meaning of interval.
Thus, *entre les leçons il y a un battement de quelques minutes* does not mean
that there is rough play but simply a short break of a few minutes.

batterie (f) Battery (artillery) and electric battery (e.g. car). Note the mean-
ing of a set of utensils, as in *batterie de cuisine*.
La batterie also means the percussion (music).
Assault and battery = *voie* (f) *de fait*.

bayer An old verb virtually used only in *bayer aux corneilles*: to (stand and)
gape.
To bay = *aboyer*.

bazar (m) Bazaar (oriental). It is also used for a general, cheap, store (more
so than in English).

béatitude (f) Beatitude, bliss, also smugness. *Vos compatriotes sont enclins à la
béatitude*: your compatriots are inclined to smugness.

bénéfice (m) Benefit, but also profit. *Sans compter les petits bénéfices*: not to
mention the little extras, the 'perks'.

bénévole Can mean benevolent, but usually means voluntary, unpaid.
Secrétaire bénévole: honorary secretary.
Benevolent often = *bienveillant*.

bénévolement Benevolently, but (usually) free, for nothing. *Elle a travaillé
bénévolement dans une sorte de colonie de vacances*: she worked for nothing in a
sort of holiday camp.
Benevolently often = *avec bienveillance*.

bénin (m) **bénigne** (f) Can mean benign (of people) but nowadays is usually
used (of things) to mean benign (benign growth), harmless, slight, mild.
Une sanction bénigne: a mild sanction.

biais (m) Angle, slant, bias. Also roundabout way (figurative).
Bias (prejudice) = *parti pris* (m).

biaiser To slant. To use evasive means.
To be biased = *être prédisposé* (*contre*).

biche (f) Does not mean bitch (*chienne* (f)), but doe.

bière (f) Beer, also coffin.
Bier = *civière* (f).

bif (m) Beefsteak. Popular abbreviation of *le bifteck*.
Bif(f): *pain* (m), *marron* (m) and many others (popular usage).

biffer To cross out, strike out. *Biffez-le!*: Strike it out!
To bif(f) = *cogner, flanquer un marron* (popular usage).

bigot (m) **bigote** (f) Bigot (with regard to religion). Bigot in a more general sense needs a word like *fanatique* (m/f).

bigot Bigoted, zealously holy. In a more general sense bigoted = *fanatique*.

bigoterie (f) Bigotry (religious sense). In a more general sense = *fanatisme* (m).

bile (f) Bile, but much used in some familiar expressions as *se faire de la bile*: to worry, to get het up.

bilieux Bilious, and for obvious reasons also cross, surly (note *bileux* – different spelling – is said familiarly of someone who worries a lot).

billard (m) Billiards and billiard-table. French quite often combines the activity and the place in one word. *Nous avons un billard chez nous*: we have a billiard-table at home.
In familiar French it can also mean the operating table!
And *billard électrique*: pin table.

billet (m) (Written) note, (bank) note, ticket. *Il cherche son billet*: he is looking for his note (or banknote or ticket).
Billet = *cantonnement* (m).

biscotte (f) Rusk. *N'oubliez pas d'acheter quelques biscottes*: don't forget to buy some rusks.
Biscuit = *biscuit* (m).

biscuit (m) Biscuit, but sometimes cake. *Biscuit de Savoie*: sponge cake.
For the expression 'that takes the biscuit' there are a number of equivalents, including *ça c'est le comble!*

bisness (m) Implies shady business. The spelling may vary. It belongs to popular usage.
Business = *affaires* (f).

bistro(t) (m) In English this word currently suggests a small French-style restaurant, but in French (where it is somewhat familiar) it really means pub, bar, café, with the emphasis more on drink than on food. Thus *le bistro du coin*: the 'local'. Nevertheless *bistrots* may be found that pride themselves on their menus.

blâme (m) Blame, disapproval, also reprimand.

blâmer To blame, but also to reprimand, criticize. *'Sans la liberté de blâmer, il n'est pas d'éloge flatteur'* (Beaumarchais – and the motto of the newspaper *Le Figaro*).

blanchir To turn white, whiten. *Ses cheveux ont blanchi*: his hair has turned white.
To blench (go pale) = *blêmir*.
       (flinch) = *broncher*.

blanquette (f) The usual meaning is a culinary one. A meat (usually veal) stew with white sauce.
Blanket = *couverture* (f).

blêmir To turn pale, wan, to blanch.
To blemish = *ternir, souiller*.

blesser To wound, hurt. *Ce prêtre a blessé beaucoup de personnes*: this priest has hurt a lot of people.
To bless = *bénir*.

bleu Blue, but if you come across a *conte* (m) *bleu* it is not a 'blue' story but on the contrary a sentimental, romantic one. (This concept of romance is in the French expression *fleur bleue* (*être fleur bleue*: to be romantic) and the German *die blaue Blume*.)
'Blue' = *porno*. *Un film porno*: a 'blue' film.

bleu (m) The colour blue, but has other meanings. A bruise (compare the phrase 'black and blue'), workmen's overalls and a beginner, novice or raw recruit, for whom we would choose a different colour – a greenhorn. The latter is familiar usage.

blindé Armoured, with armour plating, with protective reinforcement. *Le président descend de sa voiture blindée*: the president gets out of his bullet-proof car.
The familiar meanings should be noted, too. *On finit par devenir blindé*: one eventually becomes hardened.
Le pauvre était blindé hier soir: the poor fellow was blind drunk last night.
Blind = *aveugle*, blinded = *aveuglé*.

blocage (m) Blocking, freezing (as of prices).
Blockage = *obstruction* (f).

blond (m) Blonde colour, which can mean flaxen, light gold as well as fair, blonde.

blond A reminder that the colour is a light golden brown (e.g. of sand, beaches) as well as blonde, fair.
Cigarettes blondes: mild cigarettes.

blonde (f) Can mean a blonde, but also light beer (*bière blonde*). *Demandez une blonde!*: ask for a lager! (A school examiner would be inviting confusion with such an example in the text!)

blottir To nestle, snuggle (*se blottir*).
To blot = *sécher* (*l'encre*).
To make a blot = *faire un pâté*.

blouse (f) Smock, loose overgarment, surgeon's white coat, but also blouse. *Le dentiste met sa blouse blanche*: the dentist puts on his white coat.

bombe (f) Bomb. Also a kind of ice cream. It means too a spray (e.g. deodorant, paint).
Note the sense of a hunting-cap. '*Avec sa bombe de chasse, sa veste noire très*

ajustée, ses culottes de peau blanche et ses bottes à revers, elle avait vraiment fière allure' (Pierre Daninos, *Les Carnets du Major Thompson*, Hachette).
Faire la bombe: to go on the spree, paint the town red (familiar usage).

bomber To bulge, stick out. *Il bombe la poitrine en bon soldat*: he sticks out his chest like a good soldier.
To bomb = *bombarder*.

bond (m) Bound, leap, jump. The word is not the same as 'bond' in spite of the phrase *faire faux bond à quelqu'un*: to let someone down, not to turn up.
Bond (fetter) = *lien* (m).
    (money) = *bon* (m), *obligation* (f).
    (word) = *parole* (f).

bonnet (m) Bonnet, cap. It comes into a number of idiomatic expressions such as *avoir la tête près du bonnet*: to be quick-tempered; *un gros bonnet*: a bigwig; *c'est blanc bonnet et bonnet blanc*: it comes to the same thing (it's six of one and half-a-dozen of the other).
But it is not bonnet of a car = *capot* (m).

bonneterie (f) Hosiery.
Bonnet-making = *fabrication* (f) *de bonnets*.

bonnetier (m) Hosier. *Je l'ai acheté chez le bonnetier*: I bought it at the hosiers.
Bonnet-maker = *fabricant* (m) *de bonnets*.

bonté (f) Kindness.
Bounty = *générosité* (f).

book (m) Bookmaker, being the familiar abbreviation of *le bookmaker*. *Il faut consulter les books*: you must consult the bookies.
Book = *livre* (m).

boom (m) Financial boom (*boom pétrolier*: oil boom).
Familiarly, a word for a teenagers' party (= *le boom*). *Il y aura un boom chez moi*: there'll be a party at my house.
Boom (harbour) = *barrage* (m).
    (noise) = *bruit* (m) (*de canon*).
    (ship) = *bout-dehors* (m).

bosser Popular French for to work hard, slave away. *Il aime bosser, celui-là*: there's a chap who likes slaving away.
To be bossy = *être affairé et autoritaire*.

botte (f) A (large) boot. *Botte de cheval*: riding boot.
Can also mean a bundle or truss (e.g. hay).
And can mean a thrust (with a sword).
(Small) boot = *bottine* (f).
Boot (car) = *coffre* (m).

boucherie (f) Butchery, slaughter, but has also the more pleasant sense of butcher's shop.

boucle (f) Buckle. Also a loop, a bow (that one ties), loop, bend (of a river), curl (of hair), and ear-rings (*boucles d'oreilles*).
Boucler la boucle: to loop the loop.

boulet (m) Cannon-ball. *Partout des boulets, partout des morts*: Cannon-balls and dead people everywhere.
Bullet = *balle* (f).

boulingrin (m) Not all may recognize this word as the English word 'bowling-green' (just as some may forget that cul-de-sac is a French word meaning literally 'bottom of the sack'). It now means a plot of grass, usually with trees at the side.
Bowling-green = *terrain* (m) *pour jeu de boules*.

bouquet (m) Bouquet, bunch of flowers; bouquet, aroma, of wine, as we use it. But it has a number of other meanings, such as a clump (as of trees). It also refers to the crowning-piece of a firework display, hence the familiar expression *c'est le bouquet!*: that's the limit!
And it is a word for prawn.

bout (m) End. *Venir à bout de quelque chose*: to overcome something. From the meaning of 'end' it can be used to mean a scrap – *un bout de craie*: a bit of chalk.
Bout (fever) = *attaque* (f), *accès* (m).

bouter An old word meaning to put, to push (out). *Ils ont bouté l'ennemi hors du pays*: they drove the enemy out of the country.
To boot = *flanquer des coups de pied (à quelqu'un)*.
(What's more) = *par-dessus le marché*.

boutique (f) Can mean 'boutique', but there is nowadays a dangerous tendency for young pupils always to translate it thus. It usually just means (small) shop.
Surprisingly, perhaps, to talk shop is *parler boutique*.

bouton (m) Button, but also handle, knob (as of a door), also bud, as well as pimple. *Couvert de boutons*: covered with pimples (or buds).

bowling (m) Bowling alley. *Il y a plusieurs bowlings dans ce quartier*: there are several bowling alleys in this district.
Bowling = *jeu* (m) *de boules, les boules* (f).

box (m) Horse-box in a stable, also lock-up garage. Sometimes large covered parking lot. *Je cherche toujours un box, en attendant ma voiture couche dehors*: I am still looking for a lock-up; meanwhile my car stays out at night.
It also can mean box-calf, being the common abbreviation of *box-calf* (m).
Note *le box des accusés*: dock (court).
Box = *boîte* (f)
and popularly (for TV) = *boîte à images, télé* (f).

boxer (m) Boxer (dog).
Boxer (sport) = *boxeur* (m).

boy (m) Boy, young native servant (Africa, etc.).
'Il s'arrêta et la regarda d'un air inquisiteur.
Whisky, John? demande Patricia . . . Boy!

Voilà, mem, dit le boy en apportant le plateau déjà préparé' (Pierre Boule, *Les Voies du salut*, Julliard).
Boy = *garçon* (m).

bracelet (m) Is bracelet, but also the word for watch-strap. (*Un bracelet montre*: a wristwatch.)

branche (f) Branch (tree), branch of a subject, but surprisingly not branch of a firm = *succursale* (f), *filiale* (f).

brande (f) Heath or heather.
Brand (sort) = *marque* (f).

braquer To lock, turn the steering wheel, turn (of cars). *Soudain le conducteur braque à gauche*: suddenly the driver puts the wheel over to the left.
Also to aim, point (guns, etc.).
To brake = *freiner*.

brasier (m) Mass of heat, fire, blaze, glowing coals.
Brazier = *brasero* (m).

brasse (f) Stroke (swimming). *Nager la brasse*: to swim breaststroke.
Also means fathom.
Brass = *cuivre* (m) (*jaune*), *laiton* (m).

brassière (f) Baby's vest with long sleeves. A good example of English using a French word, but with an entirely different meaning.
Brassiere = *soutien-gorge* (m).

brave Brave. *Un homme brave*: a brave man. *Un brave homme*: a good sort. *Eh bien, mon brave?*: Well, my old friend?

break (m) In spite of the spelling, this means shooting-brake and not 'break'; i.e. *rupture* (f), *pause* (f) or, at school, *récréation* (f).

brevet (m) Patent. Also brevet, certificate, exam (similar to O levels) or a certificate as for a pilot, mariner.

bribes (f) Scraps, bits. *Il sait maintenant ce que vous avez fait, il l'a appris par bribes, de-ci, de-là*: he knows now what you have done, he found out from scraps of conversation here and there.
Bribe = *pot de vin* (m).

brick (m) Brig (sailing-ship).
Brick = *brique* (f).
To drop a brick = *faire une gaffe*.

bride (f) Bridle. *Aller bride en main* does not therefore mean to carry the bride over the threshold, but to lead a horse.
Lâcher la bride is often used figuratively meaning to give vent, to give freedom, full rein, and *tourner bride* is to turn round and retrace one's steps or (figuratively) to do a U-turn.
Bride = (*nouvelle*) *mariée* (f).

brigade (f) Brigade (military) but also squad, shift. *Une brigade d'ouvriers regardaient le fossé*: a gang of workmen were looking at the ditch.

brigadier (m) Corporal (cavalry, artillery). Also foreman, and *brigadier de police* is a police sergeant.
Also the stick for *les trois coups* to announce the beginning of a theatrical performance.
Brigadier = *général* (m) *de brigade*.

briquer To scrub (deck, etc.). *Il faut briquer l'appartement*: the flat must be scrubbed out.
To brick = *briqueter, murer*.

broche (f) Brooch, also spit (cooking).

brocher To stitch, bind (books) with paper. Also to brocade.
But not to broach = *entamer*.

brosser To brush, but do not be misled by the figurative expression *brosser un tableau*: to paint a picture. *Il a brossé un tableau de cette situation difficile*: he painted a picture, gave a broad outline, of this difficult situation.

brun Brown, but often dark (skin, etc.).
Un jeune homme brun: a dark young man.

brushing (m) One of the words seen on the hairdresser's list, the equivalent of blow-dry.
Brushing = *coup* (m) *de brosse*.

brut Usually means unrefined, rough and, occasionally, brute. *Champagne brut*: extra dry champagne.
If a salary is quoted as so many francs *brut*, it means gross.

brutal Can be brutal, but also rough, hard, blunt. *Il est brutal avec les gosses*: he is very rough with the kids. *Une rencontre brutale entre un cyclomoteur et une camionnette*: a violent collision between a moped and a van.

brutalement Brutally, roughly, bluntly. Also abruptly, fiercely, violently.
'*Il fit brutalement marche arrière, heurta un talus, rebroussa chemin, s'engagea dans la piste la plus directe*' (Raymond Jean, 'L'Oeil de verre', *Nouvelles 10*, Julliard).

brutaliser The French sense is to bully, ill-treat. *On l'a questionné mais cela ne veut pas dire qu'on l'ait brutalisé*: they questioned him, but that does not mean he was roughly handled.
To brutalise (to turn into a brute) = *abrutir*.

brutalité (f) Brutality, also lack of polish, coarseness. Also violence, force, as in *la brutalité de la collision*: the force, shock, of the collision.

brute (f) Can mean brute (of animal or man). But its sense is sometimes less strong, such as boor or bully.

buffet (m) Buffet as in English (the food, and the place where you eat).
But also means sideboard, dresser. *Je l'ai laissé sur le buffet*: I left it on the sideboard.

bugle (m) Key bugle, cornet.
Bugle usually = *clarion* (m).

building (m) Large modern building such as a block of flats. A good example of French using an English word but with a slightly different meaning.
Building = *bâtiment* (m).

bulbe (m) Bulb (plant).
Bulb (light) = *ampoule* (f).

bulle (f) (Papal) Bull or (soap) bubble.
Also 'balloon' in comic strips.
Bull (animal) = *taureau* (m).

bulletin (m) Bulletin, and *le bulletin météorologique* is the weather forecast. *Le bulletin* is also used for a school report; *bulletin de vote* is a ballot-paper.

bureau (m) Office. *Je l'ai vu au bureau*: I saw it at the office.
Also writing-desk. *Je l'ai vu sur le bureau*: I saw it on the desk. It also has special meanings such as *Deuxième Bureau* for (Military) Intelligence.

but (m) Goal (both senses), target, aim, object. *Aller droit au but*: to go straight to the point.
De but en blanc: point blank.
But = *mais*.

butte (f) Butts (shooting).
Hillock, mound (*la Butte Montmartre*).
Etre en butte à: to be exposed to (ridicule, etc.), (sometimes) to be the butt.
English 'butt' has various other meanings which include rifle-butt: *crosse* (f), cask: *futaille* (f) and, with the head, *coup* (m) *de tête*.
Butt (ridicule) also = *risée* (f).

butter To earth up (e.g. plants, trees).
To butter = *beurrer*.

C

cab (m) Hansom cab. *Il hèle un cab*: he hails a hansom.
Cab (taxi) = *taxi* (m).

cabane (f) Hut, log cabin. (*'Ma cabane au Canada'* in the words of the song.)
Also rabbit-hutch.
Cabin (ship's) = *cabine* (f).

cabaret (m) The modern meaning is of a smart night club (with a show).
The original and now dated meaning is tavern.
Cabaret = *attractions* (f).

cabinet (m) Cabinet (political sense, sometimes furniture), but often means a (small) room. *Cabinet de travail*: study.

Also a doctor's consulting room, surgery and dentist's surgery. *Soudain il a décidé de fermer son cabinet et de prendre sa retraite*: suddenly he decided to close his surgery and retire.

Les cabinets means lavatory but, on the other hand, *cabinet de toilette* is a dressing-room or bathroom.

cabriolet (m) The horse-drawn cabriolet has changed with the times. From cab to car, it now means a convertible.

cachet (m) Used in English to mean an air of distinction, and sometimes a dose (e.g. aspirin tablet).

In addition, the French word means a seal, also postmark.

Also fee of performers such as actors.

caddie (m) Golf caddie, and also now (supermarket) trolley. *Elle a cogné tout le monde avec son caddie*: she banged into everyone with her trolley.

cadet (m) Not just cadet, but commonly used for younger, junior. *Mon frère cadet*: my younger brother.

C'est le cadet de mes soucis: it is the least of my worries.

café (m) Café, but also coffee. *Un bon café dans un bon café*: a good coffee in a good café. The French café is very different from the English one.

Note too the useful *café complet* (two words that can save a lot of bother) for continental breakfast.

cake (m) English-type fruit cake. *Du cake pour toi?*: A piece of fruit cake?

Cake (large) = *gâteau* (m).

    (small) = *pâtisserie* (f).

It's a piece of cake! = *C'est du gâteau!*

calcul (m) Calculation, calculus. *Calcul de tête*: mental arithmetic.

Also means (gall) stone: *calcul (biliaire)*.

calculateur (m) Computer, or someone who calculates (like an accountant), or a calculating person.

(Pocket) calculator = *calculatrice* (f).

calculatrice (f) (Pocket) calculator. Could also be a female person who makes calculations, or a calculating female!

calleux Callous in the literal sense, 'hard of skin'. *Un homme aux mains calleuses*: a man with callous (hardened) hands. He is not necessarily lacking in feeling!

Callous (insensitive) = *insensible, dur*.

caméra (f) Cine-camera or TV camera. *J'ai acheté une belle caméra*: I have bought a nice cine-camera.

Camera = *appareil* (m) *(photographique)*.

campagne (f) Country (as opposed to the town), as well as campaign.

camper To camp.

Also to put (firmly). *Je campe mon chapeau sur sa tête*: I plonk my hat on his head. Also to bring out vividly a character as an author or artist might do.

Voilà notre homme bien campé: there's our man well described (hit off).

camping (m) Camping. *Avez-vous jamais fait du camping?*: have you ever been camping? Also camp site. *J'aime ce camping*: I like this camp site.

canadienne (f) *Une Canadienne*: a Canadian (woman).
But *une canadienne* (with a small c) is a short fur-lined jacket, a sheepskin coat. *Je vais porter ma canadienne*: I am going to wear my sheepskin jacket.

canal (m) Canal, also channel. Sometimes TV channel.
English Channel (because of its so-called sleeve shape) = *Manche* (f).

canapé (m) Cocktail canapé also sofa, couch. *J'ai laissé les canapés sur le canapé*: I left the cocktail snacks on the sofa.

cancan (m) Cancan (dance), also gossip.

candeur (f) Innocence, artlessness, not candour. Much care is needed because the latter may very well make sense.
'– *Qu'est-ce qui t'a décidée à venir?*
– *Rien, répondit Yvonne.*
Elle leva les yeux et offrit à sa mère un regard dont la candeur n'était pas à discuter.
– *Absolument rien, ajouta-t-elle, et elle se remit à regarder les images'* (Raymond Queneau, *Pierrot mon ami*, Gallimard).
Candour = *franchise* (f).

candide Ingenuous, naïve, artless (compare Voltaire's *Candide*).
Candid = *franc*.

candidement Innocently, artlessly.
Candidly = *franchement*.

cane (f) Female duck.
Cane (school) = *verge* (f).
    (walking-stick) = *canne* (f).
Sugar-cane = *canne à sucre*.
Cane (chairs) = *rotin* (m).

can(n)ette de biere (f) Bottle of beer (with patent stopper).
Can = *boîte* (f), *cannette en métal*.

canon (m) Cannon, gun and canon (Church). Also (rifle) barrel. *Baïonnette au canon*: with fixed bayonet. *'Une dizaine d'hommes, on voyait déjà luire le canon de leurs armes'* (Henri Queffélec, *Sous un Ciel noir*, Mercure de France). And familiarly, it is used for a glass of wine.

canot (m) Small boat such as a rowing-boat, speedboat (*canot automobile*), lifeboat, rubber dinghy (*canot pneumatique*).
Canoe = *canoë* (m).

canoter Not 'to canoe', but just to go boating, to go out in a boat. *On aura l'occasion de canoter*: there will be a chance to go boating.
To canoe = *faire du canoë*.

cantine (f) Canteen, restaurant (school, etc.).
Also has the sense of a chest, (tin) trunk. *'L'ingénieur pointa l'index vers deux valises de paille et une cantine'* (Henri Queffélec, *Sous un Ciel noir*, Mercure de France).

cantique (m) Canticle, but also often hymn. *J'adore les cantiques de Noël*: I love Christmas carols.

le Lac des Quatre Cantons We call it Lake Lucerne.

cap (m) Cape (geographical).
Is also used figuratively (as well as literally) in a number of expressions such as *changer de cap*: to change direction; *mettre le cap sur*: to head for. Note *de pied en cap*: from head to foot. (The word derives in fact from Latin *caput* = head.)
Cap (to wear) = *casquette* (f).
(But to 'cap' someone at sport is *caper*!)

cape (f) Cape (to wear), but cape (geographical) is *cap* (m). *Cape* comes from the Italian *cappa*.
Note *rire sous cape*: to laugh up one's sleeve.

capon (m) Coward (dated). *Il m'a traité de capon*: he called me a coward.
Capon = *chapon* (m).

capsule (f) Capsule (pill), also capsule (space capsule) and the cap of a bottle (hence *un décapsuleur*: a bottle-opener).

capucine (f) Capuchin nun, or nasturtium.

car (m) Common abbreviation for *autocar*, meaning long-distance bus, coach or out-of-town bus. *Pour y aller vous pouvez prendre le car*: to go there, you can take the bus. *Il a été renversé par un car*: he was knocked down by a coach.
It can sometimes mean van – *car de police*: police van.
Autocar in English is now the name of a magazine.
Car = *auto(mobile)* (f), *voiture* (f).

caractère (m) Character in various senses, but also means just temper. *Il est de mauvais caractère*: he is bad-tempered.
He's a character: *c'est un original*.
Character (theatre) = *personnage* (m).

caravane (f) Caravan as in English, including the one that a car tows. Except that a gipsy caravan is (strictly speaking) *roulotte* (f).

carcasse (f) Carcass.
Also frame, as of an umbrella.
Is also used for tyres. *Pneus à carcasse radiale*: radial tyres.

cargo (m) Cargo boat. (This is the standard word, although it is really an abbreviation of *le cargo-boat*.) *Le cargo est arrivé ce matin*: the cargo boat came in this morning.
Cargo: *cargaison* (f).

carnation (f) May be an art term meaning flesh tint. *L'artiste approuva. Une belle carnation, dit-il*: the artist approved. 'A beautiful flesh tint,' he said.
Or can have the sense of complexion. *'Le rouge de la honte vint teinter la*

blanche carnation de la gross Lalie, qui ne sut trouver rien d'autre à dire que: ah oh ah' (Raymond Queneau, *Un Rude Hiver*, Gallimard).
Carnation = *oeillet* (m).

carpette (f) Rug (on the floor).
Son caniche dort toujours sur la carpette devant le feu: her poodle always sleeps on the rug in front of the fire.
Carpet = *tapis* (m).

carrière (f) Both career and quarry. *Suivre une carrière*: to follow a career; *exploiter une carrière*: to work a quarry.
La carrière can refer specifically to the diplomatic service.

carte (f) Card, map and menu. *Passez-moi la carte*: hand me the menu.
Cart = *charrette* (f).

carter (m) One may wonder what a carter has to do with cars or bicycles. It is a technical word for casing, housing (such as in crank-case). (The name of the person has become the object – compare Macadam.)
Carter = *charretier* (m).

carton (m) Carton. Also cardboard. Also invitation card (*carton d'invitation*).
Carton à chapeaux: hat-box.
Rester dans les cartons: to be shelved.

case (f) Hut (*La Case de l'oncle Tom: Uncle Tom's Cabin*). Also compartment, locker.
Also a 'box' (printing). *Cochez une case*: tick one of the boxes.
Case (suitcase) = *valise* (f).
Case (in this case) = *cas* (m).

casque (m) Helmet, headphones.
Cask = *tonneau* (m), *fût* (m), *baril* (m).

casquette (f) Cap.
Casket = *coffret* (m).

casserole (f) Saucepan. *Par la fenêtre on voyait les casseroles de la vieille dame*: through the window you could see the old woman's saucepans.
Casserole (food) = *ragoût* (m) *en cocotte*.

cassette (f) It is sometimes tempting to think only of modern meanings, i.e. recording cassette. But the word also means casket (so the context is important) as here – '*Après l'avoir dégagé, Fournier remplit de terre et de cailloux la crevasse qui avait servi de cachette, replaça le mieux possible la pierre de margelle, et, réunissant toutes ses forces, transporta chez lui la précieuse cassette*' (Emile Souvestre, *Au Coin du feu*).

castor (m) Beaver.
Castor (furniture) = *roulette* (f).

casualité (f) Fortuitousness (rare).
Casualty = *mort* (m), *blessé* (m).

casuel Casual in the sense of 'by chance', 'fortuitous'.
Casual (indifferent) = *indifférent, négligent, insouciant*.

catapulte (f) Either the large ancient catapult machine or the modern catapult for launching aircraft.
Catapult (of a youngster) = *fronde* (f), *lance-pierres* (m).

catch (m) All-in wrestling, catch-as-catch-can.
Catch (a good catch to marry) = *un beau parti*.
      (latch) = *loquet* (m).
      (snag) = *anicroche* (f).
      (haul) = *coup de filet* (m).
      (trap) = *attrape* (f).

catholique Catholic (Church) and catholic, universal.
Familiarly, *ce n'est pas catholique*: it's a bit fishy.

cause (f) Cause, in various senses. *Il n'a rien dit, et pour cause*: he did not say anything, and for a good reason. It is also a legal word for trial, case, brief. *Mettre en cause*: to question, accuse, suspect. *La télévision mise en cause* . . . : television attacked . . .

causer To cause, but also chat. *Si vous êtes libre, venez causer un peu*: if you are free, come and have a chat.

caution (f) Guarantee, surety, bail. Deposit (money). (English has the same idea in the expression 'caution money'.)
Guarantee in the sense of reliability – *sujet à caution*: unreliable, cannot be vouched for. *Ce mot n'a pas encore la caution des dictionnaires*: this word has not yet been confirmed by the dictionaries.
Caution = *précaution* (f), *prudence* (f).

cavalier (m) Horseman, rider. Partner at a dance. Knight at chess.
Also staple.

cave (f) Cellar. *On a trouvé la victime dans la cave*: the victim was found in the cellar. *J'ai une bonne cave*: I have a good (wine) cellar. But on the other hand *une cave à liqueurs* is just a liqueur cabinet.
Cave = *caverne* (f).

caviar (m) Is caviar, but you might come across *passer au caviar*, which means censoring (of a passage).

céder To cede, yield, give up, give way, give in. But note that it can mean to dispose of, sell – *magasin à céder*: shop for sale; *céder à bail*: to lease.

cellier (m) Storeroom. *La bouteille est dans le cellier*: the bottle is in the storeroom.
Cellar = *cave* (f).
Salt-cellar = *salière* (f).

censeur (m) Censor (Roman), critic, censor. Also, in *lycées*, deputy head responsible for discipline and organization.

censure (f) Censure, criticism, also censorship.

censurer To censure, criticize, also to censor.

centimètre (m) Is both centimetre and tape-measure.

cercle (m) Circle, and used as 'club' more than 'circle' (luncheon circle), as in English – *Je l'ai vu au cercle*: I saw him at the club.
(Theatre) circle = *balcon* (m) or *galerie* (f).

certifié Not 'certified' (i.e. as a lunatic)! Refers to teachers with the CAPES (*Certificat d'Aptitude Pédagogique à l'Enseignement Secondaire*) certificate for education.

cession (f) Not session nor ceasing, but a technical word, 'transfer' (legal).
Session = *séance* (f).
Ceasing = *cessation* (f).

chagrin (m) Is more grief than chagrin – *chagrin d'amour*: unhappy love-affair.
Is also shagreen (leather).
Chagrin = *dépit* (m).

chaîne (f) Chain, also channel (television). *Je préfère la deuxième chaîne*: I prefer channel two.

chair (f) Flesh.
Chair = *chaise* (f).

chaire (f) Chair, throne, pulpit, chair (university), teacher's platform and chair, desk. *L'élève hésite avant de s'approcher de la chaire*: the pupil hesitates before going up to the teacher's desk.
Chair = *chaise* (f) (derived from *chaire*).

chalet (m) Swiss chalet, sometimes used for a house in that style. If you ever come across *un chalet de nécessité*, it is a public convenience.

Champagne (f) (the region of) Champagne.
The drink is *le champagne* (masculine, as are all French wines).

chance (f) Chance. *Il y a peu de chances qu'il gagne*: he has not much chance of winning. *Ses chances sont infimes*: his chances are minute. Often it means luck. *J'ai eu la chance de dénicher ce petit cendrier en argent*: I was lucky enough to unearth this little silver ashtray. It is sometimes used for chance or opportunity, but this is usually *occasion* (f).

chandelier (m) Candlestick. *Le voleur a tout pris – même les chandeliers*: the thief took everything – even the candlesticks.
Chandelier = *lustre* (m).

change (m) Change, exchange (financial), hence *le bureau de change* for changing money.
But *je lui donne le change*: I am putting him off the scent (or track). This was originally a hunting term.
Change (loose change) = *monnaie* (f).
       (of situation) = *changement* (m).

chant (m) Singing, song, melody, canto. *C'est son chant du cygne*: it is his swan song. Also crowing. *Au chant du coq*: at cock-crow.
Chant = *psalmodie* (f).

chanter To sing, (rarely) chant. Is used of certain birds and insects – *le coq chante*: the cock crows.
Faire chanter quelqu'un has, though, a sinister meaning – to blackmail someone.
And there is a familiar use as in *si ça vous chante?*: if you like the idea?
To chant (in church) = *psalmodier*.

Chantilly May be found on the menu as well as the map. In the former case means whipped cream. *Des fraises avec un peu de Chantilly – miam! miam!*: strawberries with a little whipped cream – yum! yum!

chaperon (m) Not, as one might expect, a feminine noun, although its normal meaning is 'chaperone'.
Chaperon can also mean hood, hence *le Petit Chaperon rouge*: Little Red Riding Hood.

char (m) Chariot, and now used for (military) tank (*char d'assaut*).
Also float (carnival).
Char (charwoman) = *femme* (f) *de ménage*.

charge (f) Charge in various senses, also burden, load. *Charges de famille*: dependants.
And it can have the idea of exaggeration, hence caricature. *Un dessin ou plutôt une charge*: a drawing or rather a caricature.
Note that *prendre quelqu'un en charge* can mean to take care of, responsibility for, someone; or to pick up, take aboard (e.g. taxi). *Le chauffeur de taxi est avant tout . . . un homme de plume! A peine vous a-t-il pris en charge qu'il se jette sur son carnet pour noter l'heure et votre destination'* (Patrice and Leila Blacque-Belair, *New York*, Seuil).
To take charge = *être responsable, s'occuper de*.
No charge = *gratuit*.
What's the charge? = *Qu'est-ce que cela coûte?*

charger To charge in various senses, also to load, burden. *Je suis chargé de paquets*: I am laden with parcels.
To charge (money) = *demander* (*un prix*), *coûter*.
(legal) = *inculper*.

chargeur (m) Contains the basic idea of loading (from *charger*). The usual meaning is a magazine for a (hand) gun. Also shipper, loader (person). Charger (for batteries).
Charger (horse) = *coursier* (m).

chariot (m) (Hay) wagon. Also a luggage-trolley at stations, or can be a trolley in a restaurant (for the *hors-d'oeuvre*, for example).
Chariot = *char* (m).

charleston (m) Charleston (dance). Also the name of a loaf (one of 36 kinds of French bread?) – a specialist term.

charme (m) Charm. *Un chanteur de charme*: a crooner. Also charm, spell.
Je suis sous son charme: I am under his spell. Also a hornbeam.
Se porter comme un charme: to be as sound as a bell, very fit.

charte (f) Charter.
Chart = *carte* (f) (usually qualified by some word such as *marine*).

chasse (f) Chase, but usually shooting or hunting.
To move to the very practical, if not from the sublime, to the ridiculous, *chasse d'eau*: flushing (lavatory), should be noted perhaps.

chasser To chase away, hunt, shoot. *J'ai chassé les voleurs*: I chased away the thieves.
To chase (after) = *poursuivre*.

chat (m) Cat.
Chat = *causerie* (f).
To chat = *bavarder, causer*.

château (m) Castle, palace, country mansion.
Château d'eau: water-tower.

chauffeur (m) Chauffeur or driver. The feminine is *chauffeuse*, which in addition can mean a low comfortable chair. Do not confuse *chauffeur* with *chauffard* (road-hog). On the railway, *chauffeur* is not the driver but the fireman or stoker (*chauffer*: to stoke as well as to heat).

chef (m) Chef (head cook), chief, boss, leader.
Chef de gare: station-master.
Also the old French word for head (Latin *caput*), and is used in some expressions such as *sous plusieurs chefs*: under several headings, *faire quelque chose de son propre chef*: to do something off one's own bat, and sometimes literally in a literary or humorous style. *Il agite le chef* does not mean that he upsets the chef, but that he shakes his head.

cheftaine (f) A scouting term. Cub-mistress.
Chieftain = *chef* (m).

cheminée (f) Chimney, funnel, fireplace, mantelpiece. *Plus il fait froid, plus je m'approche de la cheminée*: the colder it is, the closer I get to the fireplace.

chenal (m) Channel (as at a harbour).
(English) Channel = *Manche* (f).
Channel (TV) = *chaîne* (f).

chérir To cherish; but to cherish a hope: *caresser un espoir*.

cherry (m) This word may be doubly misleading unless one remembers the French habit of abbreviation. It is not cherry, not even sherry, but cherry brandy (familiar for *le cherry-brandy*).
Cherry = *cerise* (f).
Sherry = *sherry* (m).

chic (m) Smartness, but also knack, gift. *Elle a le chic pour arranger les fleurs*: she has a gift for arranging flowers.

chic Chic, smart but also, in more familiar usage, decent, kind. *C'est très chic de ta part*: it's jolly decent of you.

chicorée (f) Chicory (coffee) or endive.
Chicory (salads) = *endive* (f).

chiffon (m) Rag, duster. *Que de poussière! Passe-moi le chiffon*: What a lot of dust! Pass me the duster.
Causer chiffons: to talk dress.
Chiffon = *mousseline* (f) *de soie*.

chimiste (m) Chemist, who is concerned with chemistry. *C'est un chimiste célèbre*: he is a famous chemist.
Chemist (shop) = *pharmacien* (m).

chips (m) Potato crisps. *André adore les chips!*: Andrew adores crisps!
Chips = (*pommes*) *frites* (f).

choc (m) Can mean shock, but has many nuances and can mean bang, knock, jar, even clink (glasses). *Tâchez de fermer la grille sans choc*: try to close the gate gently (without banging it). A slight sound (tapping, knocking) is meant when H. Bernay writes in *La Montagne du silence*, '*des chocs répétés qui faisaient penser au travail d'une multitude de petits marteaux*'.
Prix choc! are not shocking prices but, on the contrary, greatly reduced ones.
Chock = *cale* (f).
Choc (for chocolate) = *choco* (m) (popular usage).

choquant Might be shocking, but often displeasing, upsetting. Shocking (also) = *affreux, scandaleux*.

choquer To bump, clink, as well as to shock or displease. *Nous avons commencé par choquer nos verres*: we began by clinking glasses. *Cette phrase avec tous ces longs mots choque un peu*: this sentence with all these long words displeases (jars) somewhat.

chrétienté (f) Christendom.
Christianity = *Christianisme* (m).

chute (f) Fall (literal and figurative) in a wide sense. *La chute des feuilles en automne*: the fall of the leaves in autumn. *Chute d'eau*: waterfall.
Chute (swimming-pool, playground) = *toboggan* (m).
    (domestic rubbish) = *vide-ordures* (m).

circonscription (f) Circumscription, but also district, parliamentary constituency.

circonstanciel Usually a grammatical term. *Complément* (m) *circonstanciel*: adverbial complement.
Circumstantial (detailed) = *circonstancié*.
Circumstantial evidence = *preuves* (f) *indirectes*.

circulation (f) Circulation, also traffic. *La circulation est intense*: the traffic is heavy.

citadin (m) **citadine** (f) City-dweller. *C'est une question importante pour tous les citadins*: it is an important question for all who live in big towns.
Citizen = *citoyen* (m), *citoyenne* (f).

cité (f) Not always city or large town, sometimes much smaller. It can be a students' hostel (*cité universitaire*) or a housing estate (*cité ouvrière*).

Note the expression *gagner droit de cité*: to gain acceptance, recognition. City (often) = *grande ville*, rather than *cité*.

clairet *Vin clairet*: light red wine.
Claret = *bordeaux* (m) *rouge*.

clairvoyance (f) Clairvoyance, that is to say clearsightedness, perspicacity. Clairvoyance (with special gifts of perception) = *voyance* (f).

clairvoyant Shrewd, perceptive, clear-sighted ('clairvoyant' in this sense). *'Il y avait là beaucoup de gens clairvoyants, avisés, faisant partie du Tout-Paris . . .'* (Edmond Jaloux).
Sometimes means able to see, as opposed to blind.
Clairvoyant (with a special gift of sight) = *doué de seconde vue*.
As a noun: *voyant(e)* (m/f).

clamer To proclaim (but not to claim). To clamour, shout out. *'Déjà, des coups précipités retentissaient à la porte d'entrée. Voilà, voilà! clama l'aubergiste, j'arrive!'* (Georges Bayard, *Michel et les routiers*, Hachette, Bibliothèque Verte).
To claim = *réclamer*.

claque (f) Claque (theatrical sense as in English) but also familiarly used for slap, clout.
Claque (m): opera-hat.

classe (f) Class. Classroom. Age-group.

clerc (m) Meant cleric, then learned person, hence the phrase *être grand clerc*: to be bright. *Pas besoin d'être grand clerc pour comprendre cela*: you don't have to be very bright to understand that.
Now usually used in the sense of clerk (as in a lawyer's office), whence another phrase *faire un pas de clerc*: to make a blunder.
Clerk (usually) = *employé* (m).

clergyman (m) Clergyman but, curiously, you may possibly find the word used to describe the clothes (clerical dress), and not the person.

cliché (m) Cliché, trite phrase, also negative (photography), and sometimes photograph.

clip (m) Brooch (clip-on).
Clip = *pince* (f), *attache* (f).
   (ammunition) = *chargeur* (m).
   (slang sense) = *baffe* (f).

clique (f) Clique, but also drum and bugle band. A description of the trooping of the colour – *'Après une demi-heure d'attente, la nouvelle garde arrive par la grande avenue* (the Mall), *précédée de sa clique'* (Jean Oger, *Les Anglais chez eux*, Arthaud).

cloaque (m) Cesspool.
Cloak = *manteau* (m), *cape* (f).

cloque (f) Blister.
Clock = *horloge* (f), *pendule* (f).

clos Closed. But *une maison close* may be open. It is a brothel.
Closed (often) = *fermé*.

club (m) (Social) club, but can mean a club used in playing golf.
Club (weapon) = *matraque* (f).

cocktail (m) Cocktail, and cocktail party. *Il y aura un grand cocktail ce soir à 6
heures*: there will be a big cocktail party tonight at 6. *Une grande salle pour
banquets, cocktails etc.*: a large room for banquets, cocktail parties, etc.

coco (m) Coconut (*noix* (f) *de coco*). Also, a child's word for egg and,
familiarly, chap, sort – *un drôle de coco*: an odd type.
May also be a term of endearment, and is familiarly used for cocaine.
Cocoa = *cacao* (m).

code (m) Code (of law), code (Highway). Elliptical use for dipped head-
lights. *Se mettre en code*: to dip one's headlights. *Codes en ville* (headline in
Le Figaro, 18 December 1979).
Code (secret). *Mettre en code*: to put into code.

coffre (m) Coffer, chest. Also boot of a car.
Un coffre-fort: a safe.

coi (m) **coite** (f) *Se tenir coi*: to lie low, remain quiet. In Gide's *La Porte étroite*
his hero overhears a conversation – '*et ce fut bein plutôt la gêne et la timidité,
que la curiosité d'en entendre davantage, qui me tinrent coi.*'
Coy = *timide, farouche*.

coin (m) Corner.
Coin = *pièce* (f) *de monnaie*.

col (m) Collar. Both languages talk about *col blanc*: white-collar worker.
Also col or pass (mountains) and neck (bottles).
Collar (for dogs) = *collier* (m).

collaborateur (m) **collaboratrice** (f) Collaborator (in a good or a pejorative
sense), also often colleague or contributor.

collecter To make a collection (church).
Can also mean to (go and) collect something.
To collect (e.g. stamps) = *collectionner*.

collecteur (m) Can mean a collector (as of taxes), but care is needed as it is
often used in a technical sense, including that of sewer (drain). *Un
collecteur de Paris*: a Paris sewer. *Un grand collecteur*: main sewer.
Collector (of stamps, etc.) = *collectionneur* (m).

collection (f) Collection (stamps, etc.), but collection in a church = *quête* (f)
and for mail = *levée* (f).

colon (m) Colonist or settler. Also a child at a holiday camp (*colonie de
vacances*).
But colon (medical) = *côlon* (m).
The punctuation sign is *deux points* (m).

combinaison (f) Combination, but as regards clothes it usually means

overalls or a pilot's type suit; for women it can mean a slip. *Le pilote ôte sa combinaison*: the pilot takes off his (flying) suit.
Combinations = *combinaison-culotte* (f).

combiner To combine, but familiarly to contrive, wangle, scheme. *On pourrait combiner quelque chose?*: could we fix, wangle something?

comédien (m) **comédienne** (f) Not only comedian (actor), but also actor (actress), as the *Comédie Française* suggests. This National Theatre is not concerned just with comedies. *J'ai débuté comme comédien en 1960*: I started as an actor in 1960.
Comedian (e.g. variety show) = *comique* (m).

commandant (m) Commander in the Navy but Major in the Army and Squadron Leader in the Royal Air Force. Also Captain of an airliner. Commander, commandant.
Commander (sometimes) = *chef* (m).

commande (f) Order (for goods). *Passer une commande*: to put in an order. *Le carnet de commandes*: order book.
Can also mean control. *Il cherche les commandes*: he looks for the controls.
Command (order) = *commandement* (m), *ordre* (m).

commander To command, also to order, as in a restaurant. *Je vais commander*: I am going to order.

commenter To comment (on something, someone), also commentate.
To comment (that . . .) = *remarquer que*.

commettre To commit (crime, etc.).
But in legal language can mean to nominate, appoint (someone). *'On commit un médecin qui constata la folie'* (Maurice Garçon, *Voltaire et la tolérance*, La Table Ronde).
To commit (to prison) = *emprisonner, envoyer en prison*.
To commit oneself (risk) = *se compromettre*.
(undertake) = *s'engager*.

commissaire (m) May mean commissar. It is also used for a variety of officials, e.g. a member of a commission, police inspector or superintendent, auditor, purser on a ship, a steward. *Un commissaire de la piste a failli mourir*: a track marshal nearly died.

commissariat (m) Police station. Also purser's office (ship).
Commissariat (military) = *intendance* (f).
(Russia) = *ministre* (m).

commission (f) Commission (as opposed to omission), commission (business order), also sales commission, commission (enquiry). Also errand, shopping. *J'ai encore quelques commissions à faire*: I've still some shopping to do.
Also board, committee. *Tous les membres de la commission médicale sont d'accord*: all the members of the medical board agree.
Commission (quite often) = *ordre* (m), *commande* (f).

commissionnaire (m) Usually used in business for an agent or broker, or for a messenger.
Commissionaire = *portier* (m).

commode (f) Chest of drawers. *Je l'ai trouvé derrière la commode*: I found it behind the chest of drawers.
Commode = *chaise* (f) *percée*.

commodité (f) Convenience, comfort.
Commodities = *marchandises* (f), *produits* (m).

commotion (f) Might be commotion (usually upheaval).
Medical term for shock, concussion.
Commotion = *émoi* (m), *brouhaha* (m) (among several words).
What a commotion! = *quelle histoire!*

commun Common in various senses. Poor (of material). *Un manteau de laine commune*: a coat of poor wool.

en commun In common, but *les transports en commun*: public transport. *Pendant la grève les transports en commun ont souffert*: during the strike public transport suffered.

communication (f) Communication in various senses, also telephone call.

compas (m) Pair of compasses or mariner's compass.
(Pocket) compass = *boussole* (f) (*de poche*).

compensation (f) Compensation, balance, setting off of losses.
En compensation de . . .: to make up for . . .
Compensation (often and especially in legal context) = *indemnité* (f), *dédommagement* (m).

compenser To compensate for something, make up for, balance, adjust. *Pour compenser, je vous offrirai un verre de vin*: to make up (for it), I'll give you a glass of wine.
And *une semelle compensée* is a wedge heel. To compensate someone for something usually = *dédommager quelqu'un de quelque chose* (e.g. loss, injury).

compère (m) Now usually means an accomplice.
Compere = *animateur* (m).

complainte (f) Comes from an old French verb, *complaindre*, but it now has the rarer meaning of complaint in English – a lament, a plaintive ballad.
The normal meaning of complaint = *plainte* (f).

complémentaire Complementary (colours, etc.), also 'additional' as in *pour renseignements complémentaires*: for further information.
(Do not confuse with complimentary = *flatteur*.)

complet Complete. *Pain complet*: wholemeal bread. *Café complet*: continental breakfast.
C'est complet!: that's the limit!
Also full. *Complet!*: No room!

complexion (f) Temperament, constitution (the old meaning in English). *Si pâle! C'est un garçon de complexion délicate*: So pale! He is a delicate boy. Complexion usually = *teint* (m) (but may sometimes = *complexion*).

composer To compose in various senses, including music.
Also (at school) to do a test, exam. *Cet après-midi les élèves composent*: this afternoon the pupils are doing a test.
Composer un numéro: to dial a (telephone) number.
Note that it can also mean to come to terms with (*avec*). *Ce seront des adversaires formidables, mais je n'ai pas l'intention de composer avec eux*: they will be tough opponents, but I don't intend to compromise with them.
To compose oneself = *se calmer*.

composition (f) Composition, and used at school for essays, tests and (end of term) exams.

composter To compost, but one should also know the common current meaning: to frank, stamp a railway ticket. Travellers should heed the notice *N'oubliez pas de composter*: do not forget to stamp your ticket (for which you look for the machine, the *composteur* (m)).

compréhensif The French word embraces the full meaning. Not only comprehensive, but also understanding. *Un père compréhensif*: an understanding father.
Comprehensive school = *collège* (m) *d'enseignement secondaire*.

compréhension (f) Comprehension (ability to understand) and also understanding, tolerance. *On compte sur la compréhension de tout le monde*: we are relying on everybody's tolerance.

compteur (m) Commonly means a meter (gas, etc.).
Compteur de vitesse: speedometer.
Counter (shop) = *comptoir* (m).
         (token) = *jeton* (m).

concilier Is to conciliate, reconcile, but can also mean to win (over). *Il a pu se concilier la confiance de son beau-père*: he was able to win the trust of his father-in-law.

concret Concrete, real, actual. *Sa vie, c'est du concret*: he deals with realities (not abstractions).
Concrete (material) = *béton* (m).
         (reinforced) = *béton armé*.

concussion (f) Misappropriation (of public money). *La concussion est toujours une affaire grave*: misappropriation of money is always a serious matter.
Concussion = *commotion* (f).

condamner To condemn.
Also to block up a door or window. '*Il pouvait être onze heures quand nous entendons frapper à la petite porte du jardin: c'était une porte condamnée. Jamais on n'entrait ni ne sortait par là . . .*' (Bergeret and Herman Grégoire, *Messages personnels*, Bordeaux, Editions Bière).

Condamner sa porte: 'to sport one's oak', to lock oneself in one's room.

conducteur (m) Driver. *Attention! Il ne faut pas parler au conducteur*: Be careful! You must not speak to the driver.
Conductor, guide, leader.
Conductor (on tram, etc.) = *receveur* (m).
   (orchestra) = *chef d'orchestre* (m).
   (lightning) = *paratonnerre* (m) (or *conducteur de paratonnerre*).

conduire To conduct, guide, lead.
To drive (vehicles).
To carry (e.g. water in pipes).
Se conduire: to behave (to conduct oneself).
To conduct (orchestra) = *diriger*.

conduite (f) Conduct, behaviour. Direction, guidance. Driving (vehicles).
Une conduite intérieure: saloon car.
Pipe (gas, water, etc.).

confection (f) 'Making' in a fairly general way, but particularly used of ready-made clothes. *Maison* (f) *de confection*: outfitters (you would look in vain for sweets).
Confectionery = *confiserie* (f).

confectionneur (m) The usual meaning is outfitter (selling ready-made clothes).
Confectioner = *confiseur* (m).

conférence (f) Conference. *Une conférence de presse*: a press conference.
Also means lecture. *Je vais donner deux conférences par semaine*: I am going to give two lectures a week.
Conference also = *congrès* (m).

confesser Often to confess (one's sins), confess to a wrong.
In a general sense, to confess, admit = *avouer*.

mettre en confiance (f) *Il m'a mis en confiance*: he won me over.
Note *un homme de confiance* for somebody's right-hand man.
To let somebody into the secret = *mettre quelqu'un dans la confidence*.
To give someone confidence = *donner confiance à quelqu'un*.
A confidant = *confident* (m), *confidente* (f).

confidence (f) *Il m'a mis dans la confidence*: he let me into the secret.
So it does not mean confidence (trust or assurance) but confidence (secret), and care is needed, as this example shows:
'– *Tu es plus grand que moi, Désiré. Et tu es seulement dans la classe de Laurent?*
– *Oh! moi, répliqua Désiré, moi, je suis un mauvais élève. Ferdinand gloussa doucement. Cette confidence l'étonnait*' (Georges Duhamel, *Le Notaire du Havre*, Mercure de France).
Confidence (trust or assurance) = *confiance* (f).

confiner Can mean to confine, but *confiner à* is to border on, touch on. *Ce livre confine au génie*: this book borders on the brilliant.

To confine oneself (to doing something) = *se borner*.
To be confined to bed = *devoir garder le lit*.

confirmé Confirmed, also experienced. *Un professeur confirmé*: an experienced teacher.
A confirmed bachelor = *un célibataire endurci*.

confondre To confound, stagger, confuse, disconcert. Also to confuse, muddle. Also to merge together. *Un petit bouquet avec des fleurs rouges et jaunes confondues*: a little bunch with red and yellow flowers mixed together.

confondu Confounded, nonplussed, also abashed.

confortable Indeed means 'comfortable' (of things).
Thus do *not* say: '*Je suis confortable*', as though you were a chair or a bed! One can say (among other things): *Je suis à mon aise*.

conforter Rarely, if ever, used now in the sense of to comfort, or even in the medical sense of to fortify.
The modern meaning is to confirm, reinforce. *Cette confession de stupidité a conforté les ouvriers dans leur opinion du patron*: this admission of stupidity confirmed the workmen in their opinion of the boss.
To comfort = *consoler*.

confronter To confront, usually as here – *On a confronté le voleur avec son complice*: the thief was confronted with his accomplice.
To be confronted by (a difficulty) = *se trouver en face de*.
To confront (a danger) = *faire face à*.

confus Confused, and often in the sense of abashed, embarrassed. *Je suis tout confus*: I don't know what to say.

confusion (f) Confusion, and often in the sense of embarrassment.
Confusion de peine: sentences to be concurrent (legal).

congestion (f) Congestion (medical sense). *Congestion cérébrale*: stroke.
Congestion (crowd) = *encombrement* (m), *embouteillage* (m).

congestionné *Visage congestionné*: flushed face.
Can also (unlike the noun – so far) have the sense of congested, crowded.
A cette époque les rues deviennent de plus en plus congestionnées: at this time the streets become more and more congested.

conjoncture (f) Conjuncture, but also has a common topical meaning of the economic state. *En ce qui concerne la conjoncture*: concerning the economy . . .

conjuguer To conjugate (verbs), also to pair, combine. *Ils ont réussi à force de conjuguer leurs efforts*: they succeeded by dint of combining their efforts.

conjurateur (m) Conspirator, or sometimes exorcist.
(Conspirator often = *conjuré* (m).)
Conjuror = *prestidigitateur* (m).

conjurer To plot, scheme. Also to avert, ward off. *Comment conjurer ce péril, c'est là la question*: how can one ward off this danger, that is the question.

Also to entreat, urge. *Je vous en conjure*: I entreat you.

To conjure = *faire des tours de passe-passe*.

To conjure up = *évoquer*.

conscience (f) May mean conscience, also awareness. Can also mean consciousness and conscientiousness.

consécutif Consecutive, also consequential, resulting from. *La fatigue consécutive à un travail si dur*: tiredness from such hard work.

conseil (m) Counsel, advice, also counsel (law).

Also council, cabinet, committee.

Note *conseil de guerre*: court-martial as well as council of war. The latter might also be *délibérer ensemble*.

conséquent Consistent. *On ne peut pas dire qu'elle soit conséquente avec ses théories*: one cannot say that she is consistent in her theories.

Consequential = *consécutif*.

conservatoire (m) Museum or academy, conservatoire.

But not conservatory in the sense of greenhouse, which = *serre* (f).

considération (f) Consideration in various senses, but note the sense of 'respect'. *Il a de la considération pour sa tante*: he thinks highly of his aunt.

Consideration in the sense of being considerate usually = *égards* (m), and in a monetary sense can = *rémunération* (f).

considérer To consider, but also to respect (consider highly). *Je considère beaucoup ma mère*: I have a great respect for my mother. *Un professeur considéré*: a respected teacher.

To be considerate = *être plein d'égards*.

consigner To consign (goods).

Also to pay a deposit, hence *une bouteille non consignée*: a non-returnable bottle.

To put (pupils) in detention (compare consigned to barracks). *Il s'agit des élèves consignés*: it is to do with the pupils in detention.

To put something out of bounds, to forbid entrance.

En attendant, la police a consigné le café: meanwhile the police have closed the café.

Can also mean to record something in writing; put one's cases in the left luggage office – *consigner ses bagages*, means to leave them at *la consigne*.

To consign (often) = *livrer, confier, reléguer*.

consistant Well founded (argument, rumour). Also solid, substantial. *Pour fêter son arrivée, on avait préparé un repas plus consistant*: to celebrate his arrival, a more substantial meal had been prepared.

Consistent = *logique, conséquent*.

Consistent (steady) = *régulier*.

consommateur (m) **consommatrice** (f) Consumer, also customer (restaurant, café).

Il entra dans un café où quelques consommateurs bavardaient au bar: he went into a café where a few customers were chatting at the bar.

consommation (f) Consummation, also consumption. *Société de consommation*: consumer society.

In a café or bar it means a drink. *Je n'ai pas payé les consommations parce que je n'avais pas d'argent, dit-il*: I didn't pay for the drinks because I hadn't any money, he said.

consommer Can mean to consummate or consume, but in a café or bar it means to drink. *Les voyous sont entrés dans le café où quelques clients étaient en train de consommer*: the hooligans entered the cafe where some customers were drinking.

consomptif Wasting (away) in a medical sense.
Consumptive = *phtisique, tuberculeux* (the former is dated).

consomption (f) Nearly always used in a medical sense for wasting away, decline.
Consumption (as in fuel consumption) = *consommation* (f).
　　　　(disease) = *tuberculose* (f) *pulmonaire*.

consumer To consume, devour (e.g. of flames), use up (energy, etc.).
Not to consume, eat, which = *consommer, dévorer*.

contact (m) Contact. Also switch, ignition.
Clé (f) *de contact*: ignition key.

contempler To contemplate, gaze at. *Il contemplait la vue avec grande joie*: he was gazing at the view with great joy.
To contemplate (reflect) = *méditer* (occasionally *contempler*).
　　　　(doing something) = *projeter de faire quelque chose*.

contenance (f) Countenance. *Il a tâché de faire bonne contenance*: he tried to put a good face on it.
Also contents. *La contenance du réservoir est importante de nos jours*: the capacity of the petrol tank is important nowadays.

contester To contest, and very much a contemporary word for to protest, argue against, question. *A cette époque il contestait tout*: at that time he was 'anti' everything.

contingent (m) Contingent, also quota. *Le contingent de chacun*: everyone's share.

contour (m) Outline, line, circumference.
Also bend, twist (as of a road).
Contour (map) = *courbe* (f) *de niveau*.

contrée (f) Occasionally country, usually is the equivalent of region. *C'est une contrée plus chaude que la nôtre*: it is a warmer region than ours.
Country (geographical) = *pays* (m).
　　　　(as opposed to town) = *campagne* (f).

contribution (f) Contribution. Also means tax. *Après avoir payé mes contributions, je ne me sens pas très riche*: after paying my taxes, I don't feel very rich.

contrôlable May mean controllable, but often verifiable.

Advertisements for posts may ask for references that can be checked = *références* (f) *contrôlables*.

contrôle (m) Control. Checking. Testing. *Un espion craint toujours un contrôle aux gares*: a spy is always afraid of station check-points.
Control = *autorité* (f), *maîtrise* (f).
Controls = *commandes* (f).

contrôler Sometimes, and probably increasingly (under English influence), to control, but usually to check. *Pouvez-vous le contrôler?*: can you check it? To control = *maîtriser*.

contrôleur (m) Controller, ticket-inspector.

convenir To suit, be convenient, agree, acknowledge. *Il convient que vous le fassiez*: it would be proper for you to do it.
To convene = *convoquer*.

convers Converse (a term in logic), but usually means lay. *Frère convers*: lay brother.

convertible (m) Convertible settee-bed. *Tu sais ce que mon mari a fait? il vient d'acheter un convertible*: Do you know what my husband has done? He has just bought a settee-bed.
Convertible (car) = *décapotable* (f), *cabriolet* (m).

conviction (f) Conviction, belief. Although *pièce* (f) *à conviction* means evidence produced in court as proof, conviction (in the legal sense) = *condamnation* (f).

convoi (m) Convoy, also train. *Deux convois se heurtent*: two trains collide.

convulser To convulse (e.g. with fear, pain).
But the colloquial English 'I was convulsed' = *'Je riais à me tordre.'*

coopération (f) Co-operation, but also has the meaning of work such as voluntary service overseas. *Il est allé en coopération l'an dernier*: he went abroad on voluntary service last year.

cop (m) Not a cop, but a pal, chum; i.e. the popular abbreviation of *copain* (m). *Il est parti avec les cops*: he has gone off with the lads.
Cop = *flic* (m).

copie (f) Copy. Also exercise, piece of work at school. *J'ai beaucoup de copies à corriger ce soir*: I have a lot of work to correct this evening.

coq (m) Cock. *Etre comme un coq en pâte*: to be in clover.
But *coq* also means ship's cook. *'Le maître coq vint passer le nez à la porte: Aujourd'hui, je descends à terre. Tu feras la cuisine pour les deux marins qui restent à bord. Tu mangeras seul ici'* (André Dhôtel, *Le Pays où l'on n'arrive jamais*, Pierre Horay).

cor (m) **anglais** Is cor anglais but a French horn is *cor d'harmonie*.

corde (f) A reminder that it means rope just as much as (or more than) cord. Also refers to strings of instruments (or of a tennis racquet) as well as to vocal cords.

Ce n'est pas dans mes cordes: it's not my line.
Chord = *accord* (m).

cordon (m) Can be cordon (e.g. police cordon).
Other meanings include strand (rope), cord, bell-pull, door-pull, ribbon (of a decoration).
Cordon bleu: a very good cook.
Cordon Bickford is a slow safety-fuse for explosives (from the name of the inventor).

cordonner To twist together (silk, etc.).
To cordon off a street would need a paraphrase (e.g. *établir un cordon d'agents pour fermer la rue*).

corne (f) Horn in various senses. *Prendre le taureau par les cornes*: to take the bull by the horns.
But hunting-horn is *cor* (m) *de chasse*.
Corn (foot) = *cor* (m).
      (crop) = *blé* (m).

corner To sound the horn (motorists) (but more usually *klaxonner*). To trumpet, ring.
Ce chauffeur aime corner!: this driver likes to sound his horn!
To turn down the corner of a page.
To corner (motorist) = *virer, prendre un virage*.
       (someone) = *acculer*.

corporation (f) Corporation, guild.
But corporation (of a town) = *municipalité* (f).
In the sense of a (fat) stomach = *bedaine* (f).

corps de garde (m) Not bodyguard, but guard-room. *'L'autobus s'arrête devant le corps de garde de l'aérodrome'* (Pierre Clostermann, *Le Grand Cirque*, Flammarion).
Bodyguard = *garde du corps* (m), *gorille* (m).

correct Correct, right, proper. Also reasonable, adequate. *C'est un petit hôtel sans luxe mais correct*: it is a little hotel with no luxury, but adequate. *La cuisine est correcte*: the food is all right.

correction (f) Correction and correctness. Also punishment, thrashing. *Tu parles d'une correction!*: what a thrashing! *Après une correction sévère*: after being severely chastised.

correspondance (f) Correspondence, also an important word for connection (travel). *C'est embêtant si on manque la correspondance*: it is annoying if you miss the connection. *La correspondance est assurée avec toutes ces villes*: there is a connection with all these towns.

corsage (m) Bodice.
Corset = *corset* (m).

costume (m) Costume, dress (*en grand costume*: full dress), also suit. *Il portait un costume bleu*: he was wearing a blue suit.
Woman's costume = (*costume*) *tailleur* (m).

cosy-corner (m) Divan bed in a corner with shelves. Also called *un cosy*. *C'est petit mais confortable – j'ai deux fauteuils, une table et un cosy-corner*: it is small but comfortable – I have two armchairs, a table and a nook with divan and shelves.
Cosy corner = *petit coin* (m) *confortable*.

côtelette (f) Cutlet, chop or (in the plural), mutton-chop whiskers. (A near similarity in the two languages.)

coton (m) Cotton. Can also mean cotton wool. *Tu t'es coupé, il te faut du coton*: you have cut yourself, you need some cotton-wool.

cottage (m) Little house in country style.
(Thatched) cottage = *chaumière* (f).

cotte (f) Coat, as in coat of mail (*cotte de mailles*).
But can also mean workmen's overalls.
Coat = *manteau* (m).
Cot = *lit* (m) *d'enfant*.

couche (f) couch (in literary style) and more frequently layer or bed, and classes, as in *couches sociales*: social classes. Also baby's nappy. *Fausse couche*: miscarriage.

coucou (m) Cuckoo but has a number of other meanings, including cuckoo clock and a cowslip, and familiarly an old aeroplane, old 'kite'.

coupe (f) The same word as 'cup' but with a limited meaning. It is used for an ornamental cup, a sporting trophy. *La coupe Davis*: Davis Cup. On the other hand *soucoupe* (f) is a saucer, and the idea of drinking-cup is retained in the proverb 'There's many a slip . . .': *il y a loin de la coupe aux lèvres*. Furthermore, champagne has the distinction of being drunk out of *la coupe*. It is used for a glass of champagne, for example, on cocktail lists.
La coupe (from *couper*) has the meaning of cutting (*coupe de cheveux*: hair-cut) or cut of clothes.
Cup (drinking) = *tasse* (f).

couplet (m) Verse of a song.
Couplet = *distique* (m).

coupon (m) Coupon. Sometimes ticket or part of a ticket (e.g. return half).
Coupons d'étoffe: remnants.

couronne (f) Coronet or crown, also wreath of flowers. *Couronne mortuaire*: funeral wreath. *Ni fleurs ni couronnes*: no flowers (funeral request).
Couronne is also a type of loaf.

courrier (m) Courier, also mail, post. *Est-ce qu'il y a du courrier pour moi?*: Are there any letters for me? *Par retour du courrier*: by return of post.

cours (m) In the academic sense means not only course (holiday course, course of lectures) but also a lesson. *J'ai mon cours de latin ce matin*: I have my Latin lesson this morning.

courtier (m) Broker. *Est-ce que les courtiers sont toujours riches?*: are brokers always rich?
Courtier = *courtisan* (m).

courtine (f) Formerly, a (bed) curtain. Also refers to a wall (joining bastions) in old fortifications.
Curtain = *rideau* (m).

cousin (m) Cousin, also gnat. *Les cousins commençaient à l'embêter*: the gnats were beginning to annoy him.

couvert (m) Cover, shelter, protection. *Le vivre et le couvert*: board and lodging.
A number of meanings are connected with the table. It can mean cutlery–knives, forks, spoons. Also a place at table, cover. *Un petit restaurant de luxe de vingt couverts seulement*: a small luxury restaurant only seating twenty. *Mettre le couvert*: to lay the table.
Can mean cover charge.
Cover (often) = *couverture* (f).
Under separate cover (letters) = *sous pli séparé*.

crack (m) Expert (compare 'crack shot'). *On cherche des cracks*: we are looking for experts. Crack player (sport), as in English.
But crack also often = *fente* (f), *fissure* (f), *fêlure* (f) or (of noise) *craquement* (m), *coup* (m) *sec*.

cracker (m) Cracker (biscuit).
But (Christmas) cracker is *diablotin* (m).

crâne (m) Cranium, skull.
Crane (bird and mechanical) = *grue* (f).

craquer To crack (noise), also to split (seams, coat).
Can also mean to crack (up) (of a person). *Il a craqué quand il était sur le point de gagner*: he cracked when he was about to win. And can mean to strike (a match). *Il sortit deux allumettes et il en craqua une*: he took out two matches and struck one. Note *plein à craquer*: bursting at the seams.
To crack (split) = *fendre, fêler*.

crash (m) This may be found (perhaps particularly among pilots) with the meaning of crash landing. And a *franglais* meaning is a crash course, which leads to some (seemingly alarming) announcements such as *business crash* (but which means only a crash course for business purposes; e.g. in English). Almost as alarming as the headmaster who announced that he was organizing a crash course in driving lessons.
Crash (noise) = *fracas* (m).
(accident) = *collision* (f).
(financial) = *krach* (m).

cravate (f) Tie, formerly cravat. *Il noue sa cravate*: he knots his tie.
Now cravat = *foulard* (m).

crayon (m) Pencil.
Crayon = *crayon de couleur*.

crèche (f) A creche for children, day nursery, also crib (Christmas).

crème (m) A white coffee (with cream). Stands for *un café crème*. *Un crème!* a

crié le garçon: one white coffee! shouted the waiter.
Cream = *crème* (f).

crème (f) Cream. *Crème fouettée*: whipped cream, but *crème anglaise* is custard.
Crème is also used figuratively in the sense of the best, the pick of the bunch. *La crème des patrons*: the best of bosses. (The full phrase *la crème de la crème* is not a normal French expression.)

crêpe (m) Crepe. Also a mourning-band on the arm.

crêpe (f) Pancake.
Crepe = *crêpe* (m).

crevasse (f) Crevasse, but also crack on skin or walls.

cric (m) Jack (car).
Crick (in the neck) = *torticolis* (m).

crier To cry, to shout. *Ne criez pas!*: don't shout!
To cry (weep) = *pleurer*.

criquet (m) Locust. *Je pense au temps chaud et aux criquets*: I think of the hot weather and the locusts.
Cricket = *grillon* (m).
  (game) = *cricket* (m).

crise (f) Crisis; and often extended to mean shortage (*crise pétrolière*: oil shortage).
Also frequently used for attack, fit. *Crise cardiaque*: heart attack. *Crise de larmes*: fit of tears.

critique (f) Often criticism. *Que pensez-vous de cette critique?*: What do you think of this criticism?
Critic = *critique* (m) (f).

crochet (m) Crochet is one of many meanings. *Elle fait du crochet le soir*: she does crochet-work in the evenings.
Also means a hook. *Il faut deux crochets pour ce grand tableau*: we need two hooks for this big picture.
Hook, too, in the boxing sense (*un crochet du gauche*: a left hook).
Still influenced by the curved shape, it can mean a picklock (implement) and also a sudden turn. *Là où la route fait un crochet*: where the road bends sharply.
If something (printed) is *entre crochets* it is within square brackets.
On TV it can mean a talent contest.
Finally, there is a familiar phrase *vivre aux crochets de quelqu'un*: to live off someone (at his expense).

cross (m) Cross-country run or running, being the typical familiar abbreviated form of *le cross-country*. *J'aime le cross*: I like cross-country running.
Cross = *croix* (f).

crosse (f) (Bishop's) crook, crozier. *L'évêque a perdu sa crosse*: the bishop has lost his crook.

Also stick as for hockey and – of course – lacrosse. Also rifle-butt.
Cross = *croix* (f).

crudité (f) Crudity, crudeness, but do not be put off eating *les crudités,* which are raw fruit and vegetables (*on commence par des crudités?* is a suggestion to have them as a first course and no cause for offence).

cube (m) Cube, and building-block (toy).
In modern popular usage *un gros cube* is a powerful motorbike. *Il soupira, écarquillant les yeux – Si j'avais seulement un gros cube comme ça!*: he sighed, opening his eyes wide – if only I had a big bike like that!

culte (m) Worship, as well as cult. *Le culte des héros*: hero-worship. Protestant service. *Il assiste au culte chaque semaine*: he goes to the (Protestant) service each week.

culturisme (m) Not improvement of the mind, but the body! Bodybuilding (practised by *les culturistes*).

cumulus (m) Cumulus (cloud).
(Electric) hot-water heater (trade name).

curateur (m) Trustee, guardian, administrator (to look after someone's interests).
Curator (museum) = *conservateur* (m).

cure (f) Cure of souls (the function of the *curé*). Sometimes means parish or vicarage.
Also medical cure, especially in the sense of to take a cure, to take the waters.
Note the old phrase *je n'en ai cure*: I do not care.
Cure (healing, remedy) = *guérison* (f).

curé (m) Parish priest, vicar. *En regardant par la fenêtre, j'ai vu un curé descendre la rue*: looking out of the window I saw a priest coming down the street.
Curate = *vicaire* (m).

curer To clean out. To clean (one's nails), pick (nose, teeth). (Hence *un cure-dents*: tooth-pick.) *Le médecin se cure les ongles*: the doctor cleans his nails.
To cure = *guérir*.

curiosité (f) Curiosity, as in English, also with the sense of sights.
Les curiosités de la ville: the sights of the town.

cycle (m) Cycle (events, change).
Can mean cycle (bicycle), too, but is used officially rather than familiarly – *chez le marchand de cycles*: at the bicycle (cycle) shop.
Cycle, bike = commonly *vélo* (m) (which goes back to a Latin origin rather than the Greek origin of *cycle*).

cynique (m) Cynic (in the philosophical sense), also shameless person.
Cynic = *railleur* (m), *sceptique* (m).

cynique Cynical, in the philosophical sense, otherwise shameless, brazen.
Cynical = *railleur, sceptique*.

cyniquement Brazenly, with effrontery.
Cynically = *d'un ton railleur, sceptique*.

cynisme (m) Cynicism (in the philosophical sense), but usually shameless-
ness, impudence.
Cynicism = *raillerie* (f) *sceptique*.

D

dada (m) A child's word for horse – gee-gee. Also used for hobby-horse,
pet theme. *Les ovni? Attention, il va enfourcher son dada!*: UFOs? Look out,
he'll get on to his pet theme.
Daddy = *papa* (m).

dais (m) Canopy.
Dais = *estrade* (f).

dam (m) This is an old word, sometimes used in literary style, which is
basically the same word as English 'damage' and French *dommage*. It
means prejudice, harm, detriment. *Ceci se passe au grand dam des passants*:
this is happening much to the detriment of the passers-by.
Dam (river) = *barrage* (m).

dame A mild exclamation. *Dame oui!*: Well, yes! Should not be confused
with English damn (different origin), which could = *Sacré nom d'un chien!*

dancing (m) Dance-hall. *J'aime ce dancing*: I like this dance-hall. (It is
interesting to note that we do not use the word in this way and the French
do not use *palais de danse!*)
Dancing = *la danse*.

darne (f) Steak (fish).
Darn = *reprise* (f).

date (f) Date (calendar).
Date (e.g. with girl or boy) = *rendez-vous* (m).
The fruit = *datte* (f).

daube (f) Stew (*boeuf* (m) *en daube*: braised beef).
Daub = *barbouillage* (m).

dauber To stew (beef, etc.).
There is a dated sense of to poke fun at, mock (literary style).
To daub = *barbouiller, peinturlurer*.

débarrer To unbar.
To debar = *exclure, interdire*.

débâter To unsaddle (by taking off the pack-saddle).
To debate = *débattre*.

se débattre Not to debate (*débattre*), but to struggle. *Ses parents se débattaient toujours contre la vie*: his parents were always struggling against life.

débauchage (m) Enticing people away from work, or laying off of workers. Debauchery = *débauche* (f).

débaucher To debauch, corrupt. From the moral idea of leading astray comes the practical meaning of enticing someone away from his work, encouraging him to strike.
It can also mean to lay off (workmen). *On a dû débaucher pas mal d'ouvriers*: quite a lot of workers had to be laid off.

débit (m) Debit, but also (retail) selling. *Un débit de tabac*: a tobacconist's.
Also flow, rate, output. And (familiarly) long utterance, words, speech.

débiter To debit, but there are various other meanings. To retail, to sell, to discharge a given amount. *Ces pompes débitent pendant la journée des quantités énormes*: enormous quantities come from these pumps during the day. To saw up, cut up. *On se chauffe facilement. On abat des arbres pour les débiter plus tard*: keeping warm is easy. We cut down trees and saw them up later. The word also has a familiar meaning, to utter (often in a long and boring way). *Le professeur se lève et débite les mêmes faits de la même façon*: the teacher gets up and pours forth the same facts in the same way.

débonnaire Good-natured, easy-going. *'Les deux officiers, aussi débonnaires que les précédents étaient enragés, escortent Lucien Neuwirth, qui peut à peine se traîner, jusqu'a un village heureusement proche'* (Paul Dreyfus, Histoires extraordinaires de la Résistance, Fayard). In English it may mean cheerful. But it often has with it the sense of being casually elegant (*élégant, suave et gai*).

débris (m) Not only rubbish, but also left-over bits, remnants; fragments.

début (m) Debut (as in English) but also much more widely used.
Au début: at the beginning. *Dès le début de la guerre*: from the beginning of the war.

débutante (f) A beginner (feminine of *débutant*), as well as sometimes a (social) debutante. *Pour une débutante, elle skie drôlement bien*: for a beginner, she skies jolly well.

décade (f) Period of ten days. Sometimes used for decade (ten years) but, properly speaking, this = *décennie* (f).

décadence (f) Care is needed to decide whether decadence or decline (fall) is meant. *La décadence de l'Empire*: the fall of the Empire.

décanter To decant, also become clear, as in *la situation se décante*.

décent Decent, proper, seemly. *Je ne sais pas s'il est décent de vous remercier, après trois mois, de votre cadeau*: I don't know if it is proper to thank you, after three months, for your present.
Decent (kind) = *chic*.

déception (f) The idea of deception has faded, and it means disappointment. *Le dîner était horrible! Quelle déception!*: the dinner was horrible! What a disappointment!
Deception = *tromperie* (f).

décevant Can mean deceptive, misleading, but usually disappointing. *Les ventes sont décevantes*: the sales are disappointing.

décevoir To disappoint (if you deceive yourself, you disappoint yourself). *Je suis très déçu*: I am very disappointed.
To deceive = *tromper*.

décharge (f) Discharge (various senses), unloading, hence *une décharge publique*: a rubbish dump.
Also a legal term (compare discharge in English) for defence – *à la décharge de ce monsieur*: in this gentleman's defence.
Discharge (employer) = *renvoi* (m).

décharger To discharge, unload. To discharge, let off (weapon).
To vent (anger). To discharge, release.
But to discharge (dismiss) someone = *congédier*, or *libérer* (prisoner, soldier).

décidément Decidedly, firmly, definitely, certainly. Sometimes used as an exclamation – Well, really! *'– Ah ça? décidément! vous me logez chez vous, près de vous comme cela! Avez-vous bien fait toutes vos réflexions? Qui est-ce qui vous dit que je n'ai pas assassiné?'* (Victor Hugo, *Jean Valjean*).

déclaration (f) Declaration, in varying senses, including declaration of love. *Tu lui as fait une déclaration?*: You told her you loved her?

décliner To decline. *Il a décliné mon invitation*: he declined my invitation.
To decline (grammatical term).
To give particulars. *Il décline son identité*: he gives his name and address.
To decline, sink, go down, fade. *Le soleil déclinait lentement*: the sun was slowly going down.

décomposé Can mean decomposed, rotten, but (of features) it means very drawn or distorted. *Une homme aux traits décomposés*: a man with distorted features.

décomposer Can mean to decompose, rot, also to distort (features); also to break up, split, analyse.

déconfiture (f) Discomfiture, check, failure. But note particularly that it often has the meaning of bankruptcy.

découvert Discovered, but often used as an adjective to mean open, exposed, bare.
(Note *à découvert*: overdrawn (money).)

découvrir To discover, also to uncover. Hence (in the right context) *il se découvre*: he takes off his hat, he bares his head.

défait Means drawn (of features).
Can also be dishevelled (e.g. a bed).

But could mean defeated (of an army).

défectif Defective, in the grammatical sense.
Defective = *défectueux*.

défection (f) Defection, and has also come to mean cancellation (hotels). *Il n'y plus rien pour cette période, sauf défections*: there is no more room left for this period, apart from cancellations.

défendeur (m) **défenderesse** (f) Defendant (legal).
Defender = *défenseur* (m).

défendre To defend, and (familiarly) *il se défend*: he copes all right, he manages.
Also just as commonly means to forbid. *Je vous défends de sortir*: I forbid you to go out.

défense (f) Defence, and *les défenses d'un éléphant* are (not surprisingly) the tusks.
It also means prohibition, and is common in notices. *Défense de fumer*: no smoking.

déférer Can mean to defer, in the sense of to submit (e.g. to someone's wishes).
Also a legal term, usually used in the sense of bringing to court, handing over to a judge.
To defer (put off) = *remettre, différer*.

défiance (f) Distrust, suspicion (from the verb *se défier*). *Il a un air de défiance et il ne me répond pas*: he looks distrustful and does not answer me.
Defiance = *défi* (m).

défiant Mistrustful, suspicious. *Un paysan défiant*: a suspicious countryman.
Defiant = *réfractaire*.
          (expression) = *de défi*.

défier To defy, but often just to challenge. *Je vous défie au billard*: I challenge you to a game of billiards.

défiler Can mean to unstring (as of beads).
Défiler son chapelet (rosary) is a familiar expression meaning to say one's piece, speak out.
But the verb commonly means to file past, go past, march past (military). *Toute la journée des touristes défilent vers la plage*: all day tourists stream towards the beach.
To defile = *souiller*.

définitivement Definitely, i.e. permanently, irrevocably. *Il va rester définitivement en France*: he is going to stay in France for good. *Et puis en septembre, je pars définitivement*: and then in September, I'm off for good.
Definitely (usually) = *sûrement, sans aucun doute*.

déformé Out of shape, twisted, distorted. '*Une ombre se profila sur le rideau. Bien que déformée, on reconnaissait la silhouette de la jeune fille qui traversait la*

salle à manger à pas pressés' (Georges Simenon, *Maigret et l'Inspecteur Malgracieux*, Macmillan).
Deformed = *difforme*.

dégradation (f) Dismissal (from rank, rights).
Degradation of a person.
Damage, deterioration. *En entrant dans la ville, on est bouleversé de voir les dégradations des bâtiments*: on entering the town, one is stunned to see the state (damaged state) of the buildings. *Beaucoup de dégradations ont été commises dans l'église par des vandales*: a lot of damage has been caused in the church by vandals.

dégrader To degrade, lower, dismiss. Also to degrade in a figurative sense.
To damage, often as the result of weather.
To shade off (of colours) (hence *le dégradé*: range of colours).
La situation se dégrade: the situation is worsening.
To degrade oneself (sometimes) = *s'abaisser*.

degré (m) Degree. Also step. *Sur les degrés du musée*: on the museum steps.
(Academic) degree = *grade* (f), *diplôme* (m), *licence* (f).

dégustation (f) Sampling, tasting. *Un moment de dégustation*: a moment for sampling, relishing.
Disgust = *dégoût* (m).

déguster Not to disgust, but on the contrary to sample, taste, relish. *On va déguster des huîtres*: we shall go and sample some oysters.
To disgust = *dégoûter*.

déjection (f) Evacuation (as of the bowels). In the plural it means excrement.
Dejection = *abattement* (m).

déjettement (m) Not dejection, but warping, being lopsided.
Dejection = *découragement* (m), *abattement* (m).

délai (m) Sometimes means delay (*sans délai*: without delay). Often has a meaning which is almost the opposite – time limit, time allowed. Thus a shop or business may advertise *délais rapides*, meaning that the job can be done in a short period. Or again it can speak, proudly and properly, of *des délais respectés*, meaning that it will keep to the time agreed, and may even say *Vous pouvez compter sur nos délais*: you can rely on our keeping to the time schedule.
To ask for *un délai* is to ask for extended time.

délayer Not to delay, but to water, thin (something solid).
To delay = *retarder*.

délivrance (f) Deliverance, freeing, or in the sense of giving out. Thus *lieu* (m) *de délivrance*: place of issue (e.g. documents).

délivrer To deliver, release. To deliver (birth). To hand over, issue.
To deliver (goods) = *livrer*.

déloyal Disloyal, also unfair. *Cette concurrence déloyale*: this unfair competition. *Un avantage déloyal*: an unfair advantage.

demande (f) Sometimes demand, but often request – a much milder meaning. Thus *sur demande*: on request; *faire une demande d'emploi*: to apply for a job (not to demand one!); *faire sa demande en mariage*: to propose.
Also bid (cards).
Demand(s) = *exigence* (f).

demander Sometimes to demand, but frequently just to ask (for). *Le garçon a demandé encore dix francs*: the waiter asked for another ten francs. *Le prisonnier demande à boire*: the prisoner asks for something to drink.
Je me demande si . . .: I wonder whether . . .
Also to bid (cards).
To demand (often) = *exiger*.

démanteler Can be to demolish (walls, fortifications) but usually means to break up (Empire, etc.). *La police a démantelé un réseau de call-girls*: the police have broken up a call-girl ring.
To dismantle (often) = *démonter*.

démarier To unmarry. To thin out (plants).

démenti (m) Denial, contradiction. *Un démenti de l'hôpital*: a denial from the hospital.
Demented person = *dément* (m).

démentir To give the lie, contradict, prove wrong.
To be demented = *être dément*.

démonstrateur (m) Demonstrator, usually in a commercial sense of showing a product.
Demonstrator (political) = *manifestant* (m).

démonstration (f) Demonstration of something by someone.
Demonstration (political) = *manifestation* (f).
                    'demo' = *manif.* (f).

démonter Surprisingly, not to dismount. It means to dismantle or, familiarly, to upset, put out.
To dismount = *descendre*.

dent (f) Tooth. Prong.
But *une roue dentée* need not cause alarm – it is a cogwheel. *Une roue voilée*: a buckled wheel.
Dent = *bosse* (f), *bosselure* (f).
To dent (e.g. car wing) = *cabosser*.

dental Dental (linguistic term).
The more common meaning connected with dentistry is *dentaire*. *Carie* (f) *dentaire*: tooth decay.

denture (f) (Natural) teeth. *Un beau garçon aux yeux bleus et à la denture étincelante*: a handsome lad with blue eyes and sparkling teeth.
Denture = *dentier* (m).

départ (m) Departure, but note the figurative sense of beginning. *Au départ c'était très difficile*: initially it was very difficult.

départir To share out (one's possessions), allot.
(*Se départir* can mean to depart from (e.g. an attitude).)
To depart = *partir*.

dépendance (f) Dependence, also (in the plural) outhouses, annexe. *Un manoir avec de grandes dépendances*: a manor with large outbuildings.

dépendre To depend. *Cela dépend de vous*: it depends on you.
Also means to belong to. *Un parc qui dépend de la municipalité*: a park belonging to the council.
And can mean to be under the authority of someone. *Cet employé dépend de son patron à Paris*: this employee is under his boss in Paris.
Furthermore it can mean to unhang, take down (*dé* + *pendre*).

déplacement (m) Displacement, travel, and often means movement, travel, in quite a limited sense. *Quelquefois nous allons au théâtre mais ça ne vaut pas toujours le déplacement*: sometimes we go to the theatre, but it isn't always worth the journey.
Note *être en déplacement*: to be away on business, to be on a business trip.

déplacer Sometimes to displace, often just to move. To transfer a person.
Se déplacer frequently has the mild sense of to move, travel, get around. *Il se déplace difficilement*: he gets around with difficulty.
To displace (often) = *remplacer*.

déployer To deploy, display, also unfurl, open out. *Il a déployé tous les journaux dominicaux*: he spread out all the Sunday papers.
Rire à gorge déployée: to laugh uproariously.

déportement (m) Can mean swerve, the skidding of a car, or (in the plural) misconduct.
Deportment = *conduite* (f).

déporter To deport, but also to carry away. *On a déporté quelques parachutistes*: some parachutists were deported. *Le vent a déporté quelques parachutistes*: the wind carried away some parachutists.

déposer To deposit, put down, put. *Il m'a déposé près du casino*: he put me down near the casino.
Also to depose (a king).
Marque déposée: registered trade-mark. And in legal language, *déposer* means to give evidence.

dépositaire (f) Depositary, trustee. Agent (for goods).
Do not confuse with depository (*dépôt* (m)).

dépôt (m) Can refer to the depositing of various things.
Deposit (money, and in the sense of sediment).
Can be a dump or tip for depositing rubbish as well as a depot, warehouse, etc.
Police-station, cells.

dépotoir (m) Usually means rubbish-dump, sometimes sewage works.
Depository = *dépôt* (m).

déprédation (f) Depredation, pillaging, also damage (caused to property). *Le week-end les vandales arrivent et les déprédations sont importantes*: at the week-end the vandals arrive and the damage is considerable.
Also means misappropriation of money.

député (m) Delegate. Deputy (French politics).
Member of Parliament.
Deputy = *adjoint* (m), *substitut* (m).

déranger To derange, but mostly to disturb, upset. *Il m'a dérangé*: he disturbed me. *Je ne veux pas vous déranger*: I don't want to trouble you. *Ne vous dérangez pas*: please don't bother (trouble).
To go out of order: *L'appareil est dérangé*: the machine is out of order.
Can mean deranged (of the mind), but *mon petit est dérangé*: my little boy has diarrhoea, has an upset tummy.
Deranged (usually) = *détraqué*.

dérider To smooth (out the wrinkles), to cheer (someone) up. *Alors, vous l'avez déridé un peu?*: Well, you cheered him up a bit?
To deride = *railler, se moquer de*.

dérivatif (m) Has a topical meaning of outlet, distraction. A doctor might say: *Il faut vous trouver un dérivatif – le tennis, le rami, n'importe quoi*: you must find a distraction – tennis, rummy, anything.
Derivative (word) = *dérivé* (m).

dériver To derive. *Ce mot dérive d'un autre plus long*: this word is derived from a longer one.
To divert (as of water). Also to drift. *On dérivait et la mer commençait à bouger*: we were drifting and the sea was beginning to get up.

dérober To steal. To hide (*un escalier dérobé*: secret staircase).
Se dérober: to steal away, dodge, evade.
To give way (under a weight).
To disrobe = *se dévêtir de sa robe*.

désagrément (m) Displeasure, annoyance, being upset. *Il assistera à la réunion et j'ai peur qu'il nous cause des désagréments*: he will be at the meeting and I am afraid he will give us bother.
Disagreement = *désaccord* (m).

désarmement (m) Disarming, disarmament, but also laying up (mothballing) of a ship. *'Dans deux jours, dans trois jours, dans huit jours, le "Norway", l'ancien "France", quittera le quai où il est amarré depuis son désarmement en 1974'* (Jacques Laurent, *Le Figaro*, 9 August 1979).

désarmer To disarm.
But note *il ne désarme pas*: he does not give in (over some point), he does not relent.
Le froid ne désarme point: there is no letting up of the cold.
Désarmer is also to lay up (a ship).

descendre To descend, go down, come down, get off (vehicles), dismount, bring down.

Readers of thrillers will know that it is also 'to bump off'.
Note *descendre à un hôtel*: to put up at a hotel. *Je suis descendu à un petit hôtel près de la gare*: I put up at a small hotel near the station ('I descended to a small hotel' would be something different!).

descente (f) Descent.
Can also mean a police raid or swoop, and *descente sur les lieux* is a visit to the scene of the crime.
Can mean a hill or slope, but *une descente de lit* is just a bedside rug.

déshonnête Unseemly, indecent, a word likely to be found in literary style.
Ces mots plutôt déshonnêtes m'ont surpris: these rather improper words surprised me.
Dishonest = *malhonnête*.

déshonnêtement Immodestly, in an indecent way.
Dishonestly = *malhonnêtement*.

déshonnêteté (f) Unseemliness.
Dishonesty = *malhonnêteté* (f).

déshonorer To dishonour, also to disfigure, mark (for example a building).
Ces voyous s'amusent à déshonorer nos beaux monuments: these hooligans enjoy themselves disfiguring our fine monuments.

désigner To point out. *De le main droite il a désigné la maison*: with his right hand he indicated the house.
To designate, fix, name.
To design = *dessiner, créer*.

désister Occasionally to desist, but *il se désiste*: he withdraws (as of a candidate for office).
To desist (usually) = *cesser*.

désolé Desolate (countryside), also very upset, sorry.
Je suis désolé: I am very sorry.

désoler To desolate, ravage. To distress.

desservir Can mean to clear away (a table), also to do a disservice, harm.
Also has quite the opposite meaning – to minister (for example a clergyman to a parish) or to serve a locality with reference to transport (in particular), to link up. *C'est une localité bien desservie par les cars*: the region is well served by buses.

destituer To dismiss, remove from office. *On a destitué le juge*: the judge was dismissed.
To make destitute = *rendre quelqu'un dénué de tout*.

destitution (f) Dismissal (from a post).
Malgré sa destitution, il va toujours bien: in spite of his dismissal he is still getting on all right.
Destitution = *dénuement* (m).

détacher To detach in various senses, or may mean to clean, remove marks (*dé*+*tache*).

With reference to a car, *pièces détachées* may sound a bit alarming, but they are in fact spare parts.

détail (m) Detail, and also retail.

détailler To detail, and to sell retail. Also break up, sell separately (items).

détenir Can mean to detain (as of a prisoner), also hold, to have in one's possession. *Il détient le record du monde*: he holds the world record. To detain (I don't want to detain you) = *retenir*.

détente (f) Used sometimes in English for easing of political tension. In addition to this sense, the word means general relaxation. *Deux heures de détente sur la plage*: two hours of relaxation on the beach.
Also means trigger (guns).
Someone who is *dur à la détente* is close with his money, close-fisted (familiar).

détention (f) Holding, possession of something; in particular detention (in a legal sense).
Detention (school) = *consigne* (f).

détérioration (f) Deterioration, but also damage. *J'habite un petit appartement et heureusement ce n'est pas moi qui paie les détéroriations*: I live in a little flat and fortunately I don't have to pay for any damage (or wear and tear).

détériorer To make worse, or damage. *Il faut payer les livres détériorés*: damaged books must be paid for. *Se détériorer*: to deteriorate, to get worse, to finish in a bad state.

déterminé Determined. Also definite, specific. *Pour des raisons déterminées*: for specific reasons.

déterrer To unearth or exhume. *Je l'ai déterré chez un bouquiniste*: I unearthed it at a secondhand bookseller's.
To deter = *décourager*.

détonner To be out of tune (literally) and hence to clash, jar. *Avec son drôle d'accent, vous pensez s'il détonnait un peu*: with his odd accent, you can imagine that he jarred a bit.
To detonate = *détoner*.

détour (m) Detour, roundabout way (as in English), but also curve, bend.

détresse (f) Distress, but can also have the specific sense of financial difficulties. *Il m'a dit qu'ils sont maintenant dans la détresse*: he told me that they are now in a bad way financially.

détresser To unplait (hair)
To distress = *désoler*.

déviation (f) Deviation, but (with regard to traffic) it means a diversion. *Les déviations sont souvent agaçantes*: diversions are often annoying.

dévider To unwind.
To divide = *diviser*.

devis (m) Estimate. *Il est important de demander un devis*: it is important to ask for an estimate.

Device = *moyen* (m), *combine* (f).
    (mechanical) = *engin* (m).

deviser To chat. *Nous étions en train de deviser*: we were chatting away.
To devise = *trouver (un moyen), inventer*.

dévotion (f) Devotion in a religious sense.
But devotion to duty, etc. = *dévouement* (m). *'Je n'oublierai jamais avec quel dévouement on m'y prodigua des soins'* (René Guillot, *L'Homme de la 377*, Hachette, Bibliothèque Verte).

diaphragme (m) Diaphragm, also sound-box (gramophone).

différend (m) Difference, disagreement. *Le différend entre les deux pays*: the disagreement between the two countries.
Difference = *différence* (f).

différer To defer, put off. *Il a différé son retour*: he has postponed his return.
Also to differ.

difficile Difficult. Also (in familiar usage) fussy, for example about food. *Je ne suis pas difficile*: I am not fussy.

diffuser To diffuse. To broadcast, propagate.
To distribute (as of journals).

diffusion (f) Diffusion (of heat, etc.).
Also diffusion (compare Rediffusion) in the sense of broadcasting. *Des diffusions furent faites dans toute l'Europe*: broadcasts were made all over Europe.
Circulation, spreading of news. Distribution (as of journals).

digestif (m) Might be a digestive (medical), but is much more likely to be something more pleasant, to wit a liqueur taken at the end of a meal (as opposed to an *apéritif* before the meal). *Je peux t'offrir un digestif? Un cognac?*: May I offer you a liqueur? A brandy?

dilapidation (f) Squandering of money, or the misappropriation of it. *Après cinq mois de dilapidation, il n'est plus riche*: after five months of squandering, he is no longer rich.
Dilapidation = *délabrement* (m), *dégradations* (f).

dilapider To waste, squander (money, fortune), or misappropriate money. *Tout a été dilapidé*: all has been squandered.
To dilapidate = *délabrer*.

diligence (f) Diligence.
Faire diligence: to make haste.
Also means stage-coach.

dîme (f) Tithe, or dime (USA).

diplôme (m) Diploma, but can also be more important, i.e. a (university) degree.

direction (f) Direction, way. Running (of a business). Management, those in charge. *Offert par la direction*: With the management's compliments.

Nouvelle direction: new management. *Secrétaire de direction*: personal secretary.

Note too that it refers to steering (vehicles), hence *Accident sérieux; direction bloquée*: serious accident, steering jammed. *Direction assistée*: power-assisted steering.

directoire (m) 'Directoire' (historical), also a small group of (political) leaders.
Directory (telephone) = *Bottin* (m), *annuaire* (m).

discothèque (f) Discotheque, but also what it was originally, a record-library (compare *bibliothèque*).

discrétion (f) Discretion, and the useful phrase *à discrétion* means 'it is up to you'. *Vin blanc à discrétion*: as much white wine as you want (even if you go beyond discretion!)

discussion (f) Discussion, but also argument. *Pas de discussion!*: No arguing!

discuter To discuss, also to argue, e.g.: *'Dans la soirée il faisait ses courses, toujours souriant, ne discutant jamais les prix'* (Jean Pradeau, *Tête d'horloge*, Solar).

disgrâce (f) Disgrace, being out of favour.
Can also mean (literary style) a lack of attraction, plainness. *'Apolline rebutait par la disgrâce d'un visage aux chairs molles où s'inscrivait une résignation congénitale de bête malheureuse'* (Marcel Aymé, *Aller retour*, Gallimard).
Disgrace (sometimes) = *honte* (f).

disgracié Disgraced, or out of favour. It has also the sense of being out of favour with nature, hence ugly, plain or even deformed.

disgracier To disgrace, remove from favour.
To disgrace (often) = *déshonorer*.

disgracieusement In an inelegant, uncouth, awkward or ungracious way.
Disgracefully = *d'une manière scandaleuse*.

disgracieux Awkward, ungracious, unattractive. *Mais qui va achete chaussures disgracieuses?*: But who is going to buy these unattractive shoes.
Disgraceful = *scandaleux*.

disparaître To disappear, and a euphemism for to die. *Peu après son vieil ami a disparu*: soon afterwards his old friend passed away.

disparition (f) Disappearance, also death, passing away.

dispensaire (m) Out-patients' department. (Could be a vet's dispensary for animals.)
Dispensary (chemist) = *pharmacie* (f).

dispensation (f) Dispensation, giving out. Administration.
Dispensation (exemption) = *dispense* (f).

dispenser Sometimes to dispense, distribute.
Usually to exempt someone from something. *Je vous dispense de cette corvée*: I'll let you off this chore. *Se dispenser de quelque chose*: (usually) to let oneself out of doing something.

To dispense with someone, something (usually) = *se passer de*.
To dispense (medicine) = *préparer*.

se disperser To disperse, also to disperse, spread one's efforts. *Si vous cherchez un certain livre, il ne faut pas vous disperser ou vous perdrez beaucoup d'argent*: if you are looking for a certain book, you mustn't range too widely or you'll lose a lot of money.

disposer To arrange, lay out. To dispose, prepare someone for something. To prescribe (as of laws).
And (important) to have at one's disposal, to be free to use. *Tu peux disposer de ma machine à écrire*: you may use my typewriter.
L'argent dont il dispose: the money he has available.
Note *vous pouvez disposer*: you can go now (interview).
To dispose of (get rid of) = *se débarrasser de*.

disque (m) Gramophone record, disc. *J'ai une collection de disques chez moi*: I have a collection of records at home.
Also (in sport) the discus. And (metal) disc.
To slip a disc = *se déplacer une vertèbre*.

dissertation (f) Now used in the sense of essay (e.g. school).
Dissertation = *mémoire* (m) or (when spoken) *discours* (m), *péroraison* (f) (pejorative).

dissipation (f) Dissipation. Dispersion. Inattention (at school).

dissipé Dissipated, but happily for school-children the meaning is less strong. *Un élève dissipé*: an inattentive pupil.

dissiper To dissipate, dispel (as of clouds, fog), squander (as of time, money). *Le brouillard se dissipe*: the fog lifts.
But *les élèves se dissipent*: the pupils are inattentive.

distraction (f) The two main meanings are distraction in the sense of diversion, amusement, and the meaning of absent-mindedness. *Il faut trouver une distraction pour les enfants*: we must find something to amuse the children.
Distraction (often) = *interruption* (f).

distrayant Enjoyable, entertaining.
Distracting = *qui vous détourne l'attention*.

distributeur (m) Can be a person (e.g. film distributor), but is often a machine such as a slot-machine. *Tu n'as pas de billet? Va trouver un distributeur*: you haven't a ticket? Go and find a slot machine.

distribution (f) Distribution, and also the cast (play, film). *Avec cette distribution magnifique, on peut compter sur un grand succès*: with this magnificent cast one can be sure of a great success.
And (popular French) *une distribution* can mean a thrashing.

dodo (m) Dodo, but is more likely to be heard in the sense of sleep. It really belongs to children's language. *On va faire dodo?*: are we going to bye-byes, then?

dogue (m) Large mastiff-like dog (the word comes from the English 'dog'). Dog = *chien* (m).

domaine (m) Domain, property, or domain, province (figurative). But *le(s) Domaine(s)* can mean public property, the State (which has it in its care). '*C'est un ancien entrepôt de grains que les Domaines ont cédé à la ville pour une bouchée de pain*' (Jean Giono, *Le Moulin de Pologne*, Gallimard).

domesticité (f) Being in domestic service, or domesticity (animals). Also a general word for servants, staff. Domesticity = *goûts* (m) *domestiques, plaisirs* (m) *du foyer*.

dominer To dominate in various senses, to surpass, overlook. *Mon appartement domine la mer*: my flat looks right over the sea.
Also means to predominate. *C'est une école mixte, mais dans ma classe les garçons dominent*: it is a mixed school but in my class there are more boys than girls.

don (m) Gift (in both senses). Don (from Latin *dominus*) = *professeur* (m) *d'université*.

donjon (m) Keep (of a castle). Dungeon = *cachot* (m).

doper To dope with stimulants, and hence (familiarly) to excite, stimulate. *Le danger me dope*: danger gives me a kick. To dope (often) = *droguer, anesthésier*.

dormant Dormant, sleeping. It can mean fixed, immovable (of windows, etc.).

dossier (m) Dossier, file. Also back of a chair. *Il se leva de sa chaise et mit la main sur le dossier*: he got up from his chair and put his hand on the back.

dot (f) Dowry. Dot = *point* (m).

doter To dower (a bride), also endow. *Il a doté sa fille généreusement*: he gave his daughter a rich dowry. *Doter de*: to provide with. To dote = *radoter*. To dote on = *adorer*.

double (m) Double in various senses, including of people. Doubles (games). Also copy, duplicate. *Donnez-moi un double*: give me a carbon copy. Double (or understudy) = *doublure* (f). At the double = *au pas de course*. At the double! = *Plus vite que ça!*

doubler To double. *Doubler* (= *redoubler*) *une classe*: to stay down. Also to line a garment. *Doublé de soie*: silk-lined. Can mean too to dub (a film) and (familiarly) to double-cross. And (most important) to overtake. *Je vais doubler ce poids lourd*: I am going to overtake this long vehicle.

doublet (m) Doublet (linguistics).
Doublet (clothes) = *pourpoint* (m).

douter To doubt, but *se douter* (*de*) is to feel, suspect. *Je m'en doutais*: I thought as much. *Je me doutais qu'il le ferait*: I felt sure he would do it.

doyen (m) Doyen, senior. Also dean.

dragon (m) Both dragon and dragoon (military). '*Et mon père qui était de l'Yonne, qui avait fait son service militaire dans les dragons à Joigny précisément!*' (Marie-Madeleine Fourcade, *L'Arche de Noé*, Fayard).

draguer To dredge, drag (water).
And (familiarly) to try and pick up girls.
To drag (pull) = *traîner*.

drain (m) Drain for fields (agricultural term), or drain, tube (medical term).
Drain in the normal sense = *égout* (m).
Brain-drain = *fuite* (f) *des cerveaux*.

dresser Does not mean to dress. Can mean to erect something, draw up (plans) and train (animals) (compare dressage). So although dogs sometimes wear coats, *un chien bien dressé* is a well-trained dog.
Se dresser: to rise up (often of things such as mountains), also to sit up (people). *Soudain il se dresse*: suddenly he sits up.
To dress = *s'habiller*.

dresseur (m) Trainer (for animals).
Dresser (e.g. theatre) = *habilleur* (m), *habilleuse* (f).
(furniture) = *dressoir* (m), *buffet* (m).

dressing-room (m) A fashionable *franglais* word which may be seen in advertisements for property. *Balcon, salle de bains moderne, dressing-room . . .*: balcony, modern bathroom, dressing-room. In practice it may be only a very large cupboard.

driver (m) A driver in trotting races.
Driver (cars, etc.) = *conducteur* (m).

droguerie (f) The 'drug' scene is a little confusing. *Les drogues* (f) can refer to medicines but usually to (harmful) drugs.
But *la droguerie* is the store that sells pharmaceutical goods and, mostly, hardware.
Drug addiction = *toxicomanie* (f).
Drug store = *drugstore* (m).

droguiste (m) Owner of a *droguerie*, hardware-shop owner.
Drug addict = *drogué(e)* (m/f), *toxicomane* (m/f).

drôle (m) Can mean a rascal, sometimes, as well as an odd fellow.
Droll fellow (odd) = *drôle de type*.
        (funny) = *farceur* (m).

drôle Has a much wider use than droll. Funny; strange. *C'est drôle! Je ne le vois pas*: It's odd! I can't see it.
Droll (also) = *cocasse*.

drôlement Funnily, but the very common familiar meaning is one of intensification. *Il fait drôlement chaud*: it is jolly hot.
Drolly = *d'une manière cocasse.*

dry (m) The abbreviation for *dry martini*. It saves you three syllables, and is perhaps evocative and may have a snob appeal. *Il pleuvait toujours quand je suis arrivé à l'hôtel et j'ai demandé tout de suite un dry*: It was still raining when I reached the hotel and I immediately called for a dry martini.
(To) dry = *se sécher.*

duc (m) Duke, but some care is needed, as it may mean a (horned) owl.
Un grand duc: eagle owl (as well as a grand duke!).

duvet (m) We use the word in English in the sense of a type of warm quilt (eiderdown), and down, fluff, is the first meaning of the French *duvet*. Then it means a sleeping-bag stuffed with down or something similar.
Duvet = *couette* (f) (which in fact has the same Latin origin as the English quilt).

écho (m) Echo, and also refers to gossipy news items of a newspaper. *Je lis les gros titres, puis les échos de la ville*: I read the headlines, then the local gossip items.

éclair (m) Certainly it means a delicious kind of cream-cake, but also a flash, and *il fait des éclairs*: it is lightning, there are lightning flashes. *Visite* (f) *éclair*: flying (lightning) visit.

économie (f) Economy, also economics. *Les économies*: savings.

économique Economic (policy, etc.), or economical.

édifice (m) (Important) building. A word more widely used than English 'edifice'.

édifier To edify, enlighten, but also to build, erect. *Une statue édifiée pour la circonstance*: a statue put up for the occasion. Can even be used for tents.

éditer May be to edit (e.g. a text), but usually to publish. '*Sur la porte du réfectoire, en effet, M. Mouret avait affiché une carte des environs de Morzine, la carte que le syndicat d'initiative éditait à l'usage des touristes*' (Paul-Jacques Bonzon, *Les Six Compagnons et l'homme des neiges*, Hachette, Bibliothèque Verte).
To edit (newspapers) = *rédiger.*

éditeur (m) Can mean the editor of a text, but normally refers to a publisher of books. *Selon l'éditeur, le livre est épuisé*: according to the publisher, the book is out of print.

Editor (newspapers) = *rédacteur* (m).

éducation (f) Sometimes not only education, but more specific training, and in a general sense often manners, breeding. *Il manque d'éducation*: he has no manners, he was badly brought up. If he has no education, he is *sans instruction*.

Education (often) = *enseignement* (m), *instruction* (f).

éduquer To educate, bring up. *Il est mal éduqué*: he is badly brought up. An educated person is *instruit*.

effectif Effective in the senses of true, real, actual or of coming into effect. But effective (e.g. measures) often = *efficace*.

effectivement Effectively. *Est-ce qu'il peut agir effectivement?*: Can he act effectively?

Also means actually, in fact, indeed. '*M. Bridges était effectivement curé de ce village, mais il venait d'en partir et ne devait être de retour que dans trois semaines*' (Benjamin Constant, *Le Cahier rouge*).

And as an answer, it can mean 'Indeed', 'Quite so.'

élaboration (f) Elaboration, working out.

Elaborateness = *soin* (m).

élaboré Elaborated, worked out slowly and carefully.

Elaborate = *compliqué*.

élaborer To elaborate, work out.

But in English we often use the verb in the sense of going into detail = *entrer dans le détail*.

élan (m) Elan, dash, also spring, leap. Also a sudden show of feeling, impulse.

And can mean a moose. *En voyant l'élan, le chasseur hésite*: on seeing the moose, the huntsman hesitates.

élargir Has the sense of enlarging, but used with prisoners, it means setting free. *Il a décidé d'élargir les trois hommes*: he decided to release the three men.

To enlarge (photography) = *agrandir*.

élargissement (m) Enlargement, broadening out, but also release (of prisoners).

Enlargement (photographs) = *agrandissement* (m).

élastique (m) Elastic, also elastic rubber band. *J'ai laissé tomber tous mes papiers. Auriez-vous un élastique?*: I've dropped all my papers. Would you have an elastic band?

élément (m) Element. May be seen in newspaper crime reports meaning facts, information – *la police a très peu d'éléments jusqu'ici*: the police have very little to go on so far.

Can mean a unit (furniture).

Can refer to people, not necessarily in a pejorative way.

élimination (f) Elimination, but (in industry or medicine) waste, getting rid of. Some pill might be advertised '*pour stimuler l'élimination*'.

embarcation (f) Small boat. *Le colonel attend l'embarcation*: the colonel is waiting for the small boat.
Embarkation = *embarquement* (m).

embarras (m) Can mean embarrassment, but frequently difficulty (often financial) or difficulty of choice. *Il a des embarras d'argent*: he is in financial difficulties.
L'embarras du choix: too much to choose from.
And *un embarras gastrique* is when you have an upset stomach.
Embarrassment (often) = *gêne* (f).

embarrassant Sometimes embarrassing. Often just awkward – of a situation or even of a parcel. *Je ne peux guère monter dans l'autobus avec ces paquets embarrassants*: I can scarcely get into the bus with these awkward packages.
Embarrassing = *gênant*.

embarrassé Sometimes means embarrassed but frequently just in an awkward position, or hampered, confused. *Je voudrais vous aider . . . mais . . . je suis vraiment embarrassé*: I would like to help you . . . but . . . I am really at a loss.
Embarrassed = *gêné*.

embarrasser To embarrass, but usually to encumber, put in difficulties, puzzle. *Ça va vous embarrasser si je laisse mon pardessus là?*: Will my overcoat be in your way if I leave it there?
To embarrass = *gêner*.

embrasse (f) Curtain loop.
Embrace = *embrassement* (m), *embrassade* (f).

embrasser May mean to embrace, include, and note *embrasser une carrière*: to take up a career.
But usually means to kiss (occasionally to embrace).
In familiar French one may hear *il a embrassé un platane*: he has wrapped his car round a tree.
To embrace = *serrer dans les bras*.

embûche (f) The same word as ambush, but now means trap, snare.
Il m'a tendu une embûche: he laid a trap for me.
Ambush now = *embuscade* (f). *Il m'a tendu une embuscade*: he laid an ambush for me.

émissaire (m) Emissary, and *un bouc émissaire* is a scapegoat.
But it is also an overflow pipe, channel. '*Mais sans aucun doute le facteur essentiel, et de loin le plus grave de pollution, découle du rejet en mer des eaux usées, déchets, canaux d'évacuation divers, égouts et émissaires*' (Marcel Rovère, *Nice-Matin*, 2 April 1974).

émission (f) Emission, issue, but particularly common for transmission, broadcasting, programme.

émotion (f) Emotion, but often should be translated as shock, excitement or fuss. *Après les émotions d'hier soir*: after the excitement of last night.

emphase (f) Bombast, flowery, over-done style. *Il parle avec emphase*: he speaks in a bombastic way. *Il se mouche avec emphase*: he blows his nose too loudly.
Emphasis = *force* (f), (*insister sur quelque chose*).

emphatique Bombastic, pompous. *Je n'aime pas son style emphatique*: I do not like his pompous style. (Could be emphatic in a linguistic context.) Emphatic = *énergique*.

empire (m) Empire, but also authority, influence. *Conduite sous empire de l'état alcoolique*: driving under the influence (of drink).

empoisonnant Very annoying (familiar use).
Poisonous = *vénéneux, toxique*.

empoisonnement (m) Poisoning, stink. Also (familiarly) annoyance, pestering, tiresome bother.

empoisonner To poison, also sometimes to stink.
Has a common familiar meaning of to annoy, plague, bore. *Il empoisonne tout le monde!*: he drives everyone mad!
S'empoisonner: to poison oneself, or to be bored (familiar).

empoisonneur (m) **empoisonneuse** (f) Poisoner or (familiarly) a bore, an annoying person, a real pest.

encenser To cense (burn incense in honour) and from that can mean to praise or flatter greatly.
Also has a particular meaning with regard to horses – to toss the head (up and down).
To incense (infuriate) = *rendre furieux*.

enchanté Enchanted, bewitched. *Un pays enchanté où les animaux parlent*: a magic country where the animals speak.
Also delighted, and a normal response on being introduced to someone.

enchantement (m) Enchantment, delight, also magic. *Comme par enchantement*: as though by magic.

encore Yet or again, but not 'encore' which is *bis!* (and *un bis*: an encore). (Comes from Latin *bis*, with the meaning of twice.)

endive (f) Chicory in Britain, but endive in the USA.
Endive = *chicorée* (f) *frisée*.

énergétique Technical word meaning concerned with energy. *Est-ce que les problèmes des années 80 seront les problèmes énergétiques?*: Will the problems of the 1980s be problems concerned with energy?
Energetic (people) = *énergique*.

énervant Enervating (rare). Normally means annoying, upsetting.
Enervating = *amollissant*.

énervé Much used for on edge, nervy. *Je deviens de plus en plus énervé, je dois aller me reposer à la campagne*: I am getting more and more on edge; I must go and rest in the country.
Enervated = *affaibli*.

énerver To upset, irritate. *Cela m'énerve*: that gets on my nerves. *Il trouve la vie de famille difficile, il s'énerve vite*: he finds family life difficult; he quickly gets upset.
To enervate = *affaiblir*.

enfant (m/f) Child (although *enfant* is of the same origin as infant). It can, too, mean lad (*Allez, les enfants!*: Come on, lads!).
Can be the native (of a place).
If someone is *bon enfant*, he is good natured.
Infant = *enfant en bas âge*.

engagé Committed (to a cause). But *un engagé*: volunteer (military).
Engaged (to be married) = *fiancé*.
       (not free) = *occupé*.

engagement (m) Pawning, pledge. Engagement, agreement. Enlistment.
Engagement (to be married) = *fiançailles* (f).

engager To engage is one of the meanings (as a servant, or something mechanical). Also to pawn, pledge, bind. *S'engager* is to commit oneself to something, or to enlist. *Il s'est engagé dans les paras*: he enlisted in the paras.
Can mean to enter (a street). *Le camion s'engagea dans une rue étroite*: the lorry entered a narrow street.
To get engaged = *se fiancer*.
To engage (a room) = *réserver, retenir*.

engin (m) Might sometimes be translated by engine, but is widely used for device, apparatus, contraption. *Pour le mauvais temps nous avons plusieurs engins antineige*: for the bad weather we have several antisnow devices.
Le garçon admire sa mobylette, et avant de monter sur son engin, il répète; 'C'est formidable!': the boy admires his moped, and before getting onto his machine, he repeats: 'It's terrific!'.
Engine = *machine* (f).
       (railway) = *locomotive* (f).
       (car) = *moteur* (m).

engrosser To make pregnant (familiar usage).
To engross = *absorber*.
To be engrossed (in one's work) = *être absorbé par son travail*.
       (in a book) = *être plongé dans un livre*.

enquête (f) Inquest, but more usually inquiry, investigation.

enragé Although the word basically means mad (as of a dog with rabies), it is commonly used to denote an enthusiast, somebody who is madly keen.
Un pongiste enragé: a mad keen table-tennis player.
But *les enragés* is a term for the 'Angry Brigade', extremists.
To be enraged = *s'enrager* (or *être furieux*).

enregistrement (m) Registration. Also recording (in various senses).
Registration (letter, etc.) = *recommandation* (f).
       (for a course, etc.) = *inscription* (f).

enregistrer To register (luggage and other things).
To record (*enregistrer sur bande*: to record on tape).

To register (a letter) = *recommander*.
  (for a course) = *se faire inscrire*.

enrober To coat, cover. *Quelques pierres enrobées de sable*: some stones coated with sand. (Compare the English enrober – the machine used to coat chocolates, biscuits or ice-creams.)
To enrobe = *mettre une robe, revêtir*.

enseigne (f) An ensign (flag), Latin *insignia* being the common origin (but *un enseigne* for the person).
Often means a sign (inn-sign, luminous sign, etc.).
Nous sommes tous logés à la même enseigne: we are all in the same boat.

entailler To notch, gash.
To entail = *occasionner*.

enter To graft (e.g. trees).
To enter = *entrer*.

entraîner To train (sport), or to bring, pull along, lead.
To entrain = (*s'*)*embarquer dans un train*.

entrée (f) Entry, entrance, (entrance) hall.
Also entrée (food).

entreprise (f) Enterprise in the sense of undertaking, (daring) task.
Also a firm, business. *Je vais monter une petite entreprise*: I am going to set up a small concern.
And *un restaurant d'entreprise* may be a perk of the job – it is a staff canteen.
To show enterprise = *être entreprenant*.

enveloppe (f) Often envelope, also sometimes outward appearance.
May simply have the basic meaning of cover, covering. *'Il voulut tâter son visage, le libérer de cette enveloppe . . . mais deux mains rudes lui maintinrent les bras'* (Georges Bayard, *Michel et les routiers*, Hachette, Bibliothèque Verte).

envie (f) Envy, but often has the less strong meaning of wish, inclination.
J'ai envie d'aller le voir: I would like to go and see him. *J'ai envie d'un appareil comme ça*: I'd like a camera like that.

époque (f) Epoch, but also an everyday word for time, period. *A cette époque-là j'étais toujours à Paris*: at that time I was still in Paris.
La Belle Epoque: the Naughty Nineties.

éprouver Not usually to prove, but to try, test, feel, undergo. But for proven qualities, etc., the word is *éprouvé*.
To prove (often) = *prouver*.

errant Normal meaning is wandering. *Elle n'aime pas les chiens errants*: she does not like stray dogs.
Chevalier (m) *errant*: knight-errant.
Errant = *fautif*.

errer To wander. (Occasionally it may mean to err, to be mistaken.) *On a erré dans la forêt*: we wandered in the forest. (Compare to err from the straight and narrow path.)
To err (usually) = *se tromper*.

essai (m) In literature it is an essay, but often means trial, test. *Je vais le prendre à l'essai*: I'm going to take him on trial. *Le banc d'essai*: test bench (also used figuratively).
Can also mean attempt (from *essayer*: to try).
A try at rugby = *il marque un essai*: he scores a try (and not 'he marks an essay'!).
Essay (school) = *composition* (f), *dissertation* (f).

essence (f) Essence. Also petrol. *Je dois m'arrêter pour faire de l'essence*: I must stop to fill up.
Also refers to species of trees. *Dans cette forêt il y a des essences de toutes sortes*: In this forest there are all kinds of trees.

estampe (f) Can be a stamp (implement for stamping metal, etc.), but is usually an engraving. *Vente d'estampes précieuses*: sale of valuable engravings.
Stamp (postage) = *timbre* (*-poste*) (m).
      (rubber) = *tampon* (m).
      (imprint) = *tampon* (m).

estamper To stamp out (metal, leather, etc.).
To stamp (post) = *affranchir*.
      (with a mark) = *timbrer*.
      (feet) = *piétiner, écraser du pied*.

estimer To estimate, value, esteem, also just to think, consider. *Nous estimons que nos clients ont ce droit*: We consider our customers have this right.

étable (f) The original sense of the word has narrowed, and it is now used for cattle – a cowshed.
Stable = *écurie* (f).

étiquette (f) Label, as well as etiquette, manners. *Regardez l'étiquette*: look at the label.

s'évader To escape. *Il s'est évadé en vain*: he escaped in vain.
To evade = *éviter*.

évaporé Evaporated, but (of people) it means frivolous, scatter-brained.

évasion (f) Escape, sometimes avoidance, evasion. *Tous les prisonniers pensaient à la possibilité d'évasion*: all the prisoners were thinking of the possibility of escape. *Vacances d'évasion au soleil*: Away-from-it-all holidays in the sun.
Evasion (avoidance) = *évitement* (m) (rare).
      (excuse) = *échappatoire* (f).

éventuel Possible. *L'hélicoptère cherche d'éventuels survivants*: The helicopter is looking for possible survivors. *Une guerre éventuelle*: a possible war.
Very occasionally does mean 'eventual'.
The Air France brochure brings out the French meaning well – they refer to the paper bag *pour l'éventuel mal de l'air*: for possible air-sickness. To understand it as 'eventual' would be very depressing!
Eventual (usually) = *final*.

éventuellement Nearly always means possibly, should the occasion arise. *Après le match, il y aura un cocktail et éventuellement un dîner*: after the match there will be a cocktail party and possibly a dinner.
Eventually = *finalement, à la longue*.

évidemment Evidently, obviously, of course. If 'evidently' in English really means 'it appears', then '*il paraît que*' or something similar is required.

évidence (f) Evidence, fact(s). *C'est une évidence*: it is an obvious fact. *Se rendre à l'évidence*: to face the facts. *La police ne peut pas nier l'évidence*: the police cannot deny the facts.
Evidence (legal) = *preuve* (f), *témoignage* (m).

évincer To evict, get rid of someone. *Il a réussi à évincer son collègue désagréable*: he was able to push out his unpleasant colleague.
To evince = *révéler*.

exact Exact, also punctual. *Tâchez d'être exact*: try to be punctual.
Also correct, right. *C'est exact*: that's right.

exalté Excited, uplifted. *Un exalté*: a fanatic. *La foule s'approche pour écouter cet exalté*: the crowd approaches to listen to this fanatic.
An exalted person (VIP) = *haut personnage* (m).

exalter To exalt, praise, but also means to excite, rouse.
S'exalter: to be fired with enthusiasm.

excéder To exceed, also to tire out, upset. *Excédé de fatigue, il monte dans sa chambre*: worn out, he goes up to his room.

excentrique Eccentric, odd, but the literal meaning is used more in French than in English, thus *quartiers excentriques*: outlying districts (away from the centre).

exclusif Exclusive, one and only. *C'est une marque exclusive*: this is the only brand.
Exclusive (select) = *très select*.

excursionniste (m) Tripper, but may refer specifically to a hiker.

excuse (f) Excuse, but also (in the plural) apology. *Mille excuses!*: a thousand apologies. *Il ne peut pas venir, et il m'a fait ses excuses*: he cannot come, and he has made his apologies.

s'excuser Can mean to make an excuse or make something an excuse, but usually means to apologize. *Je m'excuse*: I am sorry.
May I be excused? (school) = *Puis-je sortir?*

s'exécuter To comply with an unpleasant request, carry something out. '*Bac-Lan ne bougeait pas: il écoutait le bruit de la pluie sur la bâche. Sellier lui enjoignit de descendre à son tour et de dégager les roues à la pelle. Il s'exécuta sans enthousiasme*' (Raymond Jean, 'L'Oeil de verre,' *Nouvelles 10*, Julliard).
To execute oneself (to commit suicide) = *se donner la mort, se suicider*.

exemple (m) Example (note the French spelling).

Prêcher d'exemple: to practise what one preaches.
Par exemple: for example.
But *Par exemple!*: Well I never! *Par exemple! Je ne m'attendais pas à te voir là!*: Well I never! I didn't expect to see you here.

exercice (m) Exercise in various senses.
Also a financial term for a period of figures (such as a balance-sheet for a year or month).
En exercice: in office. *Pour le capitaine en exercice, c'est toujours un problème*: for the captain in office, it is always a problem.

exhaustion (f) Exhaustion (of gas, etc. Compare exhaust pipe).
Exhaustion (tiredness) = *épuisement* (m).

exhibition (f) Usually means showing in the sense of production (for example of documents) or making visible. *Je n'aime pas cette exhibition de leur richesse*: I don't like them showing their wealth like that.
Exhibition = *exposition* (f).

exhilarant The French word has a specific and limited meaning. *Gaz exhilarant*: laughing-gas (perhaps more frequently called *gaz hilarant*).
Exhilarating = *émoustillant*.

exonérer Not normally to exonerate, but rather to exempt. *Heureusement je suis exonéré de cet impôt*: fortunately I am exempt from this tax.
To exonerate (someone) = *disculper*.

expédier To expedite, hurry, also to send, post. *L'employé m'a conseillé d'expédier le colis deux semaines avant Noël*: the official advised me to post off the parcel two weeks before Christmas.
With reference to people, means to dispatch, send (out of the way).

expédition (f) Expedition. *Ils partent demain pour trois mois dans la jungle. Ce sera une expédition importante*: they leave tomorrow for three months in the jungle. It will be an important expedition.
Another common meaning is that of sending, dispatching. Shops (which have nothing to do with travel!) may advertise *Expéditions pour tous les pays*: Goods dispatched anywhere.
Can also mean expedition, in the sense of dealing with business.

expérience (f) Experience, but also experiment. *Il en a fait l'expérience*: he has experienced it. *Il a fait une expérience*: he has carried out an experiment.

expérimenter To experiment in various senses, to try out, test.
But note *expérimenté*: experienced.

expert (m) Although the adjective means expert, skilled, the noun usually has the more precise meaning of a valuer. *Il a fait venir un expert*: he got a valuer to come.
But can mean an expert. Note *expert-comptable* (m): chartered accountant.
Expert (sometimes) = *spécialiste* (m).

expertise (f) Expert opinion, valuation. *Expertise gratuite*: free valuation.
Expertise (often) = *grande habilité* (f).

explétif (m) Expletive, that is to say a redundant word to fill out a sentence (such as *ne* in *avant qu'il ne réponde*).
Expletive (swear-word) = *juron* (m).

exploit (m) Exploit, also a legal term for writ, summons.

exploitation (f) Exploitation (working), and unfair exploitation. English has these two senses, but, for the former, other words are often more suitable, e.g. working, development, mining.
L'exploitation des touristes: exploitation of tourists; *l'exploitation touristique*: tourist development.

exposer To expose, but frequently to show, exhibit, reveal. *Ses tableaux seront exposés dans trois semaines*: his pictures will be exhibited in three weeks.

exposition (f) Can be exposition (of ideas, etc.) but commonly refers to a show, exhibition. *Exposition canine*: dog show.
Also means exposure (danger, sun, photography).
Of a house, it means aspect, so that a well-placed house may be advertised as *toutes expositions*.

express (m) Fast train rather than express.
Also means an espresso (coffee). *Deux express! cria le garçon*: two expressos! the waiter shouted.
Express (train) = *rapide* (m).

extensif Has specialized meanings. Tensile; or extended with reference to sense or meaning of words; or with reference to agriculture, where extensive means getting a low return from a wide area worked cheaply (as opposed to 'intensive').
Extensive (usually) = *étendu*.

exténuant Exhausting.
Extenuating = *atténuant*.

exténuer Now usually means to exhaust. *'Les hommes ne regardaient rien, exténués, dormant à moitié'* (Roland Dorgelès, *Les Croix de bois*, Albin Michel).
To extenuate = *atténuer*.

extra Not just extra, but extra special. *Vins extra*: especially good wines.
Extra = *en supplément, supplémentaire*.

extra (m) *Faire un peu d'extra*: to splash out, to have a bit of a treat.
Extra can also mean an extra help (servant, waiter, etc.).
Extra (menu, travel) = *supplément* (m).
    (actor) = *figurant(e)* (m/f)
extras (expenses) = *faux frais* (m).

extrait (m) Extract, but *un extrait de naissance* is a birth certificate.

extravagance (f) Wildness, going too far. *Elle fait des extravagances*: she does absurd things.
Extravagance = *folles dépenses* (f).

extravagant (m) An eccentric person.
Extravagant person = *dépensier* (m).

extravagant Extravagant in the less common English sense of wild, immoderate, far-fetched. *Elle portait un chapeau extravagant*: she was wearing an incredible hat. *Il a des idées extravagantes*: he has wild ideas.
Extravagant (with money) = *dépensier, faire des folies* (f).

fabrique (f) Factory, or sometimes manufacture. *J'ai beaucoup admiré la fabrique*: I much admired the factory.
Fabric (material) = *étoffe* (f).

facétieux Facetious, but sometimes simply humorous, mischievous, funny.
To be facetious = *faire le bouffon*.

facile Easy, fluent, sometimes facile.
But facile is often pejorative in English with the sense of *superficiel*.

facteur (m) Postman.
Also organ- or piano-maker (*un facteur de pianos*).
Also factor, element.

faction (f) Faction, or being on guard (as of a sentry). *Il y a toujours un homme de faction à chaque porte*: there is always a man on guard at each door.

factorerie (f) Trading station (abroad). *Nous sommes arrivés à la factorerie de bonne heure*: we arrived at the trading station early.
Factory = *fabrique* (f), *usine* (f).

fade Insipid, lacking taste or colour, dull.
Une couleur fade: a dull colour.
Faded = *passé, décoloré, fané*.

fagot (m) Faggot, firewood, but the edible faggot is *crépinette* (f).
Note *une bouteille de derrière les fagots* for a specially good bottle of wine.

faillir To fail in something (*faillir à sa promesse*: not to keep one's promise).
But commonly used in expressions such as *il a failli tomber*: he all but fell.
To fail = *manquer*.
(exam) = *échouer* (*à un examen*).

fameux Famous, celebrated. But also, in a slightly familiar style, used to mean marvellous, very good. *Il est fameux, ton cognac!*: First class, your brandy!
Or it can mean downright, real, proper. *C'est un fameux voyage, ça!*: that's quite a trip!

familial Of the family. But *notre Ford familiale*: our Ford estate car (= *la familiale*).

familier Familiar.
Un animal familier: pet. *On voit plus d'animaux familiers en Angleterre qu'en France*: you see more pets in England than in France.

fanfare (f) Fanfare, flourish, but in addition the (brass) band. *Voici la fanfare du village*: here is the village band.

fantaisie (f) Fantasy, imagination, or fancy, inclination.
And goods which are *de fantaisie* are fancy goods.
Fantasy (sometimes) = *vision* (f) *étrange*.

fantasque Whimsical, capricious, temperamental.
Fantastic = *fantastique* (or colloquially *formidable*).

farce (f) Farce, also practical joke.
But in cooking it means stuffing.

fart (m) Wax (for skis). Its impolite English homonym is *pet* (m).

farter To wax (skis). A perfectly proper word! Unlike the English verb suggested which is the equivalent of *péter*.

fascinant Fascinating, but perhaps more common words to translate the English are *passionnant, séduisant, attrayant, absorbant*.

fascination (f) Fascination in the sense of being spellbound, as well as fascination in the sense of charm, interest.

fasciner The French word can still have the basic idea of hypnotize (as of a snake, *qui fascine sa victime*).
Otherwise it means to fascinate, charm, captivate.

faste (m) Show, display. *C'était une petite cérémonie sans faste*: it was a quiet little ceremony.
Fast (fasting) = *jeûne* (m).

faste Lucky, favourable. *Le vendredi est un jour faste pour moi*: Friday is a lucky day for me.
Fast (day) = *jour* (m) *maigre*.

fastidieux Dull, tiresome, irksome. *Il corrige son manuscrit – c'est un travail fastidieux*: he corrects his manuscript; it is a tedious task.
Une corvée fastidieuse: a chore.
Fastidious = *difficile*.

fat Conceited, pretentious, complacent. *Ce n'est pas mon oncle préféré, il est un peu fat*: he is not my favourite uncle; he is a bit conceited.
Fat = *gros, gras*.

fatal Sometimes means fatal (*un accident fatal*: a fatal accident), but care is needed as it frequently has the sense of inevitable (derived from the Latin for fate). *Il a perdu son argent – c'était fatal*: he lost his money – it was bound to happen. *C'est fatal qu'il y ait quelques ennuis*: inevitably there are some little problems.
Fatal (often) = *mortel*.

fatalement Inevitably. *Fatalement, ma belle-mère était là aussi*: inevitably, my

mother-in-law was there as well.
Fatally = *mortellement*.

fatalité (f) Inevitability, fate, bad luck. *Les accidents ne sont pas une fatalité*: accidents can be avoided.
Fatality (often) = *mort* (f).

fatiguer To tire. But you may come across the picturesque *fatiguer la salade*: to mix the salad.

fatuité (f) Self-satisfaction, smugness, being pleased with oneself. *'Je fermai la porte non sans avoir adressé à Mme. Marlotte et à sa bonne un sourire qu'il me fut difficile d'écheniller de toute fatuité'* (Paul Guth, *Le Naïf aux quarante enfants*, Albin Michel).
Fatuity (fatuousness) = *idiotie* (f).

faveur (f) Favour, but note such expressions as *à la faveur de la nuit*: under cover of darkness.

favori (m) Favourite, and (in the plural) sidewhiskers. *Dans le coin quelques hommes avec des favoris*: in the corner some men with sidewhiskers.

félon (m) Felon, traitor, somebody who is disloyal to a friend or superior. (Originally used of a vassal in feudal times.)
Felon = *criminel* (m).

félonie (f) Treachery (originally used of vassals and feudal law).
Felony = *crime* (m).

ferret (m) A (metal) tag (e.g. of laces). *Il se baissa pour examiner le ferret*: he bent down to examine the tag.
Ferret = *furet* (m).

ferry (m) Abbreviation of *le ferry-boat*. (Cross-Channel) ferry (able to transport cars, etc.).
Ferry (small) = *bac* (m).

férule (f) Cane (school).
Etre sous la férule de quelqu'un: to be under someone's (strict) rule.
Ferrule (of a stick) = *embout* (m).

fervent Fervent, but *un fervent* is much used for an enthusiast. *Les fervents du foot*: soccer fans.

fête (f) We use the word in a specific sense. In French it has a wider meaning: feast or festival or even holiday(s). *J'aime bien Noël chez moi, mais cette année nous allons passer la période des fêtes dans un chalet*: I love Christmas at home, but this year we are going to spend the holiday period in a chalet. Can also refer to someone's birthday (*Je vous souhaite une bonne fête*: Many happy returns).
(In a general way) display, fair, entertainment, show.

fétiche (m) Fetish, object of worship, mascot.

fièvre (f) Fever, but sometimes just having a temperature (*avoir de la fièvre*). Can mean fever, excitement.

figuratif Normally used with reference to art (representational).
Figurative (sense) = *figuré*.

figure 76

figure (f) Sometimes figure, but often means face. *Une figure à la fenêtre*: a face at the window.
    Figure (often) = *forme* (f), *silhouette* (f).
        (number) = *chiffre* (m).
        (slimming) = *ligne* (f).

file (f) A file or row. *En file indienne*: in Indian file. *Stationner en double file*: to double park.
    Chef (m) *de file*: leader.
    File (papers) = *classeur* (m), *dossier* (m).
        (metal) = *lime* (f).

filer Not to file papers or metal but has a number of meanings which include to spin (e.g. wool), to shadow (detectives), to go along at speed, to be off. *Il faut que je file*: I must be off.
    To file (papers) = *classer*.
        (metal) = *limer*.

filet (m) Fillet (food) is one of various meanings.
    Net (in general) (*filet à provisions*: string shopping-bag), also (railway carriage) luggage-rack (though metal has replaced the net).
    Can mean a trickle, a small amount.

filtre (m) Filter, also filter coffee (i.e. *un café filtre*).

fin (f) Not fin but finish, end.
    Less obvious expressions are *avoir des fins de mois difficiles*: to be (financially) rather hard pressed (at the end of the month) and *faire une fin*: to settle down. *Il faut faire une fin maintenant*: you must settle down now, *il faut y mettre fin maintenant*: you must put an end to it now.
    Fin (of fish) = *nageoire* (f).

fin Fine, delicate, clever.
    But *une perle fine*: a real pearl.
    Fine often = *beau, parfait*.

fine (f) Liqueur brandy. *J'ai payé une fine*: I paid for a liqueur brandy.
    Fine = *amende* (f).

finish (m) Finish (a sporting term. It is noticeable that a number of English – or pseudo-English – words appear in sport). *Un coureur sans finish*: a runner who fades at the end, who has a poor finish.
    Finish (end) = *fin* (f).
        (finishing touch) = *finition* (f).

five o'clock (m) Afternoon tea. Four o'clock would be more accurate, but the expression is anyhow dated and it may mean that one will no longer be able to enjoy the unintended humour of such phrases as *'le five o'clock à toutes heures'*.
    Five o'clock = *cinq heures*.

fixation (f) Fixation.
    Also fixing, deciding on (e.g. a date).
    There is also the sense of fastening, attachment (as for skis) – *fixations de sécurité*: safety bindings.

fixe (m) Fixed salary. *Je ne peux rien faire avant de toucher mon fixe à la fin du mois*: I cannot do anything until I draw my salary at the end of the month.
To be in a fix = *être coincé, être dans la purée* (among many expressions).
(In popular usage *un fixe* can mean a fix (drugs).)

fixé Fixed. *Je ne suis pas fixé*: I have nothing settled, I can't make up my mind.
Etre fixé means you know the position, you know what's what.
To be in a fix = *être dans l'embarras*.

fixer To fix (firmly).
Also to stare at someone. *Il m'a fixé pendant quelques moments*: he stared at me for some moments.
Can also mean to fix, appoint, settle. *Se fixer*: to settle (in a place).
To fix (sometimes) = *arranger, se décider pour quelque chose*.

flacon (m) *Flacon* and flagon are from (late) Latin *flasco*, but it is interesting to note that the French word is used for a small bottle (e.g. for scent), while the English refers to a large bottle – *une grande bouteille* (though English 'flask' may also come from *flasco*).

flair (m) Sense of smell. *Le flair du limier*: the bloodhound's sense of smell.
Figuratively the idea of to 'nose out' (*flairer*) gives the meaning of flair, intuition, perspicacity. *Le flair d'un bon détective*: the intuition of a good detective.
But English flair has also a wider meaning of aptitude, talent (*aptitude* (f)), etc.

flamme (f) Flame. In classical language it is love.
Can also mean passion, intensity of feeling. *'C'est beau, à cette heure-ci, dit-elle, en désignant Cransac au-dessus d'eux. – Oui, dit-il sans flamme'* (Colette, *Duo*, Ferenczi).

flan (m) Custard tart or baked custard.
Used familiarly, *J'en suis resté comme deux ronds de flan*, for which the English could be the equally picturesque, 'You could have knocked me down with a feather.'
Flan = *tarte* (f).

flanelle (f) Flannel (material).
The English face-flannel = *un gant de toilette*.
In its colloquial sense = *bla-bla* (m).

flash (m) Flashlight (photography). *J'ai peur des flashes des photographes*: I am afraid of the photographers' flashlights.
Also a news-flash. *Les flashes des radios*: radio news-flashes.
Flash (often) = *éclair* (m).
In a flash = *en un clin d'oeil*.

flatter To flatter or to please, gratify.
Also to pat, stroke. *Je flatte le chien – comme ça, nous sommes des amis*: I stroke the dog – in that way we are friends.

flic (m) A popular word for policeman, cop.
Flick (of the fingers) = *chiquenaude* (f), (often also) *petit coup* (m).
To go to the flicks = *aller au ciné*.

flinguer Slangy word for to kill, shoot.
To fling = *jeter, lancer, balancer*.

flipper (m) Pin-ball table. *On va jouer aux flippers?*: Shall we have a game of pin-ball?
Flipper (of a seal) = *nageoire* (f).
    (for swimming) = *palme* (f).

flirt (m) An interesting . . . English word. It may, though, come from the French, because *conter fleurette* (to say sweet nothings) may have given us 'to flirt', which then has gone back to French as *flirter*!
The French noun, though, has two meanings, flirtation, and boy or girl friend.
Flirt = *flirteur* (m), *flirteuse* (f), *coquette* (f).

flûte (f) Flute.
Also long thin loaf, champagne glass. *Jouer de la flûte*: to play the flute.
Jouer des flûtes: to beat it, hop it (popular usage).

folie (f) Madness or folly. There is also the idea of wildness and extravagance. *Deux bouteilles de champagne! Mais vous faites des folies!*: Two bottles of champagne! You are being extravagant!

folk (m) Popular abbreviation of *le folksong*.
Folk (often) = *gens* (m).

folksong (m) Folk music. *Tu aimes le folksong?*: Do you like folk music?
Folksong = *chanson* (f) *folk(lorique)*.

fonder To lay the basis for something. Also to found (prize, etc.).
To founder (plans, etc.) = *échouer*.
    (ship) = *sombrer*.

fondre Not to founder, but to melt, and sometimes to swoop on (*fondre sur*).
To founder (ship) = *sombrer*.

fontaine (f) Not always fountain, sometimes spring or source.

fonte (f) Melting (from *fondre*), and used for various technical expressions such as *fonte de fer*: cast iron.
Also means a saddle holster (on each side of the pommel for pistols).
Font = *fonts* (m) (*baptismaux*).

foot (m) Soccer. Familiar abbreviation of *le football. Le mot important chez nous, c'est le foot*: the important word in our house is football.
Foot = *pied* (m).

footing (m) Jogging, walking. *Un peu de footing le matin, ça fait du bien*: a bit of jogging in the morning does you good. Some French people are beginning to reject the misused English word and to use *le jogging* instead!
To lose one's footing = *perdre pied*.

forcer To force, but sometimes with a less strong sense. *Sa conduite a forcé l'estime de tout le monde ici*: his conduct commanded (compelled) the respect of everyone here.

forcing (m) Pressure (a sporting term). *Il a commencé à faire du forcing*: he began to put on the pressure, to pile it on.
Forcing = *persuasion* (f).

foret (m) Drill (for wood, metal, etc.).
    Forest = *forêt* (f).

forfait (m) A word with various meanings; can refer to a contract for work.
    Un prix à forfait is a lump sum, hence it is used for package holidays. *Visitez Paris! Notre forfait de trois jours*: Visit Paris! Our three-day package.
    Also the fine (or forfeit) payable if a racehorse scratches, and in sport in general *déclarer forfait* means to scratch. *Dommage que ces deux bons tennismen aient déclaré forfait*: a pity that these two good tennis-players have scratched.
    Forfait is also crime, outrage, misdeed. *'Alors, mon Père, je ne sais plus rien des suites de l'horrible forfait . . .'* (Gabriel Chevalier, *Saint Colline*, Le Quadrige d'Apollon).
    Forfeit (sometimes) = *amende* (f).
            (in games) = *gage* (f).

forfaiture (f) Maladministration by an official.
    Also breach (of faith, etc.).
    Forfeiture (often) = *perte* (f), *retrait* (m).

forger The first meaning is to forge (as the blacksmith does), which explains *fer forgé*: wrought iron; *'C'est en forgeant qu'on devient forgeron'* is the equivalent of 'Practice makes perfect.'
    Can also mean to make up, fabricate or to coin (a word).
    To forge (money) = *contrefaire*.

forgeur (m) Someone who invents, fabricates or coins something or (in a literal sense) the blacksmith's assistant.
    Forger (money) = *faux-monnayeur* (m).

se formaliser To take offence. *Il s'est formalisé de ce refus*: He took offence at this refusal.
    Formal (person) = *compassé*.

formation (f) Formation. Also training, schooling. *Quelles sont les possibilités pour les jeunes sans aucune formation?*: What are the possibilities for young people without any training at all?

forme (f) The meanings include form (*en forme*: in form), shape, figure.
    Also manners. *Observer les formes*: to observe the conventions.
    But form at school is *classe* (f), or it may also be *banc* (m).
    A form to fill in is *formulaire* (m).
    It is bad form = *c'est de mauvais ton*.

formel Formal, perfunctory or (more commonly) formal, categorical. *La consigne est formelle*: orders are orders. *Le président fut formel*: the president was categorical.
    Formal = *cérémonieux*.

formellement Categorically. *Il m'a dit formellement de rester chez moi*: he told me expressly to stay at home.
    Formally = *cérémonieusement*.

former To form, make, fashion. Note too the sense of to train, bring up, school.

formidable Formidable, but even more common as a popular expression – *C'est formidable!*: it's super!

formulaire (m) Normally means a form to fill in. *Il y a un tas de formulaires sur mon bureau*: there is a stack of forms on my desk.
Formula = *formule* (f).

formule (f) Formula, also a form to fill in. *Demandez la formule*: Ask for the form.
Also standard expression, use of words.
And can mean formula in a non-technical sense. *Nous recommendons notre formule 'tout compris'*: we recommend our 'all in' formula (or 'package').

fort (m) A fort or stronghold.
Based on the idea of 'strong', it has other meanings. *Au fort de l'hiver*: in the depths of winter (and similar expressions). *Ce n'est pas mon fort*: it is not my strong point.
Also means a strong person in various senses. *Un fort (des Halles)*: a market porter.

fortune (f) As in English, can mean fortune, chance (by good fortune), as well as fortune, wealth.
Care is needed sometimes to see with which meaning it is connected, as in the expression *de fortune*, which usually means makeshift. *Il faut trouver des moyens de fortune*: makeshift means must be found. *Une table de fortune*: a makeshift table.
Être en quête de bonnes fortunes is a familiar expression for trying to find and hit it off with a girl.
Fortune-telling = *bonne aventure* (f).

fortuné Usually means well off. *C'est un hôtel de luxe que fréquentent les gens fortunés*: it is a luxury hotel frequented by rich people. *Les étudiants moins fortunés restent chez eux*: the less well off students live at home.
Fortunate = *heureux (avoir de la chance)*.

fou (m) Madman. *Les fous du volant*: crazy drivers.
But in chess it means a bishop.
Also a (court) jester. *Le fou s'incline devant le roi*: the jester bows before the king.
Fool = *idiot* (m).

fou (fol) (folle (f)**)** Foolish may fit the sense, but it nearly always means mad. Schoolboys often cry to each other – *T'es fou, toi!*: You're mad!
Can have the idea of wild, out of control, as in *camion fou*: runaway lorry; in familiar language it is a common reinforcement. Thus *un monde fou*: an enormous crowd. *Un prix fou*: an exorbitant price.
Foolish = *bête, stupide*.

four (m) Has nothing to do with English numeral four (= *quatre*), but comes from Latin *furnus*, an oven.

Note two familiar expressions – *il fait noir comme dans un four*: it is pitch black, and *faire un four*: to be a flop.

fournisseur (m) Supplier of goods in a general sense. Tradesman. *C'est embêtant quand les fournisseurs vous font faux bond*: it is annoying when tradespeople let you down.
Furnishers (usually) = *marchand* (m) *d'ameublement*.

fournitures (f) Supplies, equipment, goods. *Chez qui faut-il aller pour les fournitures de bureau?*: Whom should we go to for office equipment? In other words, it means 'furnishing' in the general sense of supplying.
Furniture = *meubles* (m).
Furnishings = *ameublement* (m).

fourrier (m) Quarter-master sergeant.
Furrier = *fourreur* (m).

fox (m) Fox-terrier (common abbreviation of *le fox-terrier*). *Une vieille dame accompagnée de son fox*: an old lady with her fox-terrier.
Can also be the abbreviation for *le foxtrot* (dance).
Fox = *renard* (m).

foyer (m) In addition to foyer of a theatre, its chief meaning is home, or hearth. *Par un tel temps il est agréable de rester près du foyer*: in such weather it is pleasant to stay by the fire.
Can also mean a club or centre, and the centre of an outbreak.
Note *verres* (m) *à double foyer*: bifocals (here *foyer* means focus).

fracture (f) Fracture (of bones), but also means breaking open (as of a lock).

fracturer To fracture, as well as to break, force (a lock, etc.). *La porte a été fracturée*: the door has been forced open.

frais (fraîche) Fresh. Also cool. *Il fait frais*: it is cool.
Clear (of voices).

franchise (f) Franchise, immunity, freedom. *En franchise*: duty (tax) free.
Also means frankness. *Il faut parler avec franchise*: I must be frank.
As an insurance term (and quite often seen in advertisements) it means excess payment.
Franchise (electoral) = *droit* (m) *de vote*.
              (business) = *permis* (m).

fréquenter To frequent (places), see (of people), keep company.
But *fréquenter une jeune fille* is a little more precise – to go out (regularly) with, to date, a girl.

fret (m) Freight, not fret. Chartering.
Fret = *irritation* (f), *souci* (m).
       (guitar) = *touchette* (f).

fréter To freight out, hire out (a ship). Also to hire for your own use – *Notre école a frété deux cars*: our school chartered two coaches.
To fret = *se tracasser, se faire des cheveux* (popular), among many expressions.

friction (f) Can mean friction (between people), but more frequently has the original meaning of friction – rubbing, massage. *Une bonne friction!*: a good rub!

frisquet Chilly. *Il fait frisquet. Le chien commence à gambader*: There's a nip in the air. The dog begins to frisk about.
Frisky = *folâtre*.

froc (m) Frock, gown, cowl (monk).
A woman's frock (the words have the same derivation) = *robe* (f).

front (m) Front in various senses, but (of people) it means forehead. *Il s'essuie le front*: he mops his brow.
Il a le front de . . .: he has the cheek to . . .
Front seats (car) = *avant* (m).

frustrer To frustrate, but also to deprive, to do someone out of something.
On m'en a frustré: I was deprived of it.

fuel (m) Fuel oil (= *le fuel-oil*).
Fuel in English is more general – i.e. *combustible* (m), *bois* (m) *de chauffage*, *charbon* (m).

fugue (f) Fugue, but *il a fait une fugue à Monte Carlo* has nothing to do with music. It means an escapade – he has slipped off to Monte Carlo.

fumée (f) Smoke. Sometimes it means fumes, but these often = *les vapeurs* (f).

fumer To smoke is the usual meaning, although (familiarly) it can mean to fume, be very angry.
It is also to manure with dung.

fumet (m) A nice smell of cooking, or the 'bouquet' of wine. *'Ah! dis donc! quel est ce fumet?' dit-il en entrant dans la cuisine*: 'Mm! I say! What is this nice smell?' he said on going into the kitchen.
Fumes = *vapeurs* (f).

fuser To spread, run (light, colour) or to sound forth (laughter, etc.).
To fuse (electricity) = *sauter, faire sauter*.

fusion (f) Fusion, melting, but note the contemporary business sense of merger (between firms).

futile Pointless, trivial. *Un prétexte futile*: a trivial excuse. *Une ambiance futile*: trivial surroundings, a trivial atmosphere.
Futile (vain) = *vain*.
(silly) = *bête*.

futilité (f) Futility, pointlessness; also trifle, trivial thing, triviality. *'Elle disait des futilités avec des mots drôles, des intonations gamines'* (Marcel Aymé, *Aller retour*, Gallimard).
Futility (also) = *impuissance* (f), *inutilité* (f).

futur (m) Future, also (familiarly) husband-to-be.
Future (also often) = *avenir* (m).
In the future = *à l'avenir*.

G

gaffe (f) Gaff (fishing), or boathook. We sometimes use the word as in familiar French to mean a blunder (*faire une gaffe*: to put one's foot in it). But *faire gaffe* (popular usage) is different and means to watch out, take care.
Alors, fais gaffe!: So, watch it!

gaffeur (m) **gaffeuse** (f) Blundering fool (who puts his foot in it) (familiar). Gaffer = *vieux bonhomme, patron* (m), *bourgeois* (m).

gag (m) Used in the actors' sense. *Un film policier plein de gags*: a comedy thriller.
Gag (in mouth) = *bâillon* (m).

gainer To sheathe, cover, as in *gainé matière plastique*: plastic covered.
To gain = *gagner*.

galant It is a question of stress in English (and note spelling). Gallant (gallànt) is used as in French to suggest some sort of ladies' man, or noble, gentlemanly behaviour.
But gàllant (first syllable stressed) = *courageux, vaillant*.

gale (f) Scabies. Itch. Mange.
Gale = *grand vent* (m).

galerie (f) Gallery. Another useful meaning is roof-rack of a car. *Une valise est tombée de la galerie de la voiture devant nous*: a case fell off the roof-rack of the car in front of us.
Also circle (theatre).

galle (f) Gall (in the sense of a growth on a plant, from the Latin *galla*, oak-apple).
But the English term 'gall' also often = *fiel* (m).
He has the gall to = *il a le front de* . . .
Gall-bladder = *vésicule* (f) *biliaire*.
Gall-stone = *calcul* (m) *biliaire*.

galoche (f) Kind of clog, with wooden sole and leather uppers. *Il a chaussé ses galoches*: he put on his clogs. '*Elle avait aux pieds de grosses galoches de bois et, le long des hanches, un grand tablier bleu*' (Gustave Flaubert, *Madame Bovary*).
Galoshes = *caoutchoucs* (m).

galon (m) Braid or stripes (to denote rank). *Il avait deux galons à l'épaule*: he had two stripes on his shoulder.
Gallon = *gallon* (m).

garage (m) Garage, also used more generally, so could be a bus depot or aircraft hangar. Note *une voie de garage* is a railway siding. '*L'adresse qu'elle avait donnée était celle d'un hôtel près d'une grande gare. Le monde disparut pour*

l'homme autour de ce bloc de pierre d'aspect anodin, au pied duquel s'étalait le tissage compliqué des voies de garage' (Gisèle Prassinos, *Le Cavalier* (nouvelles), Plon).
Mettre sur une voie de garage is used figuratively with the meaning of to put on one side.

garantir To guarantee, but care is needed as it also means almost the opposite – to protect, shelter. *Ce chapeau de paille va me garantir du soleil*: this straw hat is going to keep the sun off me.

garde-corps (m) Parapet, balustrade, hand-rail. *Il s'approche du garde-corps*: he approaches the railing.
Body-guard = *garde du corps* (m), *gorille* (m).

garde-côte (m) No longer refers to the person, but means coastguard ship.
Coast-guard = *garde* (m) *maritime*.

garder To guard, but often to keep.
To guard (also) = *surveiller, veiller sur, protéger*.

gardian (m) A cowherd in the Camargue (the Rhône delta region).
Guardian (attendant) = *gardien* (m).

gardien (m) **gardienne** (f) Guardian, keeper, attendant. *Le gardien s'arrête pour parler à l'enfant*: the attendant stops to talk to the child. *Gardien de la paix*: policeman (who keeps the peace). *Gardien de but*: goalkeeper.
Guardian (young children) = *tuteur* (m).

gas-oil (m) Diesel oil, as well as gas oil, fuel for domestic heating.

gauche 'Gauche' as we use it – clumsy, awkward. *Un enfant gauche*: a clumsy child.
Also left side (which has given the idea of clumsiness as opposed to being dextrous or right-handed), but a left-handed child = *gaucher* (m), *gauchère* (f).

gaz (m) Gas. Also fizziness (drinks). If you order a mineral water, a waiter may ask '*Avec gaz?*' ('fizzy?').
To step on the gas may be translated by the popular *appuyer sur le champignon*.

gaze (f) Gauze.
Gaze = *regard* (m), *regard fixe*.

gazer To cover with gauze, also to gas.
And the word is used in familiar speech, as in *Ça gaze?*: All going fine?
To gaze = *regarder, contempler*.

gelée (f) Jelly, also frost (*geler*: to freeze).

gemme (f) Gem. Pine-resin. And note *sel* (m) *gemme*: rock salt.

gendre (m) Not gender, but son-in-law (from the Latin *gener*).
Gender =*genre* (m).

générale (f) A little care is needed, or some unlikely translations may result!
La générale is the general's wife (*La générale de Gaulle*).

But *battre la générale* means to sound the alarm.
La générale also means dress rehearsal (standing for *la répétition générale*).

génial Comes from *génie* (genius), so it means brilliant. *Une idée géniale*: a brainwave. *Un professeur génial*: a brilliant professor.
Genial = *bienveillant, jovial.*

génie (m) Genius, spirit.
But *génie de l'air* is actually quite down to earth – aviation engineers. (*Génie* is a general term for engineers, military or civil.)

gentil Nice, kind. *Qu'il est gentil!*: how nice he is!
Gentle = *doux.*
Genteel = *maniéré, distingué.* (The common origin is Latin *gentilis.*)

gentilhomme (m) A man of gentle birth, nobleman, (sometimes) gentleman.
In normal modern usage, gentleman = *monsieur* (m).

gentillesse (f) Kindness, pleasantness. *Elle a eu la gentillesse de me téléphoner*: she was kind enough to telephone me.
Gentleness = *douceur* (f).

gentiment Nicely, kindly. *La serveuse m'a souri gentiment*: the waitress gave me a kind smile.
Gently = *doucement.*

geste (m) Gesture. *Il a fait un geste et tout le monde a ri*: he made a gesture and everybody laughed.
Jest = *plaisanterie* (f).

girl (f) Chorus-girl. *C'est un spectacle avec les plus belles girls de Paris*: it is a show with the most beautiful chorus-girls in Paris. (Because many of them are, or were, English?)
Girl = (*jeune*) *fille* (f).

glacé Glacé (of fruits), but usually ice-cold, iced, frozen.

glacier (m) Glacier; or ice-cream-seller (maker) (and formerly someone who made mirrors).

glaise (f) Clay.
Glaze (sometimes) = *glaçure* (f), *vernis* (m).

glaiser To clay.
To glaze (windows) = *vitrer.*
        (pottery) = *vernir.*
To double glaze = *faire installer du double vitrage.*

gland (m) Acorn. Also tassel (for curtains, etc.).
Gland = *glande* (f).

glas (m) Knell. *Sonner le glas*: to toll the (passing) bell.
Glass = *verre* (m). (Note in popular French *un glasse*: a glass, drink.)

globule (m) Globule. Also the word for (blood) corpuscle.

glorieux Glorious, but in literary style it can mean proud, vain.

In everyday English glorious often = *splendide, magnifique* (weather, holidays, etc.).

glu (f) Not glue, in spite of the sense of sticking, but bird-lime.
Glue = *colle* (f).

goal (m) Typical French abbreviated word, hence the meaning is goalkeeper or goalie. (English usually abbreviates the other way, hence 'keeper.)
Goal = *but* (m).

gobelet (m) (Old) goblet. Also tumbler. Can also refer to a disposable plastic cup. *Jetez le gobelet après*: throw away the cup afterwards.
Goblet (with a foot) = *verre* (m) *à pied, coupe* (f).

goder To ruck, ruck up (material). *Ah! ce pantalon qui gode aux genoux!*: Ah! these trousers that go baggy.
To goad = *aiguillonner, inciter*.

golf (m) Golf, and also the golf-links or course.

Le Golfe de Gascogne The Bay of Biscay.

gomme (f) (Sticky) gum, also an eraser, rubber. *Passez-moi la gomme*: pass me the rubber.
Gum (teeth) = *gencive* (f).

gommer To gum, but also to erase, rub out.

gorge (f) Gorge, but also throat. *J'ai mal à la gorge*: I have a sore throat. *Rire à gorge déployée*: to laugh uproariously.
Faire des gorges chaudes de quelqu'un: to make fun of someone (or something).
Note that *un coupe-gorge* is not a cutthroat but a dangerous place (where a cutthroat = *un coupe-jarret* might lurk).
Cutthroat (razor) = *rasoir* (m) *ordinaire*.

gourmand (m) Gourmand, but also a horticultural word – tentacle, sucker. Speaking of London, Paul Morand in *Londres* writes: '*Ce n'est pas une plante grimpante, c'est un fraisier qui étend à l'infini ses gourmands*' (Plon).

gousse (f) Pod. *Gousse d'ail*: clove of garlic.
Goose = *oie* (f).

goutte (f) May be gout, but usually a drop (rain, drink, etc.). *Encore une goutte?*: Have another drop?
Note the colloquialisms *c'est une goutte d'eau dans la mer*: it is a drop in the ocean, and *ils se ressemblent comme deux gouttes d'eau*: they are as like as two peas.
La goutte d'eau qui fait déborder le vase = the last straw that breaks the camel's back.

gouttière (f) Gutter (on the roof).
Gutter in the road = *ruisseau* (m).

gouvernante (f) Can mean governess, but also housekeeper, as here: '*A mon retour au logis, ce sont les cris de ma gouvernante, qui m'accuse de crever mes* *poches et d'emplir la maison de vieux papiers qui attirent les rats'* (Anatole France, *Le Crime de Sylvestre Bonnard*, Calmann-Lévy).

gráce (f) Grace, elegance. Favour. Mercy. *De grâce!*: I beseech you! For mercy's sake! *Le coup de grâce*: the final stroke, the finishing blow. *Grâce à . . .*: thanks to . . .
Grace (meals) = *bénédicité* (m).

gracieusement Charmingly, graciously (perhaps gracefully).
But more often used to mean free of charge. *Ce petit porte-clefs est offert gracieusement*: this little key-ring is given free.

grain (m) Grain, corn, also grain (as of leather). Grain (of sand). *Grain de café*: coffee bean. *Grain de beauté*: mole.
A very different meaning is that of a sudden sharp shower, squall, gust of wind. Hence the expression *veiller au grain*: to keep a look out for squalls (or trouble).

graine (f) Seed (plants).
Familiar expressions include *en prendre de la graine*: to follow the example, to follow suit. *Être de la mauvaise graine*: to be a bad lot.
Grain = *grain* (m).

graisse (f) Grease, or fat.

grand Tall, big, large (but note *il ouvre de grands yeux*: he opens his eyes wide). *Un homme grand*: a tall man, *un grand homme*: a great man.
Occasionally means 'grand' (*Le Grand Hôtel*: Grand Hotel), but 'it's a grand hotel': *c'est un hôtel imposant* or *formidable*, according to sense.
Grand piano: *piano* (m) *à queue*.

grange (f) Barn. (Grange in English used to have this sense.) *Il a dû se coucher dans la grange*: he had to sleep in the barn.
Grange = *manoir* (m) (*avec ferme*).

grappe (f) Bunch. *Une grappe de raisin*: a bunch of grapes.
Can also refer to a knot, bunch, small group of people.
Grape = *raisin* (m).

gratification (f) Sometimes means gratification, but is usually a gratuity or bonus. *Et à Noël on peut compter en plus sur une gratification*: and at Christmas one can count in addition on a bonus.
Gratification (usually) = *satisfaction* (f).

gratifier To gratify (psychological term), but usually to present (generously). *On a gratifié le directeur d'un fauteuil tournant*: the headmaster was presented with a swivel chair.
Also used ironically.
To gratify (usually) = *satisfaire*.

gratuité (f) Usually refers to something being free. *La gratuité de ce petit service est quelque chose qu'on n'apprécie pas assez*: the fact that this little service is given free is not sufficiently appreciated.

Gratuity (tip) = *pourboire* (m).

grave Grave, serious.
But *une voix grave* is a deep voice.
The *Nouveau Petit Larousse* defines *alto* (its first meaning) as '*nom de la plus grave des voix de femme*'.

grenade (f) Has two very different meanings. A pomegranate, or a grenade.
Grenade sous-marine: depth-charge.
And *Grenade* is Granada.

grenadier (m) A grenadier, or a pomegranate tree.

grief (m) Grievance, grudge. *Il m'en fait grief*: he reproaches me for it. *Des griefs exagérés*: exaggerated grievances.
Grief = *chagrin* (m).

griffon (m) Griffin, as well as griffon (dog).

grill (m) Grill (room) (abbreviation of *le grill-room*). *Un hôtel de luxe avec restaurant et grill*: a luxury hotel with restaurant and grill (room). *Un grill cossu*: a plushy grill-room.
Grill (for cooking) = *gril* (m).

griller To grill, but also to toast (*pain grillé*: toast).
Note the familiar meaning of 'missing out' – *il a grillé le feu rouge*: he went through the red lights.
Griller une station: not to stop (trains, etc.).
To grill someone = *cuisiner quelqu'un*.

grippe (f) Means 'flu, but also dislike. *Je l'ai pris en grippe*: I have taken a dislike to him.
To grip someone = *s'agripper à quelqu'un*.

grippé *Il est grippé:* he has got 'flu.
Gripped (by someone) = *agrippé*.

gripper Usually means to seize up (machinery). A technical word that is sometimes used figuratively.
To grip = *saisir, empoigner*.

groin (m) Snout (of a pig). *Ça ressemble au groin d'un cochon*: it looks like a pig's snout.
Groin = *aine* (f).

groom (m) The sense of groom is now dated, and its modern meaning is that of page-boy. *A notre arrivée un petit groom nous a salués*: on our arrival a small page-boy greeted us.
Groom = *palefrenier* (m).
(Bride)groom = *marié* (m).

gros, grosse Big, fat. *Une grosse femme*: a stout woman.
Loud (voice, laughter).
Can mean coarse, but gross is stronger and = *grossier*.

grossesse (f) Pregnancy.
Grossness = *grossièreté* (f).

groupe (m) Group, but note that *groupe scolaire* may be a school party on an outing, or may refer to a group of (elementary) school buildings; school block.

gruger Is usually to swindle, take someone in (literary style). *'Le notaire ne donne pas de détails, mais il doit y avoir des champs à vendre, une maison et, dans ces affaires-là, il vaut mieux être sur place si on ne veut pas être grugé'* (Marcel Aymé, *Aller retour*, Gallimard).
To grudge = *en vouloir (à quelqu'un de quelque chose)*.

guérilla (f) Guerrilla warfare.
Guerrilla = *guérillero* (m).

guillotine (f) Guillotine, but the dramatic sounding *fenêtre* (f) *à guillotine* is a sash-window.

guise (f) Has the old sense of the word in English – way, fashion. *Agir à sa guise*: to do as one pleases.
Il me l'a donné en guise de récompense: he gave it to me by way of a reward.
Guise = *apparence* (f).

gym (f) Gym, gymnastics, P.E.
gym (building) = *gymnase* (m).

H

habit (m) Coat. Clothes. Evening dress. *Porter l'habit*: to wear tails.
Can also refer to riding and to monks, in which cases we too use the same word – riding-habit and monk's habit.
Distinguish between *prendre l'habit*: to take the habit (religion) and *prendre l'habitude*: to get into the habit (of doing something).
Habit (custom) = *habitude* (f).

hagard Haggard (in the earlier sense of the word), drawn, wild-looking (particularly of the eyes).
Il avait les yeux hagards: he had wild-looking eyes.
Haggard = *décharné*.

halle (f) A large covered area used for markets.
Hall (house) = *hall* (m), *vestibule* (m).

halo (m) A halo of light.
But for a saint it = *auréole* (f).

haltère (m) Dumb-bell. *Que ce haltère est lourd!*: how heavy this dumb-bell is!
Halter = *licou* (m).

hand (m) If you come across this, it will be an abbreviation for *le hand-ball*.
Hand = *main* (f).

hangar (m) Hangar (aeroplanes), but also a common word for a shed. *Derrière la ferme il y avait un grand hangar*: behind the farm there was a large shed.

harassant Exhausting. *Franchement, c'est une tâche harassante*: frankly, it's an exhausting job.
Harassing = *plein de tracasserie* (f).

harassé Tired, exhausted. *Harassé de fatigue, il alla se coucher*: tired out, he went to bed.
Harassed = *tourmenté*.

harassement (m) Might mean harassment or worry. Normally it means exhaustion.
Harassment (also) = *harcèlement* (m), *tracasserie* (f).

harasser Perhaps to worry or harass, but normally means to tire.
To harass (usually) = *harceler, tracasser, tourmenter*.

hardi Bold. *Cet homme hardi part aujourd'hui pour faire l'ascension de la montagne*: this bold man leaves today to climb the mountain.
Hardy (usually) = *robuste*.

hardiesse (f) Boldness. *La hardiesse de ces alpinistes m'étonne*: the boldness of these mountaineers amazes me.
Hardiness = *robustesse* (f).

harmonie (f) Harmony. Wind players (orchestra) or a wind band.

hart (m) Rope for hanging (criminals). (The word is now rarely used.)
Hart = *cerf* (m) (hart is perhaps used mostly in the names of inns, e.g. The White Hart).

hasard (m) Can mean hazard, but frequently just chance or luck. *Je l'ai rencontré par hasard*: I met him by chance.

hâte (f) The circumflex accent represents the *s*, so it means haste and not hate.
Hate = *haine* (f).

hâter To hasten.
To hate = *haïr*.

La Haye The Hague.

hectique Medical word (hectic) used for a fever that lasts a long time.
Hectic (usually) =*mouvementé*.

herbe (f) Herb. *Une omelette aux fines herbes*: a savoury omelet.
Also grass. *Déjeuner sur l'herbe* is a pleasant way of saying 'to picnic'.
Une mauvaise herbe: a weed.
Note such expressions as *un médecin en herbe*: a budding doctor.

héroïne (f) Both heroine and heroin (from Greek *heros*: hero).

herse (f) Harrow. *Le fermier suivait la herse*: the farmer was following the harrow.
Hearse = *corbillard* (m).

heurter To bang, knock, also to shock, jolt.
Le garçon est sorti du magasin en courant et a heurté une vieille dame: the boy ran out of the shop and banged into an old lady. *Ils se sont heurtés*: they collided.
Cette nouvelle m'a profondément heurté: this news upset me deeply.
To hurt = *blesser*.

hexagone (m) Hexagon. Also used to refer to France (because of its shape). Gérard Nirascou, writing in *Le Figaro* (19–20 January 1979) about the police, said that (*les policiers*) *'ont pu préserver jusqu'à présent l'hexagone de crimes tels que les rapts qui sont une des plaies de l'Italie'*.

hippodrome (m) In English the word is sometimes the name of a theatre or cinema. French has kept the original classical sense, and there it means a race-course. *Rendez-vous à l'hippodrome tous les samedis!*: Meeting at the race-course every Saturday!

hisser To hoist. *Ils ont hissé le pavillon*: they hoisted the flag. *'O! hisse!' ont-ils crié*: 'Heave-ho! they cried.
To hiss = *siffler*.

histoire (f) History, also story. *Une histoire de revenants*: a ghost story.
A common familiar meaning is that of fuss. *Quelle histoire!*: what a 'to-do'! *je ne veux pas avoir d'histoires avec la police*: I don't want any difficulties with the police.

holding (m) A holding company.
To have a holding (in a company): *être actionnaire*.

honnête Honest, but has other nuances – courteous and proper, decent, reasonable. The old idea of *un honnête homme* was of a gentleman, in its earlier sense.
Les honnêtes gens: decent people.
Des prix honnêtes: fair prices.

honnêtement Honestly, courteously, properly, reasonably.

honnêteté (f) Honesty, but also courtesy, decency, reasonableness. *C'est un film qui brave l'honnêteté*: it is a film which defies decency.

hôte (m) An interesting word because of its opposite meanings – host and guest (the sense of guest did exist in English but is now obsolete). *Mon hôte m'a accueilli*: my host welcomed me. *J'ai accueilli mes hôtes*: I welcomed my guests.

hôtel (m) Hotel, but this is not the only meaning. It can also be a large private (town) house. *Il a une belle femme, trois voitures et un hôtel particulier*: he has a beautiful wife, three cars and a large private town-house.
Also used for various public buildings.
Un hôtel de ville: town hall.

humain Both human and humane.

humeur (f) humour, mood, temper. *Il est de mauvaise humeur*: he is in a bad mood.

But note that *humeur* by itself can mean ill humour, temper. *'Assez rouge, dominant un mouvement d'humeur, l'oncle Théo se justifia non sans dignité'* (Michel de Saint-Pierre, *La Mer à boire*, Calmann-Lévy).
Humour (sense of humour) = *humour* (m).

hurler Not to hurl (throw), but to hurl, yell, shout, roar. *Ils ont hurlé des insultes*: they yelled out insults.
To hurl (throw) = *lancer*.

hystérie (f) Hysteria (medical term).
The English word sometimes has the sense of *crise* (f) *de nerfs* or *affolement* (m).

hystérique The medical word for hysterical. We sometimes use the word in the sense of being very upset (*être dans tous ses états*) or in the sense of being very funny (*c'est à se tordre*).

I

idiome (m) Idiom, (local) language. *Dans la vallée ils ont leur idiome à eux*: in the valley they have their own language.
Idiom (idiomatic expression) = *idiotisme* (m).

idiotisme (m) Usually means idiom. *Les idiotismes français sont très intéressants*: French idioms are very interesting.
May occasionally be found in the sense of idiocy.

if (m) A yew-tree. *Partout des ifs*: yew-trees everywhere.
If = *si*.

ignoré Unknown, (occasionally) ignored. *Dans sa résidence secondaire il peut vivre ignoré*: in his second home he can live without people knowing who he is.

ignorer Can mean to ignore, but great care is needed as it frequently means to be unaware, or not to know. *La police ignore son nom*: the police do not know his name.
Si elle m'aime, je l'ignore: if she likes me, I am unaware of the fact. And as Paul Verlaine wrote (*Fêtes Galantes*) – *'Est-elle brune, blonde ou rousse? – Je l'ignore.'*

illumination (f) Illumination, and often the lighting up of a special building (by floodlights).
Also a 'ray of light', an inspiration. *Illumination! Je sais ce qu'il faut faire!*: Bright idea! I know what has to be done!
Also illuminations.
Illumination (often) = *éclairage* (m).

illuminé (m) Not an enlightened person or a luminary; means either a visionary or a crank.
Enlightened = *éclairé*.
A luminary = *lumière* (f), *sommité* (f).

illuminer To illuminate (brightly) or cast a light upon.
Also used for special occasions, with floodlighting. *Le palais illuminé est quelque chose à voir*: the floodlit palace is something to see.
To illuminate (often) = *éclairer*.

illustré (m) Might mean an illustrated magazine (*un magazine illustré*) but note that it is a word for a comic. *L'enfant commença à feuilleter un illustré*: the child began to thumb through a comic.

illustrer Can – in literary language – mean to make illustrious, but normally means to illustrate.

imaginer To imagine.
But can have the idea of to invent – *C'est lui qui a imaginé la solution*: it is he who thought up the solution. And *imaginer de faire quelque chose* is to take it into one's head to do something. '*Ce fut au cours d'un de ces jeux que, pour échapper à Septembre, Aprilia, les membres visqueux des lentilles de l'étang, imagina de grimper aux branches d'un hêtre qui poussait à quelques mètres de la rive. Elle tomba et se brisa les deux jambes*' (Gisèle Prassinos, *Le Cavalier* (nouvelles), Plon).

immatériel Immaterial, of little substance, flimsy, ethereal.
Immaterial (unimportant) = *sans importance, indifférent*.

immortel Immortal.
Les immortels are the members of the Académie Française.
Une immortelle: an everlasting flower.

impartir To grant, allow (in legal or literary language). *Qui est-ce qui va leur impartir ce délai?*: who is going to grant them this extension?
To impart = *faire connaître*.

impasse (f) Impasse, dilemma, but also frequently used literally for a cul-de-sac.

impératif (m) Imperative (grammar).
Also demand, requirement. *A cause des impératifs de mon emploi du temps . . .*: because of the demands of my timetable.

impérieux Imperious, but also urgent. *Je n'ai pas de choix, c'est une tâche impérieuse*: I have no choice, the job has got to be done.

important Important, also serious, considerable. *Les dégâts sont importants*: the damage is considerable.

imposable Simply means taxable. *Le tout est imposable*: the whole thing is taxable.

imposer To impose, force, inspire, command (respect, etc.).
Imposer quelqu'un: to tax someone.
S'imposer (à quelqu'un): to impose oneself on someone.

En imposer à quelqu'un usually means to impress.
Il en impose: I find him imposing.
To impose on someone (deceive) = *duper*.

imposition (f) Imposition in various senses, and often refers to (the putting on of) tax.
Imposition (school) = *pensum* (m).
(on someone's time, kindness, etc.) = *abus* (m).

impotence (f) Helplessness, disability. *Il se plaint de son impotence*: he complains that he cannot get around.
Impotence = *impuissance* (f).

impotent Is clearly an adjective not to be misunderstood – it means helpless, having difficulty in moving, crippled. *Tennisman connu impotent*: Well-known tennis-player disabled.
Ce pauvre vieil homme impotent: this poor helpless old man.
Impotent = *impuissant*.

impression (f) Impression, literally and figuratively. Also printing (compare 'third impression' of a book).
Une faute d'impression: misprint.

impressionnant Impressive, but also upsetting, disturbing, awesome. *Des problèmes moins impressionnants*: less upsetting problems.

impressionner To impress, but also to upset, over-awe. *J'étais timide; ma mère m'a impressionné*: I was shy; my mother over-awed me.

improuvable Unprovable.
Improvable (land) = *amendable, améliorable*.

improuvé Not proven.
Improved = *amélioré*.

improuver You might still come across this word, which means to disapprove (now translated by *désapprouver*).
To improve = *améliorer*.

impudemment Brazenly rather than impudently.
Impudently (often) = *avec effronterie*.

impudence (f) Impudence, also lack of shame, brazenness.

impudent Impudent, and there is also often the sense of being brazen, shameless.

inadvertance (f) Inadvertence. *Par inadvertance*: inadvertently.
Also inadvertence in the sense of oversight, error through lack of attention.
Paul Guth, speaking of his pupils, writes – '*Leurs ruses, leurs inadvertances feintes*' (*Le Naïf aux quarante enfants*, Albin Michel).

inaltérabilité (f) Sometimes unalterableness, but often refers to non-deterioration or being deterioration-proof.
Unalterableness = *immutabilité* (f).

inaltérable Can mean unalterable, unchanging, but often has the sense of not deteriorating (metal, colours, etc.) and is the sort of word that one sees in advertisements for certain products.
Unalterable (often) = *immuable*.

inaltéré None the worse, not having deteriorated.
Unaltered = *sans changement*.

inapte Unfit, unsuitable. *Inapte au service*: unfit for service.
Inapt (remark) = *hors de propos*.

inaptitude (f) Sometimes inaptitude, often unfitness. *Mon frère a été mis à la retraite pour inaptitude*: my brother has been pensioned off as he is unfit for work.
Inaptitude (remark) = *manque* (m) *d'à-propos*.

incessamment Unceasingly, but in modern usage means without delay, at any moment. *Un train va arriver incessamment*: there will be a train at any moment.
Unceasingly = *sans cesse*.

incidence (f) Incidence (as in 'angle of incidence'), also effect, impact.
Incidence (sometimes) = *cas* (m).

incinération (f) Incineration, also cremation.

incinérer To incinerate, and also the equivalent of to cremate.

inciter To incite, but also to encourage, tempt. *Afin d'inciter les touristes à visiter notre pays*: in order to encourage tourists to visit our country.

incohérence (f) Incoherence, also inconsistency.

incohérent Incoherent, also inconsistent.

inconditionnel Unconditional. Also something of an 'in' word to describe those who follow or believe blindly, faithfully, without question.

incongru Incongruous. Also unseemly, even ill-mannered.
Incongruous (also) = *absurde*.

incongruité (f) Incongruity, unseemliness. *Dire des incongruités*: to make unseemly, ill-chosen remarks.
Incongruity (also) = *manque* (m) *d'harmonie, absurdité* (f).

inconscience (f) Unconsciousness. *Son inconscience continue*: he is still unconscious.
But often means rashness, folly. *L'inconscience de ces jeunes conducteurs me fait peur*: the lack of thought of these young drivers frightens me.
'Nous risquons notre chance. C'est de la folie. Nous avons conscience de notre inconscience' (Paul Dreyfus, *Histoires extraordinaires de la Résistance*, Fayard).

inconscient Unconscious in various senses, but it often means heedless, thoughtless, unaware.

inconséquence (f) Inconsequence, lack of relevance. Inconsistency (logic). Also a piece of thoughtlessness. *Il est jeune et il a commis une inconséquence –*

n'en parlons plus: he is young and it was a thoughtless thing to do – don't let us say any more about it.

inconséquent Inconsequential, inconsistent, also thoughtless, scatterbrained. *Un jeune homme inconséquent*: a thoughtless young man.

inconsidéré Inconsiderate in the sense of thoughtless. *Une idée inconsidérée*: an ill-considered idea.
Inconsiderate (to others) = *sans égards* (m) (*pour*).

inconsidérément Inconsiderately in the sense of without bothering to think. *Inconsidérément j'accepte l'invitation*: without thinking, I accept the invitation.
Inconsiderately (often) = *manquer d'égards* (m).

incontinent Incontinent, but do not be misled by the adverb (literary style), which means forthwith.
Il se lève incontinent: he gets up forthwith.

incontrôlable That which cannot be checked (sometimes it means uncontrollable).

incontrôlé Unchecked, as well as uncontrolled.

inconvenance (f) Unseemliness. Unseemly action or word.
'*Alice, assise, le regarda comme s'il eût proféré une inconvenance . . .*' (Colette, *Duo*, Ferenczi).
Inconvenience = *dérangement* (m).

inconvenant Unseemly, improper. *Il est inconvenant de rester assis quand une dame entre dans la pièce*: it is improper to remain seated when a lady enters the room.
Inconvenient = *incommode*.

inconvénient (m) Disadvantage, occasionally inconvenience. *Si vous n'y voyez pas d'inconvénient*: if you have no objection.
Inconvenience = *dérangement* (m).

incorrect Wrong, also improper of dress, behaviour, etc. *Il est entré sans cravate, ce qui est incorrect*: he came in without a tie, which is not the proper thing to do.

incorrection (f) Incorrectness (e.g. style), inaccuracy. Also impropriety, bad manners, bad behaviour.

indélicat Indelicate, tactless, and also a (tactful?) word for dishonest. *Ce jeune client indélicat a été pris en flagrant délit*: this dishonest young customer was caught red-handed.

index (m) Index of a book, also index-, fore-finger. *Il a levé l'index pour me dire 'attention'*: he raised his fore-finger to warn me.
Also price index, etc.
And *à l'index*: on the black list (from the Roman Catholic Index).

indicateur (m) Indicator, usually with reference to some instrument or gauge.

Also a railway timetable, or some guide. *Consultez l'indicateur*: consult the timetable.

Can mean a police-informer.

Indicator (car) = *clignotant* (m).

indicatif (m) Indicative (grammar).

Also used for call-signs. Could refer to a signature tune, and used for dialling code (telephone). *Voulez-vous me donner l'indicatif de Brighton, s'il vous plaît?*: Would you give me the Brighton dialling code, please?

indication (f) Indication. Clue. And (often) instructions. *Lisez les indications*: read the instructions.

Indienne (f) An Indian woman.

L'indienne can be a material (printed calico), originally made in India.

Also an overarm stroke at swimming.

indifféremment Indifferently. Often has the sense of equally. *Vous pouvez utiliser les deux indifféremment*: it doesn't matter which you use.

And an employer may advertise for someone to work *indifféremment en anglais et en allemand* – in English and German equally well (far from indifferently!).

Indifferently (of work, etc.) = *médiocrement*.

indisposer To make someone unwell or indisposed.

Also to antagonize people. *Vous allez finir par indisposer tous vos amis*: you'll end up setting all your friends against you.

indolence (f) Indolence or apathy.

indolent Indolent. Also has the nuance of apathetic.

industrie (f) In addition to meaning modern industry, there is the old sense of skill and activity. *Un chevalier d'industrie* is not a tycoon but a person of sharp practice who lives on his wits.

Industry (hard work) = *application* (f).

Tycoon = *brasseur* (m) *d'affaires, magnat* (m).

industrieux Both busy and skilful. A literary word.

Industrious (person) = *diligent, laborieux*.

inédit (Hitherto) unpublished. Therefore often means new, original, un-heard of.

Unedited = *non édité*.

inemployé Not being used (talent, etc.).

Unemployed (out of a job) = *sans emploi* (m).

infatuation (f) A literary word now meaning conceit, being too pleased with oneself. *Je ne peux pas supporter son infatuation!*: I cannot put up with his conceit!

Infatuation = *entichement* (m).

infatué Conceited, pleased with oneself (literary).

Infatuated (with) = *entiché (de)*.

s'infatuer Belongs to literary language and now usually has the sense of being conceited, very pleased with oneself.

To be infatuated (with) = *s'enticher (de)*.

infection (f) Infection.
Also stench, horrible smell. *Mais quelle infection partout dans les salles de l'hôpital!*: but what a stench everywhere in the hospital wards!

inférieur French keeps the full meaning of the word – lower as well as inferior – so some care is needed. *Les classes inférieures* are the lower forms in a school, though they may not necessarily have *des résultats inférieurs*: poor results.

infirme Infirm, crippled.
Has a wider use than in English, where it is particularly associated with old age. *Pour une jeune personne sportive, maintenant infirme, la vie n'est pas bien gaie*: for a young athletic person, now disabled, life is not much fun. And *voiture* (f) *d'infirme*: invalid carriage.

infirmer Means to quash (legal), invalidate. To deny (something) (the opposite of *confirmer*).
To make infirm = *rendre infirme*.

information (f) (Legal) enquiry. News (TV, wireless). *Je vais écouter les informations*: I am going to listen to the news.
Data. Sometimes information.
Information (often) = *renseignements* (m).

ingénuité (f) Ingenuousness, naïvety. *Son ingénuité est incroyable!*: her simplicity is incredible!
Ingenuity = *ingéniosité* (f).

ingrat Ungrateful in a wide sense of the word, hence also thankless, fruitless, unattractive. *L'âge ingrat*: the awkward age.
Ungrateful (also) = *sans aucune reconnaissance*.

ingratitude (f) Ingratitude, and it is also said about things which are unproductive (soil, etc.).

inhabitable Uninhabitable. *Maintenant sa maison est inhabitable*: now her house is uninhabitable.
Inhabitable = *habitable*.

inhabitation (f) State of not being occupied, empty.
L'inhabitation de ces appartements pose un problème: the fact that these flats are empty is becoming a problem.
Being inhabited, habitation = *habitation* (f).

inhabité Uninhabited. *Tu verras au loin une petite chaumière inhabitée*: you will see in the distance a small uninhabited cottage.
Inhabited = *habité*.

injure (f) Can mean injury (in the sense of wrong) but commonly means insult.
Injury = *blessure* (f).

injurier To insult. *Elle est descendue de sa voiture et m'a injurié*: she got out of her car and abused me. *Un gendarme attaqué et injurié*: a policeman attacked

and abused. *Le conducteur de l'auto a injurié le piéton*: the driver of the car insulted the pedestrian.
To injure = *blesser*.

injurieusement In an offensive way, insultingly.
Injuriously = *pernicieusement*.

injurieux Insulting.
Injurious = *nuisible*.

inséparable Inseparable, and *les inséparables* (m) are, in addition, lovebirds.

insister To insist, also persist, not to give up. *Téléphonez-moi le soir, et s'il n'y a pas de réponse, insistez!*: phone me in the evening, and if there is no answer, keep trying!
Remember that *insister sur* often has the sense of to emphasize – *J'insiste sur la politesse*: I attach great importance to politeness.
To insist on (often) = *exiger*.

insolation (f) Sunstroke, or exposure to sun(shine) (insolation).
Do not confuse it with insulation = *isolement* (m).

insolent Insolent, cheeky. Can also have the sense of something outrageous, indecent.
Can also mean arrogant, haughty – *'Après avoir épuisé mes grands airs insolents'* (Camus, *La Chute*).

inspiration (f) Inspiration, but also breathing in, inhaling. For a breathalyser test, you might be told *'Une bonne inspiration, s'il vous plaît!'*: Take a deep breath, please!

inspirer To inspire, also to breathe in (a meaning scarcely used in English).

installer To install, settle.
To fit out (a room, etc.).
Note the familiar *en installer*: to show off.

instamment Insistently, urgently. *On demande instamment le patron*: the boss is urgently required.
Instantly = *tout de suite*.

instance (f) Can mean insistence. Or (legal term) proceedings.
En instance de is used in various phrases with the sense of being in the process.
And *instance* also means authority, authorities (e.g. to apply to higher authorities).
Instance = *cas* (m).
For instance = *par exemple*.

instant Not usually instant, but insistent, pressing (e.g. requests or pleadings).
Instant (usually) = *immédiat*.
     coffee = *café instantané*.

instruction (f) Instruction, instructions.
Also education. *Il est sans instruction*: he is uneducated.
Common (legal language) for investigation. *Au cours de l'instruction sur la*

manifestation des prisonniers . . .: during the inquiry about the demonstration of the prisoners . . .

instruire To instruct, educate, inform, and (legal language) investigate. *On instruira mon cas bientôt*: my case will be investigated soon.

instrumental Instrumental (music).
But 'he was instrumental in making me happy' and similar phrases need a paraphrase (such as *il a beaucoup contribué à*. . .).

insuffisance (f) Insufficiency, also inefficiency. *Une insuffisance de professeurs*: a shortage of teachers. *L'insuffisance des professeurs*: the shortcomings of the teachers.

insuffisant Insufficient, also inefficient or not up to the job.

insulaire (m/f) An islander (people who are insular in this sense).
'*Les Anglais sont des insulaires; en conséquence, ils ne peuvent se suffire ni matériellement ni intellectuellement*' (Pierre de Coulevain, *L'Ile inconnue*, Calmann-Lévy).
Insular (often) = *qui a l'esprit borné*.

intangible Intangible, that which cannot be touched.
Also the figurative sense of 'which must not be touched', i.e. inviolable or sacrosanct.

intelligence (f) Intelligence, understanding. *Vivre en bonne intelligence*: to be on good terms. *Etre d'intelligence avec quelqu'un*: to be in league with someone. *Avoir des intelligences avec l'ennemi*: to have secret contacts with the enemy.
But (military) intelligence = *service* (m) *de renseignements* or *Deuxième Bureau* (m).

intéressant Interesting.
Often used in the sense of worth while, of good value, attractive (prices).
'*J'ai demandé ce soir à Patrick et Ann ce qu'ils pensent de la médecine socialisée, le* National Health Service. – *Quand on a plusieurs enfants, m'ont-ils répondu, c'est une chose intéressante*' (Jean Oger, *Les Anglais chez eux*, Arthaud).
Une rémunération intéressante = attractive pay.

intéressé Interested, but it can also mean interested for oneself, selfish.
Hence *l'amour intéressé*: cupboard love.

intérieur (m) Interior.
Hence can mean local home life, home scene. Also note *Ministre* (m) *de l'Intérieur*: Home Secretary.

intérim (m) Interim. *Dans l'intérim*: in the interim.
Also used in the sense of acting as a deputy, standing in temporarily (*faire l'intérim, par intérim*, etc.). '*J'ai peu d'enthousiasme pour commander même par intérim ce dépôt dont on ne me dit pas grand bien*' (Amiral Jubelin, *J'étais Aviateur de la France Libre*, Hachette, Bibliothèque Verte).

interlude (m) Interlude (music, TV).
Otherwise interlude (usually) = *intermède* (m).

interprétation (f) Interpretation, also used of artistes for rendering a part. *Une interprétation magnifique*: a marvellous performance.

interprète (m/f) Interpreter, but also used of actors, musicians, etc., who 'interpret' their roles. *Parmi les interprètes connus*: in the well-known cast.

interpréter To interpret, explain, understand. When an interpreter interprets, *il fait l'interprète*.
The verb often means to perform, render (music, singing, acting). *Interprété par* . . .: performed by . . .

interrogation (f) Questioning. *Un point d'interrogation*: question-mark.
Interrogation (police) = *interrogatoire* (m).

interroger To interrogate (usually in a fairly mild sense), question, examine (i.e. academic work). *La police m'a interrogé*: the police asked me some questions.
To interrogate someone = *faire subir un interrogatoire à quelqu'un*.

interrupteur (m) Might refer to someone who interrupts, but it is also a (light) switch. *Il cherche l'interrupteur*: he looks for the switch.

intervention (f) Care is needed, as it does mean intervention, but also a (surgical) operation (standing for *intervention chirurgicale*). So *il a dû faire une intervention*: (in the right context) he had to perform an operation.

intoxicant Poisonous (or toxic).
Intoxicating = *alcoolique, enivrant*.

intoxication (f) Poisoning, intoxication. *Intoxication alcoolique*: alcohol poisoning.
Also a word for (political, etc.) indoctrination (familiarly *l'intoxe*).
Intoxication (from drink) = *ivresse* (f).

intoxiquer To poison (food, fumes, etc.).
Une victime intoxiquée était couchée sur le trottoir: a victim overcome by the fumes was lying on the pavement.
S'il continue dans cette voie, il s'intoxiquera peu à peu: if he goes on like this he will gradually poison himself.
Can also mean to 'poison' the mind, to indoctrinate.
To intoxicate = *enivrer*.

introduire Can mean to introduce, bring into contact.
Also to show in. *Introduisez votre ami*: Show in your friend. But *présentez votre ami*: introduce your friend.
Introduire is also to insert (key, etc.).

inusable Do not be put off by the appearance of this word! It means hard-wearing, that which will not wear out. Thus it might be wise to buy *un veston inusable*: a hard-wearing coat.
Unusable = *inutilisable*.

inusité Means not (commonly) used, or unusual. *Ces visiteurs inusités*: these unusual visitors.
Unused (usually) = *inutilisé*.

inutile Useless, but also vain, pointless. *Inutile de vous dire que* . . .: I hardly need tell you that . . . (the information may in fact be very useful!).

invalide (m/f) May refer to an invalid, but *un invalide* is a term for a disabled soldier or workman. *Cette place est réservée aux invalides*: this seat is reserved for (war) pensioners.
Invalid (usually) = *malade* (m/f), *infirme* (m/f).

invalider To invalidate.
To invalid out (discharge) = *réformer*.

Islande (f) Iceland. *Au loin, l'Islande*: in the distance, Iceland.
An island = *île* (f).

isolation (f) Insulation. *Isolation phonique*: sound-proofing.
Isolation = *isolement* (m).

isolé Isolated, but also insulated. *Une porte isolée*: an insulated door.

isoler To isolate or insulate.

issue (f) Can mean the issue or outcome, but also common in a literal sense – way out, exit. *Issue de secours*: emergency exit.
Issue (often) = *question* (f).
   (copy) = *numéro* (m) (e.g. of newspaper).

jacquet (m) Backgammon. *Le jacquet pour tout le monde!*: backgammon for everyone!
Jacket = *veston* (m), *veste* (f).

jalousie (f) Jealousy, also sun-blind. *Elle a levé la jalousie*: she raised the sun-blind.

jaquette (f) Some care is needed, as it can mean a woman's short coat or jacket (compare coat and skirt), but for a man it is a morning coat. *Je dois mettre ma jaquette pour la réception au palais*: I must put on my morning coat for the reception at the palace.
Can also mean jacket, dust-cover (book).
Jacket = *veston* (m), *veste* (f).
Woman's bedjacket = *liseuse* (f).
Potatoes in their jackets = *pommes* (f) *de terre en robe de chambre*.

jarre (f) Large earthenware jar.
Jar (jam) = *pot* (m).
   (glass) = *bocal* (m).

javeline (f) Javelin, but in athletics = *javelot* (m).

jet (m) Can be a jet, spurt, stream (water, etc.), also gas jet. Also jet, nozzle (hosepipe, etc.).
Can mean throw, throwing.
Premier jet is a first draft, outline (of book, poem, thesis, etc.) and *d'un seul jet*: at one go.
Also increasingly used for a jet plane (rather than *un avion à réaction*). Not surprisingly, the expression *le jet set* is also found.
Jet (lignite) = *le jais*, hence jet-black = *noir comme du jais*.

job (m) (Temporary) job. *Beaucoup d'étudiants cherchent des jobs cet été*: many students are looking for summer jobs.
In English, can also refer to one's normal work (*travail* (m), *boulot* (m) (familiar) or to a task (*tâche* (f)).

joint (m) Joint, join.
Trouver le joint: to find the knack, way (of doing something).
Joint (body) = *articulation* (f).
  (meat) = *rôti* (m).
  ('shady') = *tripot* (m).

joli Pretty. *J'aime bien ton fils. Si joli!*: I am so fond of your son. So pretty!
Also used, like 'nice', in an ironical sense (*c'est du joli!*: a nice mess!).
Joliment could be translated by jolly – *il fait joliment chaud*: it is jolly hot. (The last two uses are familiar.)
Jolly = *jovial, gai*.

jonc (m) Is found by the water, but means rush (plant) and not junk (boat), which is *jonque* (f).
Jonc can also be a stick or cane.

joug (m) Yoke. *Ils ont secoué le joug*: they threw off the yoke.
Jug = *cruche* (f), *pot* (m).

journal (m) (News)paper, journal.
Also diary. *Je tiens un journal*: I am keeping a diary. *Un journal intime*: a private diary.
And can mean a logbook.
Also used by radio and TV for 'news', as in *journal télévisé*.

journée (f) Day, whole day. *Quelle journée! Comme je suis fatigué!*: What a day! how tired I am!
Il a passé la journée à dormir: he spent the day sleeping.
Aller en journée: to go out to do domestic work.
Can also refer to a day's work.
Can refer to distance, a day's journey, and *il voyage à petites journées* is a dated way of saying he travels by easy stages.
Journey = *voyage* (m).

au jugé Does not mean with (expert) judgment but, on the contrary, by guesswork, by rough reckoning.
Hence *tirer au jugé*: to shoot blind.

jugulaire (f) Could refer to the jugular vein, but commonly means a chin-strap. *Le soldat a mis la main sur la jugulaire*: the soldier put his hand on the chin-strap.
Jugular (often) = *veine* (f) *jugulaire*.

juguler Not to juggle (*jongler*), but to throttle, or to check, suppress.

juste Just, fair. Also right, accurate, in tune (as of piano).
Tight (clothes). Just enough, scarcely enough (*c'est juste*).
Note *au plus juste prix*: at the lowest possible price.
Just (also) = *équitable*.

justement Justly, rightly. Also precisely, exactly.

justesse (f) Not justice, but exactness, accuracy, and *de justesse* means just or a close thing. *Il a réussi de justesse à son examen*: he only just passed his exam (and not he passed with justice or as was fitting = *ce qui n'était que justice* or *comme de juste*).
Justice = *justice* (f).

juvénile Juvenile, to do with youth. *Délinquance* (f) *juvénile*: juvenile delinquency. *Son enthousiasme juvénile*: her youthful enthusiasm.
Juvenile (often) = *puéril*.

kart (m) Go-cart.
Cart = *charrette* (f).

kick (m) Kick-starter (motorcycle).
Kick = *coup* (m) *de pied*.
That gives me a kick = *ça me fait drôlement plaisir, ça m'excite*, or (popular) *je prends mon pied*.

kiosque (m) Kiosk (newspapers, flowers). *Kiosque à musique*: bandstand.
Can be the wheelhouse of a ship or the conning-tower of a submarine.
Can also be a summer-house.
Telephone kiosk = *cabine* (f) *téléphonique*.

kit (m) Kit (for building models, etc.).
Kit (usually) = *équipement* (m).

knickers (m) In *Histoires extraordinaires de la Résistance* (Fayard), the author Paul Dreyfus describes how a member of the Resistance escapes from Colditz in an inconspicuous disguise, which included knickers. One might have thought these would be highly conspicuous, to say the least! But they are in fact plus-fours – i.e. the abbreviation for *les knickerbockers*. *'Derrière la porte, s'ouvrait une cave voûtée. Alain Le Ray s'y changea: knickers,*

bas blancs torsadés, blouson ouvert sur une chemise bleue, casquette à boucle et à pont. En quelques instants, le prisonnier était devenu, selon sa propre expression "un promeneur allemand de mine acceptable".'
Knickers (women's) = *slip* (m).

label (m) Manufacturer's label. *Selon le label, cette étoffe est cent pour cent écossaise*: according to the label, this material is 100 per cent Scottish.
Label = *étiquette* (f).

laborieux Can mean laborious, 'hard going', or laboured. *'L'océan douteux des draps se soulevait à un rythme de tempête et la respiration se faisait de plus en plus laborieuse'* (Gilbert Cesbron, *'Mort d'une sorcière'* from *Les Enfants aux cheveux gris*, Robert Laffont).
Also means hard-working. *'Justin était doux, laborieux et portait un chapeau melon'* (Marcel Aymé, *Aller retour*, Gallimard).
Les classes laborieuses: the working classes.
Des vacances laborieuses: working holidays.

labour (m) Ploughing, tilling. *Regardez ces chevaux de labour!*: look at these plough horses!
Labour = *travail* (m), *labeur* (m).
              (manpower) = *main-d'oeuvre* (f).

labourer To plough, till (as 'to labour' could mean originally in English), turn over (soil). *Ce pauvre fermier est fatigué après avoir labouré toute la journée*: this poor farmer is tired after ploughing all day.
Also means to make a gash (furrow), a deep graze (e.g. face).
To labour = *travailler dur, faire quelque chose péniblement*.

laboureur (m) Ploughman.
Labourer = *ouvrier* (m), *manoeuvre* (m).

lad (m) Stable lad (who looks after racehorses). *Le lad fit sortir un beau cheval*: the stable boy brought out a fine horse.
Lad = *jeune garçon* (m), *gars* (m).

lamentable Not only lamentable, deplorable, but pitiful, doleful (a sense the English had originally). *D'une voix lamentable*: in a doleful voice.
And, as in English, lamentable in the sense of poor, feeble. *Des résultats lamentables*: pathetic results.

lance (f) Spear as well as lance.
Hose (*lance d'incendie*: fire hose).
Nozzle.
Lance (medical) = *lancette* (f).

lancer To throw, hurl.

Also to launch (ship, etc.) to launch or promote (goods). To start someone or something off. *Je n'ai pas réussi à lancer le moteur*: I couldn't get the engine started.

To lance (medical) = *percer*.

landau (m) Landau (horse-drawn carriage). Survives in modern French as a word for pram (because of the same sort of folding hood).

lande (f) Moor, moorland. *En regardant par la fenêtre, il voyait la lande désolée*: looking out of the window, he could see the desolate heath.

Land = *terre* (f), *terrain* (m).

langage (m) Language (in a limited sense). *Le langage technique*: technical language. *Le langage de tous les jours*: everyday language.

Language (general) = *langue* (f).

languissant Languishing, but also languid, listless, dull. *Après cette description languissante*: after this heavy-going description.

lanterne (f) Lantern, but can refer to the (side) lights of a car. Note *la lanterne rouge* in the sense of tail, bringing up the rear, those at the end or bottom (from the idea of being the red tail-light).

laps (m) A lapse of time, but only in the expression *un laps de temps*.

But after a lapse of several months = *au bout de plusieurs mois* (or other expressions).

Lapse (also) = *chute* (f), *erreur* (f).

larcin (m) Literary (rather than legal) word for petty thieving. *Vol* (m) is the legal term. *Vol simple*: larceny.

lard (m) Bacon.

Lard = *saindoux* (m).

large Can sometimes mean large, but very often means broad, wide. *Les larges boulevards*: the broad boulevards. *Avoir l'esprit large*: to be broad-minded.

Can also mean generous, liberal. *Il est large avec ses domestiques*: he is generous to his staff.

largesse (f) Largesse but usually generosity.

lavabo (m) A common meaning is wash-basin. *Il faut que je me lave les mains qui sont couvertes d'huile. Où est le lavabo?*: I must wash my hands, which are covered with oil. Where is the wash-basin?

Can also mean lavatory, as in *les lavabos*.

lavatory (m) Public lavatory. At one time it even had the sense of barber's shop (with lavatory). For once an English word is dropping out of use (perhaps because it is long, perhaps because of the French alternatives, not to mention another briefer English one favoured by the French).

Lavatory =*cabinet* (m), *toilettes* (f), *les W-C* (m).

leader (m) Usually used in a political sense, or in a sporting or commercial context.

Leader (often) = *chef* (m).
(newspaper) = *éditorial* (m).

lecteur (m) **lectrice** (f) General word for reader. *Avis au lecteur*: foreword.
Also a foreign language assistant at a university.
Lecturer = *conférencier* (m), *conférencière* (f).

lecture (f) A very deceptive word! It means reading, reading-matter, read-ing (from instruments), and so on. These meanings that also used to be found in English.
Quel est votre passe-temps préféré: La lecture: What is your favourite pas-time? Reading. *Lectures faciles*: easy reading passages. *Je suspends ma lecture pour le regarder*: I stop my reading to look at him. *La lectures sur les lèvres*: lip-reading.
Elle me fera la lecture: she will read aloud to me.
Il fait des lectures: he takes readings (from instruments).
Lecture = *conférence* (f).
To give someone a lecture (familiar) = *faire un sermon à quelqu'un* (among many expressions).

legs (m) Legacy. *Mon ami m'a fait un legs*: my friend left me a legacy.
Leg = *jambe* (f).
He gave me a leg up (literal) = *il m'a fait la courte échelle*.

Le Lac Léman Is Lake Geneva.

lentille (f) Lentil.
Another meaning is freckle. *Des mains couvertes de lentilles*: hands covered with freckles.
Also lens, hence *lentille de contact*: contact lens (= *verre* (m) *de contact*).
And can mean duckweed.

lézarde (f) Crack (as in wall). *J'ai regardé les lézardes dans le vieux mur*: I looked at the cracks in the old wall.
Lizard = *lézard* (m).

liaison (f) Liaison, joining, link, conjunction. Also relations between people. *Avoir une liaison*: to have a love affair, but *une liaison d'affaires*: a business connection.

libelle (m) Lampoon, satire. *Le directeur est furieux. On vient de lui montrer quelques libelles 'antiprof'*: the headmaster is furious. He has just been shown some 'down with teacher' lampoons.

libellé (m) Wording. *Il a protesté contre le libellé*: he protested about the wording.
Libel = *diffamation* (f).

libeller To word, write out, draw up. *Il a libellé mon invitation*: he worded my invitation.
To libel = *diffamer*.

libraire (m/f) Bookseller. *Il est libraire*: he is a bookseller.
Librarian = *bibliothécaire* (m/f).

librairie (f) Bookselling, or (more commonly) simply bookshop, and some times publishing house. *Il est entré dans une librairie pour trouver le livre*: he went into a bookshop to find the book.

For library, French goes back to Greek instead of Latin, giving *la bibliothèque*.

lice (f) Is the old English word 'lists' – *entrer en lice*: to enter the lists.

Also a technical word for a bitch (hound).

Lice = *les poux* (m).

licence (f) Licence (permission, authority), as well as licence (liberty).

Also a (bachelor's) degree (academic).

Une licence de pêche: fishing licence, but a driving licence = *un permis de conduire*.

licenciement (m) Dismissal. *Le licenciement de personnel*: staff dismissal.

Licensing (often) = *autorisation* (f).

licencier To discharge (workers, etc.). *On a licencié beaucoup d'ouvriers*: many workers have been made redundant. So a *licencié* could be somebody made redundant, or someone with a degree (*licence*)!

To license (often) = *autoriser*.

lie (f) Dregs, lees (wine, etc.). *La lie du peuple* means the dregs, the riff-raff.

Lie (untruth) = *mensonge* (m).

lier To bind, tie, connect. *Lier connaissance, lier conversation, avec quelqu'un*: to strike up an acquaintance, conversation, with someone.

Also to thicken (sauce).

Il est fou à lier: he is as mad as a hatter.

To lie = *se coucher, être couché, gésir, se trouver*.

(tell a lie) = *mentir*.

lieutenant (m) Lieutenant, but *lieutenant de port* is harbour-master (of a small port).

lifter Used in sport, meaning to put top spin on the ball. *Avec son revers lifté*: with his top spin backhand.

To lift = *soulever, lever*.

lifting (m) Face-lift.

Lifting = *soulèvement* (m).

ligne (f) Line. *Les grandes lignes* means the general outline, picture.

A la ligne: (start a) new paragraph (as in dictation).

Also the figure. *Je dois penser à ma ligne, je surveille toujours mon poids*: I must think of my figure, I'm still a weight-watcher.

La ligne aérienne might be overhead power line as well as airline.

Drop me a line = *écrivez-moi un mot*.

Hard lines = *pas de veine*.

That's not my line = *ce n'est pas (de) mon rayon*.

Hold the line = *ne quittez pas*.

limbe (f) Used in rather technical senses, as rim (of stars) or lamina (of leaves).

In the plural it can mean limbo.
English limb (of the body) = *membre* (m), and has not the same origin.

lime (f) (Sweet) lime or a file (implement). *Il me faut une lime*: I need a file.
Lime-juice is *jus* (m) *de limette* (f), or *jus de citron vert*.
A lime-tree is *limettier* (m), but a lime or linden-tree is *tilleul* (m).

limon (m) (Sour) lime.
Also has other very different meanings – a shaft (vehicles) and (commonly) mud, silt.
Lemon = *citron* (m).

limonade (f) Usually means a kind of fizzy lemonade, mineral water with a taste of lemon. Lemon-squash would be *une citronnade* or *un citron pressé*.

limonadier (m) He may manufacture minerals and soft drinks, but the word usually just means café- or pub-owner. If he were selling lemons, they would be *citrons* (m) and lemonade would be *citronnade* (f).

limoneux Muddy (from *le limon*: silt). *Eau limoneuse*: muddy water (not a tempting lemon drink).
Lemon = *de citron* (m).

limousine (f) May refer to motor-cars (limousine), but you may find it in the sense of a sort of cloak or coat as worn by the shepherds of the Limousin region.

lion (m) Lion. *La part du lion*: the lion's share. But it may refer to a person, not just a person of courage, but a dynamic person of drive and energy. Hence one may see modern advertisements by firms who are looking for *un lion*.

lippe (f) (Thick) lower lip. *'Lippe pendante, il regardait distraitement loin devant lui dans une glace, sa propre image qui se reflétait multipliée dans un miroir antagoniste'* (Raymond Queneau, *Un Rude Hiver*, Gallimard).
Lip = *lèvre* (f).

liqueur (f) Nowadays means liqueur, whereas liquor to drink = *boissons* (f) *(alcooliques)*.

liquidation (f) Liquidation (business), settling (financial). Also (of shops) selling off, clearance.

liquide Liquid. But *je n'ai pas de liquide chez moi*: would not mean that you are 'dry', but that you have no ready cash at home (standing familiarly for *argent* (m) *liquide*).

liquider To liquidate (business), to settle.
Also familiarly (as in English) *liquider quelqu'un*: to 'liquidate' someone.
In a shop, it means to sell off goods. *Tout doit être liquidé*: everything must be sold off.

liquoriste (m) Wine and spirit merchant (he sells *liqueurs* – but not liquorice).
Liquorice = *réglisse* (f).

liste (f) List, but not of ships, which = *donner de la bande* or *de la gîte*.

litière (f) Litter as in a stable for animals, or in which one could be carried. *Faire litière de*: to trample on (figuratively).
All English meanings of litter go back to the basic idea of 'bed', including –
Litter (rubbish) = *détritus* (m).
(of animals) = *portée* (f).

livide Commonly and colloquially used in English to mean very angry, i.e. to be *white*, *pale* with anger. In French, though, it can refer only to the colour. *'Au moment où Maria tourna le coin de la rue, il poussa un cri étouffé, et sa femme qui, plus qu'elle ne courait, volait vers lui, crut que son mari allait s'abattre. Il était livide'* (Jean-Jacques Gautier, *Maria la Belle*, Julliard).
Livid (very angry) = *furieux*.

living (m) Living-room, sitting-room (common abbreviation of *le living-room*). *Vaste living, grande terrasse*: large living-room, big terrace, as an advertisement might say.
Living (usually) = *vie* (f).

local (m) Building, room, premises (often used in the plural). *Ces gosses passent leur temps à jouer dans les rues – ce qu'il leur faut, c'est un local bien à eux*: these kids spend their time playing in the streets – what they need is a place of their own.
Not the colloquial English 'local', i.e. pub, which = (*le bistro, le café du coin*).

localiser To localize also to locate. *La police a localisé la voiture maquillée*: the police have located the disguised car.

location (f) Hiring, renting. *Location de voitures*: car hire.
Also used for box-office booking of seats. *La location est fermée*: the booking office is closed.
Location = *emplacement* (m).
(locating) = *repérage* (m).
On location (films) = *en extérieur*.

loch (m) Ship's log (apparatus for checking speed of ship).
(A logbook = *un livre de bord*.)
(Scottish) loch = *lac* (m) (or *loch* (m) can be used).

locomotive (f) Railway engine.
Also a modern expression for a dynamic personality, pace-setter, trend-setting leader, driving-force.

loge (f) Lodge, small hut, cabin. Freemasons' lodge.
Also used in two theatrical senses – actors' dressing-rooms or the 'green' room, and a box, which gives rise to the idiom *être aux premières loges*: to have a grandstand view, a front seat.

logeur (m) Landlord. *Les logeurs peuvent être difficiles*: landlords can be difficult.
Lodger = *pensionnaire* (m/f), *locataire* (m/f).

logeuse (f) Landlady. *Je cherche une logeuse sympathique*: I am looking for a nice landlady.
Lodger (feminine) = *pensionnaire* (f).

loquet (m) Latch. *Il mit la main sur le loquet avant d'ouvrir la porte*: he put his hand on the latch before opening the door.
Lock = *serrure* (f).

lorgnette (f) Opera-glasses. *Passe-moi la lorgnette, s'il te plaît*: hand me the opera-glasses, please.
Lorgnette = *face-à-main* (m).

losange (m) Rhombus (geometry). Diamond-shaped (*en losange*).
Lozenge (to suck) = *pastille* (f).

lot (m) Share, portion (as of land).
Lot, fate.
But *le gros lot* has a nice sense – the big prize, the jackpot.
Can mean 'lot' in the sense of a batch of goods. *Un lot de pullovers est arrivé ce matin*: a batch of pullovers came this morning.
A lot of = *beaucoup de*.

loupe (f) Magnifying-glass. *Examiner quelque chose à la loupe*: to examine closely (literally and figuratively).
Do not confuse with loop (= *boucle* (f)).
To loop the loop = *boucler la boucle*.

lover Not to love! To coil. *Les serpents se lovent*: snakes curl up.
To love = *aimer*.

loyal Loyal, but also sincere, frank, straight, fair.
Un adversaire loyal: a fair opponent.

loyalement Loyally, but also commonly used for frankly, fairly, properly.

lumineux Luminous, and *une idée lumineuse*: brainwave, bright idea.

lump (m) Lumpy eggs? No, *oeufs de lump(s)* on the menu refers to lumpfish-eggs – a caviar-like roe.
Lump = *grumeau* (m). Sometimes *morceau* (m) or (swelling) = *bosse* (f), *enflure* (f).

lunatique Care is needed, as the French sense is quite mild – capricious, temperamental, moody. English seems to have seen the effect of moon (*la lune*) changes more seriously, hence mad or (colloquially) stupid.
Lunatic = *de fou*, *stupide*.

lunch (m) A buffet meal, as at a reception.
But is being used increasingly to mean a light meal.
Lunch = *déjeuner* (m).

lustre (m) Lustre, also chandelier. *Nous avons admiré le lustre du salon*: we admired the chandelier in the drawing-room.
Another (literary) meaning is a period of five years, and it is sometimes loosely used in the sense of a long time, ages.

luthier (m) The sense has been extended from that of lute-maker to the maker in general of stringed instruments (violins, guitars).

luxure (f) A word not to misunderstand! It means lewdness, and not luxury. *On ne peut s'imaginer sa vie de luxure*: one cannot conceive his life of debauchery.

Luxury = *luxe* (m).

luxurieusement Lewdly.

Luxuriously = *dans le luxe*.

luxurieux Lewd. *Si vous pensez à des choses luxurieuses*: if you have lewd thoughts.

Luxurious = *de luxe, luxueux*.

macaron (m) Macaroon, but also a (round) badge, or sticker.

machiniste (m) Machinist. Sometimes (bus, etc.) driver.

Also used for a stage hand (theatre), scene-shifter.

magazin (m) Large shop. *Je l'ai vu dans le magazin*: I saw him in the shop. Magazine (store), (gun).

Magazine (journal) = *magazine* (m).

magnéto (m) A familiar abbreviation for *magnétophone* (tape-recorder), whereas *magnéto* (f) is magneto.

magnifier To magnify or glorify, to idealize. *'Il faut reconnaître pourtant tout ce que ce sens de l'Empire, magnifié par Rudyard Kipling, contenait de grandeur'* (Jean Oger, *Les Anglais chez eux*, Arthaud).

To magnify = *grossir, agrandir*.

magot (m) Familiarly, means money, a tidy pile. *On accuse le voleur d'avoir caché le magot*: they accuse the thief of having hidden away the money.

Can also mean magot in the sense of monkey (Barbary ape, macaque type), or a small grotesque Chinese figure (ornament).

Maggot = *ver* (m).

mail (m) An old word, one of whose meanings is mall or walk (compare Pall Mall).

Mail (post) = *courrier* (m).

    (armour) = *mailles* (f).

maintenance (f) Usually a military term for maintenance (service), or an industrial term.

Maintenance (usually) = *entretien* (m).

       (of law) = *maintien* (m).

maisonnette (f) A small house or cottage. (In English usage it can also refer to a flat.) Note the French spelling.

maître (m) Master (the circumflex accent replaces the English s). Primary school teacher.
Le chien et son maître: the dog and his master.
Note that *maître d'hôtel* is not only head waiter but also the word for butler.
Le maître d'hôtel m'apporta un whisky bien tassé: the butler brought me a stiff whisky.
(School)master = *professeur* (m).

major (m) Care is needed, as this word may mean the MO (i.e. *le médecin major*), or may refer to the regimental adjutant.
And *major-général* is the chief of staff (in war-time). In the navy he may be a rear-admiral attending to the running of the fleet, etc.
Major = *commandant* (m).
Major-general = *général* (m) *de division*.

malice (f) Malice, also just mischievousness, and sometimes trick, joke.

malicieusement Maliciously, but also has a milder meaning of naughtily, mockingly. *Le petit garçon a souri malicieusement*: the little boy gave a mischievous smile.

malignement Malignantly or spitefully, but can mean mischievously (in a sly way).

malignité (f) Malignancy (medical).
Also in the sense of sly mischievousness, spite. '*Il s'anima de la malignité qui possède, à regarder courir les passants sous l'averse, l'homme qui s'est abrité à temps*' (Colette, *Duo*, Ferenczi).

malingre Sickly, delicate, whereas a malingerer in English *pretends* he is ill.
Un enfant malingre: a sickly child.
To malinger = *faire le malade*.
A malingerer = *simulateur* (m), *fumiste* (m) (the latter is popular usage).

mandat (m) Mandate.
Also means a postal order, money order.
Can be a warrant (e.g. arrest, search). ' – *Dites, donc, dit le veilleur à voix basse, est-ce qu'ils ont un mandat? Vous savez, ce n'est pas normal d'arrêter quelqu'un la nuit*' (Cécil Saint-Laurent, *Ici Clotilde*, Paris, Les Presses de la Cité).

maniaque As noun or adjective it can mean maniac.
But care is needed, as it frequently means cranky, odd, with one's own peculiar ways. *Un vieux professeur maniaque*: a fussy old professor.

manie (f) Mania, obsession (in a medical sense).
Also craze. *Il a la manie des gadgets*: he is mad about gadgets.
Can have milder meanings. *Comme tout le monde il a ses petites manies*: like everyone, he has his odd little ways.

manifestation (f) Manifestation, showing and now common in the sense of (political) demonstration. *Encore une manifestation demain*: another demonstration tomorrow. Note too the topical sense of event (sporting or otherwise). A conference centre might well advertise that it has facilities *pour toutes les manifestations* (all kinds of events).

manoeuvre (m) (Unskilled) worker.
Manoeuvre = *manoeuvre* (f).

manoeuvre (f) Manoeuvre, working. *Les grandes manoeuvres*: army manoeuvres.
Les manoeuvres can also mean ropes, rigging.

manoir (m) Manor, but also country house, mansion.

manteau (m) Mantle or cloak, mostly coat.
Manteau de cheminée: mantelpiece.
Sous le manteau: clandestinely, privately (compare 'cloak and dagger').

manucure (f) Manicurist.
Manicure = *soin* (m) *des mains*.

manufacture (f) Sometimes used for a large factory or works (with the emphasis on quality products).
Manufacture = *fabrication* (f).

marc (m) Marc, residue (from pressed grapes, etc.). Hence *un marc* can be a brandy (distilled from marc – i.e. *une eau de vie de marc*).
Can also refer to coffee-grounds (*marc de café*) or tealeaves. If you can tell fortunes from them, *vous lisez dans le marc de café*.
Le marc is also the German Mark.
Mark = *marque* (f).
  (school) = *point* (m), *note* (f).

marche (f) March, also walk; also going, functioning, moving.
Faire marche arrière: to reverse.
Also step. *Attention à la marche*: mind the step.
March (month) = *mars* (m).

marché (m) Market, also bargain. Hence *bon marché*: cheap.
And the familiar 'into the bargain, what's more' is *par-dessus le marché*.

marcher To march, but very often just to walk.
Also to go, function. *Tout marche bien*: all is going well.
Used in various colloquial ways, and note in particular *je l'ai fait marcher*: I pulled his leg, and *il a marché*: he fell for it.

mare (f) Stagnant pond. Pool. *Le fermier s'arrêta près de la mare*: the farmer stopped beside the pond.
Mare = *jument* (f).

marginal Marginal. But it has a modern sense of living on the fringe of society, as in *un homme marginal*.

marin (m) Sailor, mariner.
Marine = *fusilier* (m) *marin*.

marine (f) Navy. *La marine marchande*: merchant navy. *Bleu marine*: navy blue. Also a general term for the art of navigation.

Of a painter, it means seascape. *Il est connu pour ses belles marines*: he is known for his beautiful seascapes.
Marine (m) can be a marine (soldier).

marmelade (f) Usually means a compote of (stewed) fruit.
If you want marmalade, ask for *marmelade d'oranges* or else *confiture* (f) *d'oranges*. Note the French spelling.
And if you are *dans la marmelade*, you are in a jam (familiar usage).

marmot (m) Urchin. *Je l'ai vue avec tous ses marmots*: I saw her with all her brats.
Croquer le marmot is a familiar expression for to be kept hanging around, waiting.
Marmot = *marmotte* (f).

marmotte (f) Marmot; and *dormir comme une marmotte* is one of a number of equivalents for 'to sleep like a log'.
Marmotte also has a very different meaning – the sample-case of a commercial traveller.

marmouset (m) Usually used in the familiar sense of young kid, little chap.
Marmoset= *ouistiti* (m).

marquer To mark, in various senses. Note that of to influence, to leave a mark, an impression. *Deux ou trois hommes m'ont marqué*: two or three men have had a lasting influence on me.
To mark (stain) = *tacher*.
        (correct) = *corriger*.

marquis (m) Marquis.
Marquee = *(grande) tente* (f).

marquise (f) Marchioness. But also a glass roof (e.g. of a station), porch, protective awning (usually of glass).

martinet (m) The less technical meaning is a strap or tawse.
Or, of birds, it is a swift (martin).
He is a martinet = *c'est un homme à cheval sur la discipline*.
She is a martinet = *c'est un vrai gendarme*.

martyre (m) Martyrdom.
Martyr = *martyr(e)* (m/f).

masse (f) Mass.
Also earth (electricity).
Can mean sledge-hammer. *Coup* (m) *de masse* = shattering blow.

masser To mass (as of crowds).
But also to rub, massage (compare 'masseur').

massif Massive, also solid (e.g. trees, silver). *En chêne massif*: of solid oak.
'*Ces six couverts l'obsédaient. Ils étaient là. A quelques pas. A l'instant où il avait traversé la chambre à coucher de l'évêque la vieille servante les mettait dans un petit placard à la tête du lit. Ils étaient massifs. Et de vieille argenterie*' (Victor Hugo, *Jean Valjean*).

mater To mate (chess).
To check, suppress, tame, completely subdue. *Je l'ai matée!*: I tamed her!
To mate (people) = *marier*.
　　　　(animals) = *accoupler*.
or *se marier, s'accoupler* (intransitive).

matérialiser To materialize.
But note a special use of *matérialisé* to denote an area marked off by a white line. At a car-park you may be instructed to make sure to park only *dans les cases matérialisées*: in the white boxes.

matériel (m) Material, equipment. *Matériel de pêche*: fishing tackle.
Material (raw) = *matière (première)* (f).
　　　　(fabrics) = *étoffe* (f).

maternité (f) Has the three meanings of maternity (*ses sentiments de maternité*: her feelings of being a mother); second, pregnancy or confinement; and third, maternity hospital. *Je l'ai vue hier à la maternité*: I saw her yesterday at the maternity hospital.

matière (f) Matter, material.
(Subject) matter, subject at school. *Quelle est votre matière préférée?*: what is your favourite subject?
Matter (affair) = *affaire* (f).
What is the matter? = *Qu'est ce qu'il y a?*
It doesn't matter = *Ça ne fait rien*.

matinée (f) May have the sense of matinée, afternoon performance.
But the normal meaning is (whole) morning. *Je suis allé en matinée – après avoir fait la queue toute la matinée!*: I went to the matinée – after queuing all morning! Note the idiom *faire la grasse matinée*: to have a late morning, to lie in.

matrone (f) Matron, but it is now chiefly used to mean a large common woman.
Matron (hospital) = *infirmière* (f) *en chef*.

mécanicien (m) (Car) mechanic, mechanic in general. Also engineer (ship), and on trains he is the engine-driver.

mécréant A literary word for disbeliever, one who does not believe in the existence of God. (This is an old sense of English miscreant.)
Miscreant = *misérable* (m), *gredin* (m).

médecin (m) Doctor. *Je cherche un bon médecin*: I am looking for a good doctor.
Medicine (remedy) = *médicament* (m).

médecine (f) No longer used for medicine (remedy), but is the general word for (the study of) medicine. *Mon père était médecin et la médecine m'intéresse aussi*: my father was a doctor and medicine interests me also.
Medicine (remedy) = *médicament* (m).
Woman doctor = *femme* (f) *médecin*.

meeting (m) Meeting, in a political or sporting sense.

Meeting = *réunion* (f).
   (casual) = *rencontre* (f).

melon (m) Melon.
Also bowler (hat) (*chapeau* (m) *melon*). *Un Anglais typique avec melon et pébroque*: a typical Englishman with bowler and brolly.

mémento (m) May mean memento, but also a note-book, diary. Can (old sense) also refer to a revision book with a summary of facts. A name given to certain prayers.

mémoire (m) Memorandum, account (business).
Also dissertation or thesis.
Also memoirs (plural).
Memory (general use) = *mémoire* (f). *Si j'ai bonne mémoire*: if I remember rightly.
But often = *souvenir* (m). *J'en garde un bon souvenir*: I have happy memories of it.

mention (f) Mention.
Also note, heading – *les mentions inutiles* are the headings that do not apply (on a form) and which you are invited to delete.
Also refers to exams, and to pass *avec mention* would be to do so with distinction.

menu (m) Menu. Also in particular the *set* menu (as opposed to *à la carte*). Thus a restaurant or hotel may advertise *'menu, carte'* (set meal and *à la carte*). *Je prendrai le menu*: I will take the set meal.
Note too the phrase *par le menu*: in detail. Jocularly one might say *je vais vous expliquer le menu par le menu*: I will go through the menu in detail for you.
Menu (also) = *carte* (f).

mercantile Commercial (or grabbing, when used pejoratively).
But mercantile marine = *marine* (f) *marchande*.

merci (m) Thanks.
But *merci* as a feminine noun means mercy (which also = *pitié* (f), *grâce* (f) etc.).

merlin Cleaver, poleaxe.
Merlin = *émerillon* (m).

messe (f) Mass (religious service).
Mess (officers') = *mess* (m).
   (muddle) = *gâchis* (m), *désordre* (m).

mètre (m) Metre, also metre rule.
Note *un mètre à ruban*: tape-measure.
Also metre in poetry.
Meter (gas, taxi, etc.) = *compteur* (m).

métropole (f) Metropolis.
Also mother-country, and is often the equivalent of France (as opposed to overseas territories).

meurtrir No longer now means to murder, but to bruise. *Il a serré tellement fort qu'il l'a meurtri*: he pressed so tightly that he bruised him.
But *le meutre*: murder, *le meurtrier*: murderer.
To murder = *assassiner*.

Mexico Mexico City. *Un voyage très simple – New York – Mexico – New York*: a very simple journey – New York – Mexico City – New York.
Mexico (country) = *Mexique* (m).

midship (m) Midshipman. This is a familiar abbreviation of *le midshipman*, which is more properly *aspirant* (m) (*de marine*). '*Le large sourire du midship s'épanouit*' (Marie-Madeleine Fourcade, *L'Arche de Noé*, Fayard).
Midships = *milieu* (m) *du navire*.

mignonnette (f) Mignonette lace, chicory (succory), crushed pepper, London Pride (flower) are the main meanings.
But mignonette (note spelling difference) = *réséda* (m) (*odorant*).

militer To militate. Also to take an active part. *Il milita dans la Résistance*: he was active in the Resistance.

mille (m) Is a mile, but *mille* is also a thousand (invariable in the plural). *Deux milles*: two miles. *Deux mille*: two thousand.
Mettre dans le mille: to score a bull's-eye (familiar and often figurative).

mincir To slim.
To mince (meat) = *hacher*.
      (of people) = *minauder*.
Not to mince one's words = *ne pas mâcher ses mots*.

mine (f) Mine (both senses).
Also appearance (mien), air. *Vous avez bonne mine*: you look well.
Used in numerous expressions, among them *il a fait mine de . . .*: he made as though to . . ., *mine de rien*: quite casually, innocently (the latter is popular usage).
Mine is also lead for a pencil (hence *porte-mine* (m): propelling pencil).

mineur (m) Both a miner and a minor.

ministère (m) Ministry. Sometimes government. *Où se trouve le ministère?*: Where is the ministry?
Minister = *ministre* (m).

minus (m) Familiar word for half-wit, clot (from *minus habens*).
Minus = *moins* (m).

minute (f) Minute (time).
Also minute, draft, original copy (legal). But the minutes (of a meeting) are *le procès-verbal*.
Minute is often coupled to a noun to suggest speed, as in *entrecôte* (f) *minute* (minute steak), *talon* (m) *minute* (new heels while you wait), *cocotte* (f) *minute* (pressure-cooker).

mire (f) (Line of) sight (weapons).
Figuratively, *le point de mire* is the centre of interest, attention.
Mire = *fange* (f).

misaine (f) Foresail. *Mât* (m) *de misaine*: foremast. Whereas the mizzen-mast is the aftermost of three masts!
Mizzen = *artimon* (m).
Mizzen-mast = *mât d'artimon*.

misérable Miserable, wretched, paltry. Also very poor, destitute.
Miserable (often) = *malheureux, très triste*.

misère (f) Misery.
Often used in a general sense of hard times, difficulty. *Faire des misères à quelqu'un*: to tease someone, give someone a hard time.
Another meaning is (dire) poverty. *Ils sont tombés dans la misère*: they have fallen on very hard times.
And *une misère!* means a mere nothing, a trifle!
Misery (sometimes) = *souffrances* (f).

miss (f) Was sometimes used in the sense of a (foreign) governess. It has been updated to mean a beauty queen!
(So Miss France is *Miss* (and not *Mademoiselle*) *France*.)
Miss = *mademoiselle*.
    (failure) = *coup* (m) *manqué*.

mite (f) Moth.
Mite (widow's) = *obole* (f).
Poor wee mite = *pauvre p'tit(e) gosse* (m/f).

mixture (f) Mixture of chemicals or drugs, or (in a pejorative sense) of drinks and perhaps food. *Mais qu'est-ce que c'est que cette mixture?*: But what on earth is this mixture (concoction)?
Mixture (usually) = *mélange* (m).

mob (f) *T'as vu la mob devant la maison?*: Have you seen the moped outside the house? Popular abbreviation of *la mobylette*.
Mob =*meute* (f), *foule* (f).

mobile (m) Mobile (art), also motive (crime).

mode (f) Fashion (in general), fashion (clothes). *A la mode*: fashionable.
Mode = *mode* (m).

modéliste (m/f) A model-maker in two senses – dress-designer, or someone who makes (scale) models of cars, trains, etc.

môle (m) Mole, jetty.
Mole (on skin) = *grain* (m) *de beauté*.
    (animal) = *taupe* (f).

moleskine (f) Does indeed come from 'moleskin', but its meaning now is imitation leather.
Moleskin (literally) = *peau* (f) *de taupe*.
    (material) = *velours* (m) *de coton*.

momentanément Momentarily, but not only for a moment, also for the moment, provisionally. *Il est parti momentanément pour l'Amérique*: he has gone to America for the time being.

mondain Mundane, worldly, but also fashionable, society. *'Les événements mondains les plus brillants de ces années scolaires – déjà mondainement saturées – sont les grands bals de fin d'année'* (Tony Mayer, *La Vie anglaise*, Presses Universitaires de France, Que Sais-Je?).
But note that *la (brigade) mondaine* is a familiar expression for the vice squad.
Mundane can also = *banal, ordinaire.*

moniteur (m), **monitrice** (f) The usual meaning is a coach, instructor for sports, etc. *Les élèves, accompagnés d'un moniteur, sont partis faire du ski*: the pupils, accompanied by an instructor, left to go skiing.
Also used of someone who helps to run a holiday camp, but is not used of a school pupil (other than as coach).

monnaie (f) In certain senses the French meaning and English still overlap – currency, money, such as in *monnaie de papier*: paper money (and note *la Monnaie*: the Mint). *Une pièce de monnaie*: coin.
But normally means change. *De la petite monnaie*: loose change. *Avez-vous de la monnaie?*: have you any change? *Je n'ai pas de monnaie*: I haven't any change.
Note the idiom *c'est monnaie courante*: it is common practice.
Money = *argent* (m).

monter To mount, go (come) up, climb, to mount, to fit, to bring up – *Il m'a monté les valises*: he brought the cases up for me.

monument (m) Monument in various senses, but can just mean historical buildings or building of particular interest, as when Zola writes *'les pans de murailles jaunes, les hauts monuments, couleur de rouille, flambaient avec les pétillements de brusques feux de fagots, dans l'air du soir'* (*La Débâcle*).

moralité (f) Morality, morals, good character.
Also the moral of a story (*la moralité d'une histoire*).

morgue (f) Morgue, mortuary, but also pride, arrogance.

morse (m) May be the Morse code, or a walrus.

mortification (f) Mortification, humiliation.
But you may find it in its medical sense of gangrene (mortification).

moteur (m) Engine. *Avant d'apercevoir sa Jaguar, j'ai entendu le bruit d'un moteur*: before catching sight of his Jaguar, I heard the noise of an engine. The dramatic-sounding *moteur à explosion* is an internal combustion engine, and *un moteur à deux temps* is a two-stroke engine.
Moteur is also the driving force. *Le moteur de ma vie*: the driving force in my life (not 'the car in my life').
Motor (car) = *auto* (f).

motif (m) Motive, but often just reason or cause. *Encore un motif d'irritation*: another cause for annoyance. Note *pour le bon motif*: seriously, with honourable intentions (when courting).
Also motif in art and music.
Motive (crime) = *mobile* (m).

moto (f) Motorbike (familiar abbreviation for *une motocyclette*). *Il s'est acheté une belle moto*: he has bought himself a beautiful motorbike. *Le bruit des motos*: the noise of the motorbikes.
Motor (car) = *auto* (f).

motocycle (m) A powered bicycle. A general word for mopeds and motor-bicycles.
Motorcycle = *motocyclette* (f).

mousse (m) A word that has often caused trouble in translation. Not 'mouse' (in spite of what some young pupils may think!), but cabin-boy, young sailor. *'A un certain moment, il cria: "Sauvez Clément!" Clément, c'était le mousse. Un enfant'* (Victor Hugo, *Pendant l'Exil*).
Mouse = *souris* (f).
Mousse (to eat) = *mousse* (f).
Moose = *élan* (m).

mousse (f) Can be (chocolate) mousse.
Also froth or foam (beer, sea, soap, etc.), as well as (sponge) rubber and moss. *Il s'assit sur la mousse*: he sat down on the moss.
Moose = *élan* (m).
Mouse = *souris* (f).

moustache (f) Moustache, and whiskers (*les moustaches*), as of a cat.

moutard (m) Brat, kid (familiar usage).
Mustard = *moutarde* (f).

moutarde (f) Is mustard, but note that the word is also used in a figurative and familiar sense, thus – *Pendant le dîner la moutarde m'est montée au nez*: during dinner I flared up (got very annoyed).

mouton (m) Sheep, as well as mutton.
Also a number of other meanings, which explains why *des moutons sous le lit* is not as odd as it sounds – it means fluff under the bed.
If it refers to the sea, then it is – 'white horses', white-crested waves. *'La mer secouait les galets en bavant et dans la rade deux ou trois navires flottaient en désordre sur les moutons'* (Raymond Queneau, *Un Rude Hiver*, Gallimard). The idea is similar when it means small, white fleecy clouds.
And popularly *un mouton* can mean a police-informer, a stool-pigeon (in a prison cell).
After which, one might well add *pour revenir à nos moutons*: to get back to the subject.

mouvant Moving (*sables mouvants*: quicksands), changeable, fluctuating.
Moving (often) = *en mouvement, en marche* (e.g. vehicle), *mobile*.
    (figuratively) = *émouvant*.

mouvement (m) Movement, in various senses, but it is also impulse, reaction. *Un mouvement de colère*: a burst of anger.
Allez, un bon mouvement!: be a sport!

muer Not to mew!, but to moult. *Le chat a mué*: the cat moulted.
It is also used when young voices break.
To mew = *miauler*.

mufti (m) Mufti (with reference to the Moslem religion).
Not to be confused with 'in mufti' = *en civil*.

mule (f) (She) mule, also a woman's slipper. *Où sont mes mules?*: where are
my slippers?

musculaire Muscular (of things, e.g. system, etc.).
Musclé, musculeux (of people).

muser Literary word for to dawdle, trifle, idle. The word comes in fact from
museau (m) (muzzle, then popularly face) with the idea of someone
'mooching' around, head in the air.
To muse = *méditer, rêvasser, murmurer (tout en réfléchissant)*.

muserie (f) Idling (literary word).
Musing = *rêverie* (f).

musical Refers to things – sounds, voices, etc. *Une soirée musicale*: a musical
evening.
To be musical (of a person) could = *être musicien, aimer la musique*, among
others.

musicien (m) **musicienne** (f) Can be a musician or performer in a band, etc.,
but it can also just mean someone who is musical.

musique (f) Music, but can also mean a band. *J'entends la musique qui
approche*: I can hear the band getting near.
Le chef de musique: bandmaster.

mutation (f) Mutation, change. Now often used for the transfer of personnel (or sportsmen). *J'ai demandé ma mutation à la brigade des stupéfiants*: I
asked to be transferred to the drug squad.

muter To transfer (employees, officials, etc.).
To mute = *assourdir*.

mutinerie (f) Mutiny or rebellion, but you may find it too in the sense of
impishness or disobedience (of children).

myrtille (f) Bilberry.
Myrtle = *myrte* (m).

mystifiant Misleading or deceptive.
Mystifying (often) = *incompréhensible*.

mystification (f) Mystification in the sense of hoax, deceit, joke.
Mystification (puzzlement) = *perplexité* (f).

mystifier Has the sense of to hoax, take in.
To mystify (often) = *intriguer, rendre perplexe*.

N

nappe (f) Tablecloth.
Sheet, layer (of water, etc.). *Une nappe de pétrole*: oil slick.
Nap (sleep) = *(petit) somme* (m).

natter To plait, braid.
To natter = *discuter le coup, faire la causette, papoter*.

nature (f) Nature, but some other meanings should be noted.
Nature morte: still life (painting).
Of food and drink, the word suggests plainness. *Du café au lait? Nature, s'il vous plaît*: White coffee? Black, please.
Payer en nature: to pay in kind.

navigateur (m) Navigator, but also sailor. *Que pensez-vous de ces navigateurs solitaires?*: What do you think of these single-handed sailors?

navigation (f) Navigation, also sailing or flying. *Un contrôleur de la navigation aérienne*: an air traffic controller.

naviguer To navigate, but also commonly used for to sail (and even to fly).
Un pilote qui préfère naviguer la nuit: a pilot who prefers flying at night.

négligemment Negligently, carelessly, but also indifferently, casually. *Tant pis! répondit-il négligemment*: Too bad! he replied casually.

négligent Not only negligent, careless, but also casual. *D'un air négligent*: casually.

négociant (m) **négociante** (f) A merchant (e.g. wine).
A negotiator = *négociateur* (m), *négociatrice* (f).

nègre (m) Negro. It is pejorative for *un Noir*.
Note that it can also mean a ghost-writer. *Je ne veux pas dépendre d'un nègre pour l'écrire*: I don't want to depend on a ghost-writer to write it.
Parler petit nègre: to talk pidgin.

nerveux Nervous, in a technical sense. *Une dépression nerveuse*: a nervous breakdown. Of people, it means highly-strung or on edge.
Or it means wiry, sinewy (e.g. hands, arms).
Un moteur nerveux would be a very responsive engine.
Nervous (often) = *timide*.

nervosité (f) (Feeling of) agitation, (state of) nerves, irritability.
Nervousness often = *timidité* (f).

nervure (f) Nervure, veins on leaf or insect wing.
Nerves = *nerfs* (m).

niche (f) Niche or nook.
Also (dog) kennel. *Le chien sort de sa niche*: the dog comes out of his kennel.
Can also mean a trick (that one plays on someone).

To find one's niche = *trouver exactement ce qu'on cherche dans la vie, être casé.*

Noël (m) Is indeed Christmas. *Le Père Noël*: Father Christmas. But you may also find it used for a (Christmas) carol or present.

noise (f) Quarrel, but now used only in the familiar expression *chercher noise à quelqu'un*: to try to pick a quarrel with someone.
Noise = *bruit* (m).

nominal Nominal (nominal value).
But also in the more literal sense of concerned with names, hence *un appel nominal* is a roll-call.

nominalement Nominally, in name, also by name, etc. *Je m'adresse à vous nominalement*: I am writing to you by name.

nonchalamment Nonchalantly, casually, or in a lazy way.

nonchalance (f) Nonchalance, indifference, and can also suggest indolence. *'Seuls l'allumeur de l'unique réverbère du pôle Nord, et son confrère de l'unique réverbère du pôle Sud, menaient des vies d'oiseveté et de nonchalance: ils travaillaient deux fois par an'* (Saint-Exupéry, *Le Petit Prince*).

nonchalant Nonchalant, casual, also indolent.

Normands (m) The Norsemen of history as well as the Normans of Normandy.
Note the familiar *répondre en Normand*: to give an ambiguous answer (typical of the caution of the Normans).

notablement Notably, to a noticeable or considerable extent. *Le danger est notablement moins grave*: the danger is notably less serious.
Notably, especially = *notamment*.

notation (f) Notation, but also marking (school). *Notation continue*: continuous assessment.

note (f) (Official) note, notes, jotting, note (music).
Also school marks or report.
Also bill. *Apportez-moi la note*: bring the bill.
Note (a few lines) = *billet* (m), *mot* (m).
   (money) = *billet* (m).
A person of note = *notabilité* (f).

notice (f) Short notice (e.g. obituary notice). Preface.
Also means (booklet of) instructions, short account, explanatory pamphlet. Talking of the *au pair* system, Jean Oger writes *'Pour remédier à cette situation, le ministère britannique de l'Intérieur* (Home Office) *a publié, pour la première fois dans les années 60, une notice sur le sujet à l'usage des jeunes filles et de leurs hôtes'* (*Les Anglais chez eux*, Arthaud).
Notice (often) = *avis* (m), *affiche* (f).
   (dismissal) = *congé* (m).

notoire Notorious, well-known (of things, and without a pejorative sense). If used of people, it is then like the pejorative 'notorious' in English. Notorious (of a place) = *mal famé*.

notoriété (f) Notoriety or being known (things), thus *c'est de notoriété publique*: it is common knowledge (well known). Of people, it means fame or reputation. *Dès qu'on atteint à la notoriété . . .*: as soon as you become a celebrity . . . The pejorative English notoriety needs a paraphrase (*mauvaise réputation*, *mauvaise publicité*, etc.).

nouvelle (f) (Piece) of news. Also short story. *Aimez-vous ses nouvelles?*: Do you like his short stories? Novel = *roman* (m).

nouvelliste (m/f) Short story writer. *Un nouvelliste connu*: a well-known short story writer. Novelist = *romancier* (m), *romancière* (f).

nuisance (f) (Often in the plural.) Something harmful or having harmful effects (often to the environment). *Espérons que cette sorte d'aérosol ne provoquera aucune nuisance*: Let us hope that this sort of spray will not give rise to any harmful effects. To be a nuisance (often) = *être embêtant*.

nuque (f) Nape of the neck. '*Il sentait le regard des deux autres peser sur sa nuque et cette impression désagréable lui donna froid à l'échine*' (André Frambois, *Diamants au sang*, Euredif). Neck = *cou* (m).

nurse (f) (Children's) nurse. Nurse (hospital) = *infirmière* (f). (male) = *infirmier* (m).

O

objecter To object. Often to bring up, put forward, plead. *Quand il a dit que le gouvernement n'avait rien fait, j'ai objecté ses succès récents*: when he said the government had done nothing, I put forward its recent successes. To object (to something) = *désapprouver* (among others).

objectif (m) Aim or objective, target. Also lens of a camera. *Un voleur pris en flagrant délit que l'objectif avait saisi*: a thief in the act caught by the camera's lens.

obligation (f) Obligation, in various senses, and (in financial terms) a bond. *Achetez des obligations!*: buy bonds!

oblitération (f) May mean obliteration, also obstruction (medical). *L'oblitération d'une artère*: the obstruction of an artery.

But the usual meaning is cancellation (e.g. of stamps). *Le cachet d'oblitération*: postmark.

Obliteration = *effacement* (m).

oblitérer Sometimes to obliterate, but usually used in the sense of to cancel (as of a stamp).

Also a medical term meaning to obstruct.

To obliterate = *effacer*.

observation (f) Observation, in various senses, but can also have the sense of a pointed remark, a reproof. *La mère faisait toujours des observations à ses enfants*: the mother was always finding fault with her children.

occasion (f) The normal meaning is occasion or opportunity. *Il faut profiter de l'occasion*: you must take the chance.

Can also mean occasion – *à l'occasion de son anniversaire*: on the occasion of his birthday.

Another meaning is bargain (compare the idea of opportunity), and can also mean occasion or reason (for something).

It is important to know that *d'occasion* is second-hand. *Une voiture d'occasion*: a second-hand car. *Je ne me sers pas de ma voiture d'occasion pour les grandes occasions*: I don't use my second-hand car for big occasions.

Occasion (sometimes) = *événement* (m).

occurence (f) Circumstances, occasion. *En l'occurence*: in the circumstances.

Occurrence (often) = *événement* (m).

offense (f) Offence (which offends someone), also sin or transgression.

Offence (often) = *délit* (m).

offenseur (m) Offender, the person who has offended, given offence. (A literary word.)

Offender (law, crime) = *coupable* (m), *malfaiteur* (m), *criminel* (m).

An old offender (crime) = *repris* (m) *de justice*.

offensif Offensive, i.e. attacking. *Armes offensives*: offensive weapons.

Offensive (insulting) = *offensant*.

       (e.g. smell) = *désagréable*.

offensivement Offensively, by attacking.

Offensively (often) = *injurieusement*.

office (m) Usually means office (in the sense of job, position), but can sometimes refer to the actual place – e.g. office, agency.

Also means church service (compare Divine Office). *Je l'ai vu à l'office ce matin*: I saw him at church this morning.

Les bons offices are the good offices of someone.

Office (for work) = *bureau* (m).

office (f) A pantry or staff dining-room. *Tout le monde a mangé ensemble à l'office*: everybody ate together in the staff dining-room.

Office (for work) = *bureau* (m).

officieusement Unofficially.
   Officiously = *avec trop de zèle.*

officieux Normally means unofficial or informal. *Il s'agit d'une lettre officieuse*: it is a question of an informal letter.
   Officious = *trop zélé.*
   Official = *officiel.*

offrir To offer. But note that it is also used in the sense of to give. *'Je lui ai offert un bouquet de roses'* is not 'I offered her a bunch of roses' (with the implication that she refused them), but 'I gave her a bunch of roses' (as a present). A shop assistant might ask – *C'est pour offrir?*: Is it for a present? *Je vais m'offrir un dîner à tout casser*: I am going to stand myself a slap-up dinner.
   Laissez-vous offrir une belle voiture: treat yourself to a beautiful car.

oignon (m) Onion. Used in a number of familiar or popular expressions. *Occupe-toi de tes oignons*: mind your own business. *Aux petits oignons*: first class. *En rang d'oignons*: in single file.
   It is a bulb (e.g. tulip bulb).
   Also a corn (especially under the big toe).

ombrelle (f) Woman's small parasol. English 'umbrella' seems to have lost this meaning now and is used for protection against bad weather (= *le parapluie*), except in the case of café or beach umbrellas (= *le parasol!*)

omnibus (m) A word that might cause difficulty. From the meaning of the old horse-drawn omnibus it has become *un train omnibus*, a stopping train (as opposed to a fast train). Thus, *il y a un omnibus à six heures*: there is a local train at six. *Il faut prendre l'omnibus*: you must take the train.

onéreux Onerous, i.e. costly, heavy (of charges). *Ce serait un voyage trop onéreux pour ma famille*: it would be too expensive a trip for my family.
   A titre onéreux is an official phrase meaning subject to payment or on condition of payment.
   Onerous (often) = *lourd, pénible.*

opinion (f) Opinion, but also used elliptically for public opinion or the public. *'Ce comportement lui valut d'être incarcéré dans la forteresse de Mutzig, et ses amis durent alerter le Parlement et l'opinion pour lui éviter le poteau'* (Marie-Madeleine Fourcade, *L'Arche de Noé*, Fayard).
   In my opinion = *à mon avis* (m).

opportunité (f) Opportuneness. Sometimes opportunity, but this normally = *occasion* (f).

opposition (f) Opposition, and (in financial language) *faire opposition à un chèque*: to stop a cheque.

oppressé Oppressed, usually in the sense of breathless. *Elle était là sur le lit, oppressée*: she was there on the bed, hardly able to breathe.
   Oppressed (often) = *opprimé.*

oppresser To oppress. *Cette nouvelle m'oppresse*: this news weighs me down.
   The verb can also mean that one has difficulty in breathing.
   To oppress (people) = *opprimer.*

oppressif Oppressive (of laws, etc.).
Oppressive (weather, etc.) = *oppressant, lourd, accablant.*

oppression (f) Oppression (as of a nation), also oppression, shortage of breath (as if one had a weight on one's chest).

or Now (not 'now at the present time'), and used at the beginning of a sentence. *Or, il était une fois une belle princesse*: Now, there was once a beautiful princess.
(*L'or* (m): gold.)
Or = *ou.*

ordinaire (m) The ordinary, normal routine, the normal state or situation.
But *l'ordinaire* has also a specific meaning, which could be a bit puzzling, of daily food, normal fare. *Quant à l'ordinaire des soldats . . .*: as for the soldiers' daily fare . . .
A l'ordinare: usually.

ordonner To order. To arrange.
Also to prescribe (medicine or treatment).
To ordain. *Il a été ordonné prêtre*: he has been ordained.
To order (restaurant) = *commander.*

organe (m) Organ (of the body). Also voice (e.g. of a singer).
Also has the figurative sense of agent, spokesman.
And can be a mechanical part.
Organ (instrument) = *orgue* (m) or *orgues* (f).
Barrel-organ = *orgue de Barbarie.*
Mouth-organ = *harmonica* (m).

organisme (m) Organism (as of the body).
Also body of people, organizing power. *L'organisme qui s'en occupe siège à Nice*: the body dealing with it has its headquarters in Nice.

orient (m) The Orient, but more commonly just the East. *'A l'orient, la lune touchant l'horizon, semblait reposer immobile sur les côtes lointaines . . .'* (Chateaubriand, *Voyage en Amérique*). *En extrême Orient*: in the Far East.

oriental Oriental or eastern; East. *'Je dis: – A travers l'Afrique orientale, c'est bien votre légende. – C'est la vérité, dit Bullit'* (Joseph Kessel, *Le Lion*, Gallimard).

original (m) Original (text, art, etc.). But note *c'est un original* – can mean 'he's a character, an odd fellow'.

originalement In an original way.
Originally = *originairement, originellement, primitivement.*

ornement (m) Decoration, embellishment, ornament.
(Small) ornament (for mantelpiece) = *bibelot* (m).

ostensible Open, clearly visible, conspicuous (this meaning has been lost in English). *'J'ai pris, d'un geste ostensible, mon revolver d'ordonnance'* (Amiral Jubelin, *J'étais Aviateur de la France Libre*, Hachette, Bibliothèque Verte).
Ostensible = *prétendu, sous prétexte.*

ostensiblement Clearly, openly.
Ostensibly = *en apparence*.

outrage (m) Outrage, brazen insult, offence.
Outrage (often) = *scandale* (m).

outrageant Usually means outrageous (in the sense of insulting). *Ces mots outrageants*: these offensive words.
Outrageous (often) = *scandaleux, excessif, incroyable*.

outrageusement Used to mean insultingly, but now usually excessively.
Outrageously (sometimes) = *d'une façon scandaleuse, d'une manière extravagante*.

outrageux Has the sense of insulting (the word is literary and little used).
Outrageous = *scandaleux, immodéré, excessif, extravagant*, etc.

ouverture (f) Opening, as well as overture. Also openness (e.g. of mind).

P

pack (m) May have three meanings. Pack ice (sea); pack (rugby football); pack of small bottles of beer, etc.
Pack (hounds) = *meute* (f).
     (bundle) = *ballot* (m).
     (soldier's) = *paquetage* (m).
     (cards) = *jeu* (m).
     (face) = *masque* (m) *de beauté*.

page (m) Page (boy). *Le roi cherchait son page*: the king was looking for his pageboy.
Page (of book, etc.) = *page* (f).

page (f) Page (of book, etc.). *Etre à la page*: to be up to date.
Page (boy) = *page* (m).

pain (m) Bread, or loaf. *Pain quotidien*: daily bread. *Petits pains*: rolls.
Also cake (of soap). It is used in various expressions. *Se vendre comme des petits pains*: to sell like hot cakes (an interesting culinary difference in the English expression). *Avoir du pain sur la planche*: to have plenty of work on one's hands. *Pour une bouchée de pain*: for a mere song (very cheap).
Pain (physical) = *douleur* (f).
Pains (trouble) = *peine* (f).

pair (m) Peer or equal. Hence a number of phrases such as *hors* (*de*) *pair*: unequalled. It can mean in special senses a state of equality, hence the expression *au pair* (of students, foreign girls, etc.).
Pair = *paire* (f).

pal (m) Stake (compare 'to impale').
Pal = *copain* (m), *copine* (f).

palace (m) Luxurious hotel (a number of which have this name). *Un grand palace dans un beau parc*: a large luxury hotel in fine grounds.

palais (m) Palace, but also palate.

palette (f) Palette (painter).
Paddle (of paddle-steamer).

palme (f) Palm (leaf).
Also flipper (underwater diving).
Palm (tree) = *palmier* (m).
(hand) = *paume* (f).

palpitant Palpitating, but more often means thrilling, exciting. *Un roman palpitant*: a thrilling novel.

pamphlet (m) Used for a satirical pamphlet, a lampoon.
Pamphlet = *brochure* (f), *dépliant* (m).

pan (m) End-piece of clothes, e.g. shirt-tail, coat-tail.
Also section, as in *un pan de mur*: a section of wall.
Pan = *casserole* (f).

panache (m) Panache, dash. But *faire panache* is a familiar expression meaning to overturn or take a tumble (as opposed to *avoir du panache*: to be dashing).
Panache also means plume.

panic (m) Panic grass.
Panic = *panique* (f).

panneau (m) Panel or panelling.
Also means board, hoarding (round a site). *Panneau de signalisation*: road sign.
Can also mean trap, snare.
Panel (also) = *jury* (m).

pantomime (f) Mime or miming. Not a Christmas pantomime (for which there is no equivalent) which can be translated by *une revue-féerie de Noël*.

papier (m) Paper (in general). *Avez-vous un bout de papier?*: have you a bit of paper? *Papier journal*: newsprint (as opposed to other kinds of paper). *Son bureau était couvert de papiers*: his desk was covered with papers. *Vieux papiers*: waste paper. *Papiers d'identité*: identity papers.
Etre dans les petits papiers de quelqu'un: to be in somebody's good books (familiar usage) – the slight difference in the idiom is interesting.
A paper to read (i.e. newspaper) = *journal* (m).

parabole (f) Both parable and parabola.

parade (f) Parade. Also showing off of something, exhibition. *Il fait parade de sa richesse*: he shows off his wealth.
Also means parry (fencing), answer (to a problem). *Il n'y a pas de parade*

possible à cette forme d'attaque: there is no possible answer to this kind of attack.

Hit parade = *hit* (m) *parade*.

Parade (street) = *esplanade* (f).

paradis (m) Paradise. Also the 'gods' at the theatre (perhaps less usual now than *le poulailler*).

paraffine (f) Paraffin wax, or paraffin as a chemical term.

Liquid paraffin = *huile* (f) *de paraffine*.

Paraffin oil = *pétrole* (m) *lampant*.

parallèle Parallel.

But note the quite common and quite topical meaning of unofficial. *Une police parallèle*: an unofficial police force.

parasite (m) Parasite. Also (in plural) used for interference (wireless, etc.).

parasol (m) Café umbrella, beach umbrella. *Il faut nous acheter un parasol*: we must buy a sun umbrella.

(Woman's) parasol = *ombrelle* (f).

parc (m) A word that is less innocent than it looks. Park, but often also grounds. *Situé dans un beau parc*: in fine grounds.

Used for various animals such as in *parc à moutons*: sheep pen; *parc* could also be a playpen for children.

It may be a depot.

Un parc de stationnement would be a car park (largely replaced by the *franglais 'le parking'*).

But do not be deceived by its other meaning – a total number. *Le parc des voitures aujourd'hui* would refer to the number of cars on the road. *Notre compagnie dispose d'un parc de dix Rolls*: our company has a fleet of ten Rolls.

parcelle (f) Particle, fragment. Also a portion or plot of land.

Parcel = *paquet* (m), *colis* (m).

parceller To divide up (into small bits), or parcel out.

To parcel (up) = *emballer*.

        (out) (usually) = *diviser, répartir*.

pardon (m) Pardon, forgiveness. In Britanny it is a pilgrimage.

pardonner To pardon, forgive, but *qui ne pardonne pas* (e.g. of an illness) means fatal. *Une erreur qui ne pardonne pas* is a fatal mistake rather than an unforgivable one (*impardonnable*).

parents (m) Can mean parents. *Tu dois obéir à tes parents*: you must obey your parents.

Also means relations, relatives. *Il a des parents dans le Midi*: he has relations in the South.

And *le parent pauvre* is the poor relation (figurative).

parer To parry, avert (e.g. danger).

Also to adorn.

Note *parer au plus pressé*: to see to first things first.

parfaitement Perfectly. Also used in answer to a question, to mean exactly, right, just so. *Et il a pris l'argent? Parfaitement*: And he took the money? Exactly.

parfum (m) Perfume, scent.
Also flavour (ice-cream).
Les parfums du jour: today's flavours.

pari (m) Bet.
Parry = *parade* (f).

parjure (m) Perjury or perjurer.

parking (m) Car park. *Il y a un parking tout près*: there is a car park nearby.
Can mean parking (*parking autorisé*).

parlementaire Parliamentary. If you come across *un drapeau parlementaire* (dated), it means a white flag (of truce) (from *parlementer*: to parley).

parloir (m) Visitors' room (school, etc.). *Jean-Paul! Tes parents t'attendent au parloir*: Jean-Paul! Your parents are waiting for you in the visitors' room.
The (dated) English parlour usually = *le (petit) salon*.

parole (f) Occasionally parole.
Also (spoken) word, words of a song.
Promise, speech, way of speaking. *'Ma parole!'*: 'Pon my word!' (exclamation).
A vous la parole: I invite you to speak (meeting, etc.).
Parole (often) = *liberté* (f) *conditionnelle*.

parquet (m) Parquet floor.
Also a legal word meaning roughly a (magistrates') court.

partial Partial, i.e. biased, prejudiced. *Avec un patron partial il y aura toujours du mécontentement*: with a biased boss there will always be dissatisfaction.
Partial (partly) = *partiel*.
    (liking) = *avoir une prédilection pour*.

partialement Unfairly (with partiality). *On l'accuse d'avoir jugé l'affaire partialement*: he is accused of having judged the matter unfairly.
Partially = *en partie*.

participation (f) Participation; topical in the sense of workers' participation, being involved with management and profits (an idea encouraged by de Gaulle).

particulier (m) Private person, individual. *En ce qui concerne les particuliers*: as far as private individuals are concerned.
(Can also mean the specific, as opposed to the general.)
Particulars = *détails* (m), *précisions* (f).

particulier Particular, special, also private. *Leçons particulières*: private tuition.
May also mean odd. *Mon patron? En effet, il est assez particulier*: My boss? He is certainly rather odd.
But if he is particular, he is *exigeant*, or *difficile*.

partie (f) Part.
With reference to sport, it means a game – *une partie de tennis*: a game of tennis.
Also a legal term meaning party, client.
Occasionally party in other senses, such as *une partie de chasse*: a shooting party.
Faire partie de: to belong to.
Partie is used in many expressions. Note *c'est partie remise*: another time (it's a pleasure deferred). *Prendre quelqu'un à partie*: to go for someone (literally and figuratively). *Avoir affaire à forte partie*: to have a tough opponent on one's hands.
Party (social) = *surprise-party* (f), *réunion* (f), *fête* (f).
         (political) = *parti* (m).

partition (f) (Musical) score. *Furieux, le chef d'orchestre ferme la partition et s'en va*: furious, the conductor closes the score and goes off.
Sometimes means partition, division.
Partition (in a room) = *cloison* (f).

Le Pas de Calais We know as the Straits of Dover – honour is thus evenly divided. (Also the name of a *département*.)

passable Passable, i.e. quite good, adequate.
But passable (of roads) = *praticable*.

passage (m) Passing. Crossing (river, mountains). *Le passage à niveau*: level crossing. *Le passage clouté*: pedestrian crossing.
Passage, crossing (on a boat).
Sometimes passage, alley, way – *passage souterrain*: underground passage.
Etre de passage: to be passing through. Note *au passage*: in, while passing – *'Mais il se surprit à viser au passage la lampe allumée . . .'* (Colette, *Duo*, Ferenczi).
Also passage from a book, etc.
Passage (in a house, etc.) = *couloir* (m), *corridor* (m).

passer To pass.
But some special uses should be noted. *Passer un examen*: to sit or take an exam (occasionally with the sense of 'to pass'). *Je passe mon examen en juin*: I am sitting my exam in June. *Passer colonel*: to be promoted colonel.
Can also mean to overlook – *passez-moi le mot*: forgive my using the word.
And note *passer un pont*: to cross a bridge.
To pass (an exam) = *réussir à un examen*.
         (go past something) = *dépasser, passer devant*.

passif (m) Passive (voice) (grammar).
Also (in financial language) liabilities.

passionnant Exciting. *Un film passionnant*: a thrilling film (although *la passion* is passion).
Passionate = *passionné*.

pat (m) Stalemate (chess). *Il m'a fait pat*: he stalemated me.
Pat = *coup léger* (m), *caresse* (f).
(butter) = *rondelle* (f).

pâté (m) Pâté (on the menu). Pie.
Des pâtés can mean children's sandcastles.
In addition, means a blob of ink or a block of houses. One should distinguish therefore between *pâté maison* (the restaurant's special pâté) and *un pâté de maisons* (a block of houses).

patente (f) A licence for carrying on some trade, or the tax paid to do so.
Patent = *brevet* (m).

patenté Licensed (or, familiarly of people), could be well-established, 'proper', out and out.
Patented = *breveté*.

jeu (m) **de patience** (f) Not a game of patience (although *une patience* has or had this sense), but a jigsaw puzzle.
(Game of) patience = *réussite* (f).

patient (m) **patiente** (f) Normally refers to a doctor's (or dentist's) patient who is undergoing treatment (usually surgical treatment).
Otherwise a patient = *malade* (m/f), *client* (m), *cliente* (f).

pâtisserie (f) Pastry or small cake, also the shop that sells them, tea-room.

pathétique Pathetic, i.e. touching, moving. *D'une voix pathétique*: in a voice full of emotion. *Un livre pathétique*: a book that moves you.
Pathetic (often) = *lamentable, faible*.

pathos (m) Exaggerated pathos.
Pathos = *pathétique* (m).

patron (m) Occasionally patron (saint, or patron of a living).
Normally the owner, 'boss', head. Also employer (hence *le patronat*: employers as a body). *Le patron était derrière le bar*: the owner was behind the bar.
Also the skipper of a small vessel, smack.
Can be a pattern or model for making clothes and (by extension) size (for clothes).
Patron (often) = *client* (m), *public* (m).
(of arts) = *mécène* (m).

patronage (m) Patronage.
Also a church youth club.

patronner To patronize, support, sponsor.
But to patronize a place (e.g. a restaurant) = *fréquenter, être un client fidèle*, etc.
To patronize (arrogantly) = *traiter avec condescendance*.

pavé (m) Sometimes may be pavement (or can even refer to a road).
Often means paving-stone, cobble.
Can also be a slab of meat, and is thus sometimes seen on menus.

Note *être sur le pavé*: to be down and out.
Pavement (usually) = *trottoir* (m).

pavement (m) Ornamental paving.
Pavement = *trottoir* (m).

pavillon (m) Pavilion, lodge, gatehouse, as well as a suburban house. '*On lui avait dit que le pavillon s'intitulait Mon Repos*' (Georges Simenon, *Le Client le plus obstiné du monde*).
Also a flag (ships), hence *baisser pavillon*: to give in.

payant Can mean paying (profitable), but often has an opposite sense, i.e. *you* have to pay! (compare 'paying guest').
Often used of things, though, as in *parking payant*: parking charged for.
English seems to lack as neat a word.
Paying (profitable) (also) = *rentable*.

pêche (f) Peach, or fishing. *Aimez-vous les pêches?*: do you like peaches? *Aimez-vous la pêche?*: do you like fishing?

peine (f) Care is needed. Not physical pain (= *douleur* (f)), but pain, hurt, distress.
Also pains, trouble, toil. *Cela vaut la peine*: it is worth while. *C'est peine perdue*: it is a waste of time. *Avec grande peine*: with great difficulty. '. . . en-fin, dans le sentier qui menait de la plaine à la maison de Mateo parut un homme, coiffé d'un bonnet pointu comme en portent les montagnards corses, barbu, couvert de haillons, et se traînant avec peine en s'appuyant sur son fusil*' (Prosper Mérimée, *Mateo Falcone*).
Peine can also be sentence (legal). *Peine de mort*: death penalty (compare English 'on pain of death' and 'penal').
Note *à peine*: scarcely, hardly.

penalty (m)   A penalty (football).
Penalty = *pénalité* (f), *sanction* (f).

pendule (f) Clock.
Pendulum = *pendule* (m).

pénétration (f) Penetration.
Also perception, keen judgment.

pénétré *D'un ton pénétré*: in an earnest voice, earnestly.
Not penetrating (= *pénétrant*).

pénitence (f) Penitence or penance. Punishment (especially at school). *Mettre quelqu'un en pénitence*: to put someone in the corner. *Il est en pénitence*: he is in disgrace.

penne (f) Quill, long wing or tail feather, feather of an arrow. The word is of the same origin as 'pen', but French uses for this another word for feather = *plume* (f), and *plume d'oie* for a quill (to write with).
Pen (fountain) = *stylo* (m) (*-encre*).
(animal) = *enclos* (m), *parc* (m).

pension (f) Has many useful meanings. Pension, board and lodging, small hotel or boarding-house, sometimes a boarding-school.

pensionnaire (m/f) Normally a boarder at school or a resident in a hotel, etc.
Occasionally used for pensioner.
Pensioner (usually) = *pensionné(e)* (m/f), *retraité(e)* (m/f).
      (soldier) = *invalide* (m).

pensionner Not to pension off but to give a pension to.
To pension off = *mettre à la retraite*.

perception (f) Perception.
Also collecting of taxes, taxation, tax office.

percevoir To perceive.
Also to collect taxes, etc. *Percevoir un droit d'entrée*: to charge an entrance fee.

perche (f) Perch (fish), also pole. *Le saut à la perche*: pole-vault. Note the phrase *tendre la perche à quelqu'un*: to hold out a helping hand.
Perch (to perch on) = *perchoir* (m).

perdition (f) Perdition. *Un lieu de perdition*: a den of vice, place of debauchery.
More commonly used of ships – *un navire en perdition*: a ship in distress (which is liable to be lost – *perdu*).

perfectionnement (m) Perfecting, making better, improving.
Perfection = *perfection* (f).

perfectionner To perfect (in the sense of to improve). *Alors tu as pu te perfectionner en italien?*: So you were able to improve your Italian?
To perfect = *parachever, rendre parfait*.

performance (f) Has a more limited meaning in French. Mostly used in sport (also of cars), in the sense of result, achievement. *Il a gagné 6-0, 6-1 – une belle performance!*: He won 6-0, 6-1 – a fine feat!
Performance (theatre) = *représentation* (f).
      (duties) = *accomplissement* (m).
      (success) = *exploit* (m), *réussite* (f).

performant High performing, or highly productive, competitive.
Performing (e.g. dog) = *savant*.

période (f) Period, but not at school (= *leçon* (f), *cours* (m)).

perle (f) Pearl. Can be used of people. *Ma femme de ménage est une perle*: my household help is a treasure.
Also means a howler – *une vraie perle*: a real 'gem'.

perme (f) Familiar abbreviation for *la permission*: leave (military), pass.
Perm (permanent wave) = *permanente* (f).

permission (f) Permission, also leave (military). *Il aurait volé l'argent pendant sa permission*: he is alleged to have stolen the money during his leave.

persuader To persuade or (often) convince. *Je suis persuadé qu'il est innocent*: I am certain he is innocent.

perturber Occasionally to perturb. Usually it has a stronger sense – to upset. *Le brouillard a encore une fois perturbé le trafic aérien*: fog has again disrupted air traffic.
To perturb (often) = *inquiéter, troubler*.

pervers Has a strong sense. Evil, depraved, vicious (compare 'pervert' and 'perversion'). *Un garçon pervers*: a depraved youth.
Perverse (usually) = *entêté, désobligeant*.

perversité (f) Perversity, wickedness, depravity.
Perversity (often) = *désobligeance* (f), *esprit* (m) *de contrariété*.

peste (f) Plague (pestilence). *Fuir quelqu'un comme la peste*: to avoid someone like the plague.
But also pest, nuisance (mostly of children). Familiar usage.
Pest = *insecte* (m) *nuisible*.

pester To curse, grumble away. *Il pestait contre tout ce matin-là*: he was letting off against everything that morning.
To pester = *harceler*.

pet (m) Breaking of wind (to put it politely). There is a familiar expression – *ça ne vaut pas un pet de lapin* – meaning something that is not worth a tinker's cuss – nothing to do with a pet rabbit! (The verb from the noun is *péter*. The French noun and verb are distinctly impolite.)
Pet = *animal* (m) *familier*.
    (teacher's, mother's) = *chouchou* (m).
To pet = *caresser*, (familiar) *peloter*.

pétrole (m) Petroleum, oil. *La crise du pétrole*: oil shortage. *Une lampe à petrole*: oil lamp. *Un puits de pétrole*: oil-well. *Le pétrolier*: tanker.
Petrol (cars) = *essence* (f).

pétulance (f) Requires care, as it has nearly the opposite meaning, i.e. liveliness, verve (a meaning now lost in English). *La pétulance des gens du Midi*: the liveliness of the Southerners.
Petulance = *irritabilité* (f) (*avec un peu de maussaderie* (f)).

pétulant Not petulant but, on the contrary, lively, exuberant. *Un petit gosse pétulant*: a lively young kid. '*M. Borniol, un capitaine au long cours retraité, pétulant, bavard . . .*' (Marcel Aymé, *Aller retour*, Gallimard). (Both English and French have a common Latin origin, but the English sense has gradually changed.)
Petulant = *irritable* (*et un peu maussade*).

peuple (m) The people of a country, ordinary people. *Le peuple va réagir*: the people are going to react.
People (usually) = *gens* (m).

photographe (m) Photographer. *Elle regardait le photographe*: she was looking at the photographer. Photographic shop.
Photograph = *photographie* (f).

photographie (f) Photography. *J'aime le photographie*: I enjoy photography. But also photograph. *J'aime la photographie*: I like the photograph.

phrase (f) Sentence, sometimes phrase. *Il a écrit la phrase pour moi*: he wrote down the sentence for me. *Parler sans phrases*: to speak bluntly.
Phrase is also a musical phrase.
(In phrase book) (often) = *locution* (f), *expression* (f).

physicien (m) **physicienne** (f) Physicist. *Mon père? Il est physicien*: My father? he is a physicist. (Physician used to have this sense in English.)
Physician = *médecin* (m).

physique (f) Physics.
Physique = *physique* (m) (note the gender!).

pic (m) Pick (axe).
Also mountain peak (*à pic*: sheer).
Another meaning is woodpecker.

piccolo (m) Piccolo.
Also is found in popular usage in the sense of (a light) wine. The word comes from the Italian for small.

pick-up (m) Record-player or its pick-up arm, or a combination of record-player and amplifier. *Les jours de foire un pick-up diffusait des airs populaires*: on the days of the fair a record-player relayed popular tunes.
Also pick-up (van).

pie (f) Not pie, but magpie.
Pie = *pâté* (m) (*en croûte*), *tourte* (f).

pièce (f) Can sometimes mean piece (as in to do piece-work, to sell something at so much a piece, pieces of a collection). *Une pièce de boeuf*: a piece (joint) of beef. *Une pièce d'eau*: lake, pond (in a garden). *Une pièce de monnaie*: a coin. *En pièces* can mean in bits, pieces.
Other meanings include parts of a car, a patch (for clothes), documents (*pièces d'identité*), a play at the theatre (*pièce de théâtre*), a room. *C'est petit – trois pièces seulement*: it is small – three rooms only.
Piece (very often) = *morceau* (m).

pigeon (m) Pigeon, but (familiarly) sucker, mug, fall guy. (Compare the slangy *pigeonner quelqu'un*: to fleece or con someone.)

pile (f) Pile or heap. Also battery. *La pile qu'il vous faut!*: The battery you need!
Pile ou face?: Heads or tails? (*pile*: 'tail').
Piles (medical) = *hémorroïdes* (f).

piler Not to pile, but to crush, grind. '*Au fond, deux hommes, les bottes dans la glace pilée, triaient le poisson de la cale*' (Pierre Hamp, *Marée fraîche*).
To pile = *empiler*, *entasser*.

pilot (m) Pile (in engineering).
Pilot = *pilote* (m).

pilote (m) Pilot, also driver (especially of racing-car). *Un pilote d'essais*: a test pilot or test driver.
Can also be a pilot (for ships).

pilote Pilot, experimental (as in English).
But in practice also means low-priced, as in the well-known *boissons pilotes*: low-cost drinks.
Pilot light = *veilleuse* (f), *lampe* (f) *témoin*.

piloter To pilot (aeroplanes), but also to drive (cars). *Je voudrais piloter une voiture de course*: I would like to drive a racing-car.
Also means to show, guide round. *Quand vous viendrez à Oxford, je serai là pour vous piloter*: When you come to Oxford, I shall be there to show you round.

pimprenelle (f) Burnet (flower), whereas pimpernel = *mouron* (m).

pin (m) Pine (tree), fir.
Pin = *épingle* (f).
To hear a pin drop = *entendre voler une mouche*.
Pin money = *argent* (m) *de poche*.
Pins and needles = *avoir des fourmis dans les jambes*.
Pintable = *billard* (m) *électrique*.
Pin-up = *pin-up* (f).

pipe (m) Pipeline. A familiar abbreviation for *le pipe-line* (*franglais* for the learned *oléoduc* (m)).
Pipe (to smoke) = *pipe* (f).
  (water, etc.) = *tuyau* (m).
In the pipeline = *en route, en chantier*.

piper Can mean to deceive, dupe (archaic). To load (dice).
To utter – *il ne pipe pas mot*: he doesn't breathe a word.
To pipe (water, etc.) = *amener par canalisation*.
  (instrument) = *jouer de la flûte*.
Piped music = *musique d'ambiance enregistrée*.

pique (m) Spades (cards).
Pique = *pique* (f).

pique (f) Pique, spite. Spiteful comment.
Also pike (weapon).
Pike (fish) = *brochet* (m).

piquer Among various meanings are to prick, sting, give an injection. To stitch (by machine).
Popular usage for 'to pinch'. *Il a piqué le portefeuille qui se trouvait par terre*: he pinched the wallet which was on the ground.
Il se pique le nez: he drinks a lot, boozes (popular usage).
To pick (often) = *choisir, cueillir*.
  (nose) = *curer*.

piquet (m) Strike picket (*piquet de grève*), also stake, peg.
At school you may be put *au piquet*: in the corner.

piqueter To mark out with stakes, or to dot, spot.
Piquet (m) can mean a strike picket, but to picket needs a phrase (= *installer des piquets de grève*).

pistole (f) Pistole (ancient gold coin).
Pistol = *pistolet* (m).

piston (m) Piston, but note the familiar sense of influence, 'pull'. *Pas de problème si on a du piston*: no problem if you have influence (can pull strings).

pitance (f) Scanty portion of food. *Les pauvres faisaient la queue pour recevoir leur maigre pitance*: the poor queued up for their pittance (modest ration).
Pittance is also used in English with regard to money – a mere pittance = *un misérable salaire*.

pitié (f) Pity, compassion, mercy. *C'est à faire pitié*: it is pitiful, very sad.
Pity (what a pity, etc.) = *dommage* (m).

placard (m) (Wall) cupboard, as well as placard, poster. *Cherchez dans le placard*: look in the cupboard.
Can also be an illustrated advertisement inserted in a newspaper (e.g. for a film).

place (f) Place, in certain senses. *Remettre à sa place*: to put back in its place, or to put in one's place (figurative). Room – *Il n'y a pas de place ici*: There is no room here.
Seat (train, theatre, etc.) – *Cette place est libre*: This seat is free.
Job, situation – *J'ai une bonne place que je ne veux pas quitter*: I have a good job I don't want to leave.
La place du marché: market square. *L'autobus s'arrête près de la place*: the bus stops near the square.
Place = *lieu* (m), *endroit* (m).
To take place = *avoir lieu*.

placement (m) Placing (of things, or people – e.g. for a job).
Note its meaning of investment. *Si vous cherchez un bon placement*: if you are looking for a good investment.

placer To place, put. *Placer quelqu'un*: to show someone to one's seat (cinema, theatre), or to place someone, find a job for someone.
Can mean to sell, dispose of (goods), and to invest. *J'ai une petite somme à placer*: I have a little sum to invest.

plagiste (m/f) Not a plagiarist (= *plagiaire* (m/f)), but someone who runs part of a beach (from *plage* (f) = beach), beach-holder.

plaid (m) Plaid. Also travelling rug. *Sur la plage arrière un plaid et un parapluie*: on the (car) rear shelf a travelling rug and an umbrella. '*Michel, frileux, déplia sur ses genoux le plaid brodé à jour par les mites et les étincelles*' (Colette, *Duo*, Ferenczi).

plaisamment Pleasantly, also amusingly or ridiculously.
Pleasantly (usually) = *agréablement*.

plaisant A deceptive word. Can mean pleasant, but also amusing (*plaisanter*: to joke) – a sense it used to have in English – and occasionally ridiculous.
Pleasant (usually) = *agréable*.

plan (m) Plan, and among other meanings field, area, plane – *sur le plan économique*: on the economic plane.
In cinema language it means shot – *entre deux plans*: between two shots, and *gros plan*: close-up.
Au premier plan: in the foreground.
Laisser quelqu'un en plan: to leave someone high and dry (familiar usage).

planer To glide, hover. Also to dream, be in the clouds.
Can mean to plane (wood, etc.), though this usually = *raboter*.
To plan = *arranger*, *projeter*, also *planifier* (economy, etc.).

planning (m) Used in industry and economics, etc., for planning or schedule.
Planning (general) = *organisation* (f).
          (economics) = *planification* (f).

plant (m) Plantation, (cabbage) patch. Also seedling, plant (young vegetables).
Plant (flower) = *plante* (f).

plante (f) Plant (flower), also the sole of the foot.

plaque (f) Plaque (on wall).
Other meanings include slab, metal sheet, plate. Also *plaque minéralogique*: number plate and *plaque d'identité*: identity disc.
The familiar expression *mettre à côté de la plaque* has the sense of someone getting it all wrong, being wide of the mark.
Dental plaque = *plaque dentaire*.

plastic (m) Could be a dangerous word! It means plastic explosive and not plastic material (= *plastique* (m)).

plat (m) A dish or course (food). *Un plat de frites*: a dish of chips. *Attention, le plat est chaud!* Be careful, the dish is hot. *Pour le troisième plat*: for the third course. *Le plat du jour*: today's special.
Note the two idioms – *mettre les pieds dans le plat*: to put one's foot in it, and *mettre les petits plats dans les grands*: to go to great trouble, push the boat out (of meals).

plateau (m) Geographical plateau. Also a tray. *Un plateau d'argent*: a silver tray.

plate-forme (f) Platform. There are a number of technical uses, but note its use for a bus (when it had a platform) and *une plate-forme de forage*: oil-rig.
Platform (station) = *quai* (m).
          (rostrum) = *estrade* (f).

plausible Plausible (excuse, etc.). For a plausible person, one needs some such word as *baratineur* (m), *beau parleur* (m).

plonge (f) *Il fait la plonge* does not mean he is taking the plunge, but simply that he is doing the washing-up (in a restaurant).
Plunge = *plongée* (f), *plongeon* (m).
To take the plunge (figurative) = *se jeter à l'eau* (among other expressions).

plongeur (m) Diver. Or the washer-up in a restaurant.
Plunger (to unblock pipes) = *ventouse* (f).

plum (m) May be found as a familiar abbreviation for *le plum-pudding*. This usually has the sense of plum-pudding (though some might think of it as a fruit (plum) cake).
Plum = *prune* (f).

plume (f) Feather. Pen. Sometimes plume (but this often = *plumet* (m) or, if it is larger, *panache* (m).

pocher To poach (cooking).
Also, less pleasantly, means to black an eye. *Un oeil poché*: a black eye.
To poach (steal) = *braconner* (*le braconnier*: poacher), and both languages have the same idiom – *braconner sur les terres de quelqu'un*: to poach on someone's preserves.

point (m) Point, dot, full stop.
Also a stitch in needlework or in one's side.
Used in various expressions – *être sur le point de faire quelque chose*: to be about to do something. *Faire le point*: to take stock (of a situation). *Mettre au point*: to perfect, to bring into line, settle. *A point*: medium (of a steak).
Point (tip, end) = *pointe* (f).
What's the point (use)? = *à quoi bon?*
There is no point = *cela ne sert à rien*.

pointer Sometimes to point (e.g. a weapon).
Other meanings include to appear (as of dawn on the horizon), to soar, rise up (as of a church tower), to clock in (to work), to tick off – *il pointe le nom sur la feuille*: he ticks off the name on the paper.
To point (at) = *indiquer*.

poker (m) Poker (card game). *Un coup de poker* is thus a gamble (and not a physical assault).
Poker (fire) = *tisonnier* (m).

pôle (m) *Le pôle nord*: the North Pole.
Pole (telegraph) = *poteau* (m). Long, thin pole = *perche* (f).
   (from Poland) = *Polonais* (m), *Polonaise* (f).

poli Either polite, or polished.

police (f) Police (but note *salle* (f) *de police*: guard-room), policing, keeping law and order, regulations.
Also means policy, as in *police d'assurance*: insurance policy.
Police station = *commissariat* (m).

policier (m) A policeman.
Also a thriller (film or book), being the abbreviated form of *le film* (*roman*) *policier*. *J'ai acheté un policier*: I bought a thriller (though it could mean 'I bribed a policeman').

polir To polish, but note that for shoes or floor, etc. it is *cirer*.

politicien (m) **politicienne** (f) Politician, usually used in a pejorative sense. Politician = *politique* (m).

politique (f) Policy (government), also politics.

polo (m) Polo.
Also sweat-shirt. *Le gosse portait un polo et un short*: the kid was wearing a sweat-shirt and shorts.

pomme de pin (f) Fir cone.
Pineapple = *ananas* (m).

se pommeler To become dappled (often of the sky with small clouds).
To pummel = *bourrer de coups*.

pompe (f) Pomp, ceremony. *Un entrepreneur de pompes funèbres*: undertaker (funerals).
Also is a pump, in various senses. *Une pompe à incendie*: fire-engine.

ponce (f) *Pierre ponce*: pumice-stone.
Ponce = *maquereau* (*m*), *souteneur* (m).

ponctualité (f) Punctuality, sometimes punctiliousness.

ponctuel Punctual, sometimes punctilious.
But also has a technical but quite common sense of individual, limited, specific, pin-point. *L'atterrissage ponctuel des hélicoptères*: the pin-point landing of helicopters.

ponctuellement Punctually (or sometimes punctiliously).

pondre Not to ponder (*méditer*), but to lay (eggs) or (familiarly) to produce – e.g. a paper on something.

pope (m) You may not meet the word frequently, but it could be deceptive. He is not the Pope (who is *pape* (m)), but priest in the Greek Church (in Russia, etc.) – pope in this sense.

porc (m) Pig, as well as pork (English usually uses different words when it is a question of eating the animal), also pigskin.

port (m) Port, harbour.
Also carrying, wearing (from *porter*) – *Le port des jeans est défendu le dimanche*: jeans may not be worn on Sundays.
Port (drink) = *porto* (m).
      (side) = *bâbord* (m).

portable Portable, also wearable. *Ce veston n'est guère portable*: this coat is hardly wearable.
Portable (also often) = *portatif*.

portemanteau (m) In English the word (dated) meant a kind of suitcase.

This meaning has also been lost in French, and the word is now used for a hat and coat stand, or rack, or else coathanger. *Il enleva son pardessus et chercha le portemanteau*: he took off his overcoat and looked for the hat and coat stand.

porteur (m) Porter, but also with the basic meaning of bearer. *Il fit entrer le porteur de la lettre*: he showed the letter-bearer in.

portier (m) Really a gatekeeper, but in practice a janitor, caretaker, commissionaire, hotel porter (at the door).
Porter (station) = *porteur* (m).

poser To pose (e.g. model).
But commonly means to put, place.
Also to ask (a question) – *poser une question*.
Can mean to put up, put down, put in (such things as curtains, carpets, windows).

posséder To possess. Notice the sense of knowing thoroughly. *Pour quelqu'un qui possède le français*: for someone knowing French well.

poste (m) Post (to be at one's post). *Poste (de police)*: police station.
Can mean a wireless or television set. *J'allume le poste*: I switch on the set.
Also post (job).
Post = *poteau* (m)
    (office) = *poste* (f).
    (letters) = *courrier* (m).

poster (m) Decorative poster, whereas a large advertising poster = *affiche* (f).

pot (m) Pot, but also jar. *Un pot à confiture*: a jamjar.
Could also be a jug, mug, tankard. But *un pot-de-vin* (familiar) is a bribe.
Dîner à la fortune du pot: to take pot luck.
Le pot d'échappement: car exhaust.
Used in many other expressions, including its popular meaning of luck – *manque de pot*: no luck.

poudreux Powdery. *La belle neige poudreuse!*: lovely powder snow!
Often just means dusty, as here in Leconte de Lisle – '*Une ondulation majestueuse et lente s'éveille, et va mourir à l'horizon poudreux*' (*Poèmes barbares*).

poule (f) Hen.
But *chair* (f) *de poule* is the equivalent of 'goose-flesh'!
Quand les poules auront des dents: when pigs have wings (i.e. never).
Also sweepstake, pool, and pool (in sport).
Pool (pond) = *étang* (m), *mare* (f).
    (puddle) = *flaque* (f).

poulpe (m) Octopus, not to be confused with pulp (= *pulpe* (f)).

pourchasser To pursue, chase after (people, sometimes things). *Il pourchasse les médailles*: he is after medals.
To purchase = *acheter*.

To buy on hire-purchase = *acheter à crédit* (m).

pourpre (m) Crimson.
Purple (royal purple, etc.) = *pourpre* (f).
(colour) = *violet* (m).

pourpre Scarlet, crimson, sometimes purple.
Purple (also) = *violet*.

poursuite (f) Pursuit, also (legal) proceedings. *Il menace d'entamer des poursuites*: he is threatening to start legal proceedings.
Pursuit(s) in English also = *passe-temps* (m).

poursuivre To pursue, continue or sometimes carry on with (e.g. a project). Also common (in legal language) meaning to take proceedings (against someone). *Je veux la poursuivre*: I want to prosecute her.

pousser Is used in various ways. Its main meaning is to push.
Also to grow. *Il fait pousser des légumes*: he grows vegetables.
And to utter (a cry, a sigh). *Il a poussé un cri*: he uttered a cry.

prairie (f) Prairie, in the right context, but normally a meadow. *La prairie est semée de pâquerettes*: the meadow is dotted with daisies.

praticable Practicable, feasible. Also (roads, etc.) passable. *Cette route n'est plus praticable pour les camions*: this road is no longer passable for lorries.

pratique (f) Practice. *Dans la pratique*: in practice.
Custom. Practice, experience, the doing of something. *La pratique du golf*: the playing of golf.
May be found in its older meaning of custom, or even customer, as here – '*Familier et cordial, le meunier fait la conduite à ses pratiques debout sur le seuil*' (Emile Pouvillon, *Césette*, Alphonse Lemerre).
Practice = *usage* (m), *coutume* (f).
(training) = *entraînement* (m).

pratiquer Sometimes to practise (religion, also medicine).
To go in for, play. *Il pratique le rugby*: he goes in for rugby. *Pratiquer une opération chirurgicale*: to perform an operation (surgeon).
Also to construct. *Il a pratiqué une chatière dans le mur*: he made a cat-door in the wall.
To practise (piano, etc.) = *s'exercer*.
To practise what one preaches = *prêcher d'exemple*.
Practice makes perfect = *C'est en forgeant qu'on devient forgeron*.

précieux Precious, in various senses, but also (in)valuable. *Le temps m'est précieux*: time is valuable for me.
Votre aide précieuse: your invaluable help.

précision (f) Precision, accuracy.
Also used (mostly in the plural) to mean further particulars, exact details. *Si vous voulez bien me donner des précisions*: if you would be kind enough to give me further information. '*Malheureusement, ajouta le directeur, je ne puis, pour l'instant, apporter d'autre précision*' (Paul-Jacques Bonzon, *Les Six Compagnons et l'homme des neiges*, Hachette, Bibliothèque Verte).

préjudice (m) Can mean prejudice, i.e. detriment, harm.
Much used in the sense of damage(s). *Le préjudice atteint 800 francs*: the damage amounts to 800 francs.
Prejudice (usually) = *parti pris* (m), *préjugé* (m).

prescription (f) Directions, instructions. *Il faut suivre les prescriptions du médecin*: you must do as the doctor says.
Prescription (doctor) = *ordonnance* (f).

présentement At present, or at the moment (literary word).
Presently = *tout à l'heure, bientôt*.

préserver To preserve, protect, safeguard.
But to preserve food is *conserver*.

presser To press, also to hurry. *Ça ne presse pas*: there's no hurry, it's not pressing.

pressing (m) Dry cleaner's, dry cleaning. *Si par hasard vous avez besoin d'un pressing*: if by any chance you want some dry cleaning done.
Pressing (pressure) = *pression* (f).
(of grapes, etc.) = *pressurage* (m).
(clothes) = *pressage* (m).
He needs no pressing = *il ne se fait pas prier*.

pressurer To press (grapes).
Also to press someone (financially), bear on, exploit.
To put pressure on someone = *exercer une pression sur quelqu'un, presser quelqu'un*.
To pressurize (aircraft) = *pressuriser*.

prétendant (m) Pretender (to the throne). Candidate (for something), also suitor.
Pretender (sometimes) = *simulateur* (m).

prétendre A deceptive word, as 'pretend' will often make sense.
The usual meaning is to claim, assert (the Young Pretender claimed the throne). *Il prétend qu'il est malade*: he claims to be ill. *Je ne prétends pas qu'il vous aidera*: I am not saying he will help you.
To pretend = *faire semblant de*.

prétention (f) Pretension. Claim. *Prétentions* is also topically used in advertisements for jobs. *Envoyer photo et prétentions*: send photo, and state what salary you expect (i.e. you lay claim to).

prévaricateur (m) **prévaricatrice** (f) Someone who betrays a trust, or is corrupt in his official duties.
Prevaricator = *tergiversateur* (m), *tergiversatrice* (f).

prévarication (f) Breaking of trust, serious misdemeanour (of an official in his duties).
Prevarication = *tergiversation* (f).

prévariquer To break one's trust, be corrupt (of an official).
To prevaricate = *tergiverser*.

prévenir To forestall, avert (occasionally to prevent). Also to bias.
And commonly to (fore)warn. *Il est arrivé – je n'ai pas pu le prévenir*: He has arrived – I wasn't able to warn him.
To prevent = *empêcher*.

prévention (f) Does not mean prevention, except in a few cases such as *prévention routière*: road safety.
Otherwise means either custody (prison) or prejudice. *Il a pu agir sans prévention*: he was able to act without prejudice.
Prevention = *empêchement* (m).
Prevention is better than cure = *mieux vaut prévenir que guérir*.

prier To pray, hence also to pray, beg, beseech, ask.
Je vous en prie: Please, or Don't mention it, Not at all.
To pry = *fureter*.

prime (f) Premium (insurance, etc.). Also bonus. Also free gift (as a commercial offer).
Prime = *les beaux jours*.
In the prime of life = *à la fleur de l'âge*.

primer To excel, come out on top.
Or to award a prize or bonus.
To prime (weapons) = *amorcer*.
  (someone) = *mettre quelqu'un au courant* or (popular usage) . . . *au parfum*.

primerose (f) Hollyhock.
Primrose = *primevère* (f) (*à grandes fleurs*).

primeur (f) Refers to a state of being new, fresh. *Vous avez la primeur de cette nouvelle*: you are the first to hear this news. Also refers to early vegetables and fruits.
Primer = *premier livre* (m).

primitif Primitive, but also original. *Le sens primitif a disparu*: the original sense has disappeared.
Le cinéma primitif: the early cinema.

primitivement Primitively or originally. *Ma maison avait primitivement un toit de chaume*: my house was originally thatched.

priser Has two distinct meanings. To prize or value, or to take snuff.
To prise (open) = *forcer*.

procédé (m) Action, way of going about something. Process (manufacturing).
A different meaning is billiard-cue tip.
Proceedings (legal) = *procès* (m).

procès (m) Legal term for proceedings of various sorts. *Le père va intenter un procès*: the father is going to start proceedings.
Process = *processus* (m), *cours* (m).

procureur (m) Procurator (who has the right to represent people in legal matters, etc.) or (more commonly) (public) prosecutor (*procureur de la République*). *Procureur général*: Attorney-General.
So care is needed, since 'procurer' in English means something very different =*proxénète* (m).

profane (m) As a religious term, it may be somebody who does not believe. Can mean a layman, non-expert, even a philistine. *Je sais que le concert va être bon, mais pour un profane comme moi, ça ne me dit pas grand-chose*: I know the concert is going to be good, but to a philistine like me, it doesn't appeal much.
A profane person = *une personne grossière* (*qui jure beaucoup*).

proférer Not to proffer (which = *offrir*), but to utter. *Il a proféré quelques mots insultants*: he uttered some insulting words.

professeur (m) Professor, also (school)master, teacher. *A l'entrée du professeur, tous les élèves se turent*: when the master came in, all the pupils fell silent.

professoral Professorial. Pedantic. But also just means concerned with teaching. *Le corps professoral*: the teaching profession.

programme (m) Programme, in various senses, also syllabus. *Il n'y a pas assez d'auteurs modernes au programme*: there are not enough modern authors on the syllabus.

progrès (m) Progress, but not always with the idea of improvement. *La délinquance juvénile est en progrès*: juvenile delinquency is on the increase.

projecteur (m) Projector, also floodlight, often searchlight. '*Dans le ciel de la Ruhr, les premiers projecteurs devaient fouiller les ténèbres pour y cueillir l'avant-garde des bombardiers*' (Jules Roy, *Le Navigateur*, Julliard).

projection (f) Normally used for projection, or showing of films or slides.
Also means projection, throwing (e.g. shadows), and throwing out (liquids, etc.).
The *mot juste* to describe what a volcano throws out.
Projection (which juts out) = *saillie* (f).

projet (m) Project, plan.
Projet de loi: Bill (Government).

projeter To project, throw. Also to show (films, slides).
Also to plan (compare 'a project'). *Qu'est-ce que vous projetez de faire maintenant?*: What are you planning to do now?

prolongation (f) Prolongation, extension, and also tidily translates 'extra time' (e.g. football). *Il faudra jouer les prolongations*: extra time will have to be played.

promenade (f) Promenade, walk, avenue. More frequently the action of walking, but also drive, outing. *Une promenade en mer*: a boat trip.

promotion (f) Promotion (to higher things), also promotion of goods (business).
Can also mean year or class of students – *de la même promotion*: of the same year.

propre (Sometimes) proper.
The main meanings are clean (*une cravate propre*: a clean tie), and own (*ma propre cravate*: my own tie).
Sometimes means characteristic (of). *Propre à*: fitted, suitable, right for.
Proper (often) = *correct, comme il faut, bienséant*.

propreté (f) Cleanliness, tidiness.
Property = *propriété* (f).

propriété (f) Propriety (of expression).
Also property, in various senses. *En toute propriété* may be seen in advertisements – sole ownership.
Propriety (also) = *bienséance* (f).

prospecteur (m) Prospector. Canvasser (business).

prostration (f) Prostration, i.e. exhaustion.
Prostration (often) = *prosternement* (m), *prosternation* (f).

prostré Prostrate, quite exhausted. *Il n'avait pas mangé depuis trois jours, et il était prostré dans son bateau qu'il ne pouvait plus diriger*: he had not eaten for three days, and he was exhausted in his boat which he could no longer steer.
Prostrate (often) = *étendu (à terre), prosterné*.
            (sometimes) = *accablé*.

protection (f) Protection.
Also has the meaning of influence, having friends in high places. *Il a obtenu cette place par protection*: he got this job through influence.

provence (f) Do not confuse *en Provence* (in Provence) with *en province*: in the provinces, country (particularly as opposed to Paris, the Big City).

provoquer To provoke, but often to induce, cause, bring about. *Mais qu'est-ce qui a provoqué cette chute de pierres?*: but what caused this rock-fall?

prune (f) A deceptive word! You may be missing something you like, as it means plum. *Pour le dessert, quelques belles prunes?*: for dessert, some nice plums?
Une tarte aux prunes: a plum tart.
Prune = *pruneau* (m).

pub (f) Familiar abbreviation for *la publicité*. Thus *il aime trop la pub*: he is too fond of publicity (and not 'he is too fond of the pub'!).
Pub = *bistro* (m).

public (publique) Public – but not always! *Une école publique* would mean a state school and *une maison publique* is one of a number of expressions for a brothel – *not* a public house!
Public school = *collège privé* (m).
Public house = *bistro* (m).

publicain (m) Publican, tax-gatherer.
Publican (in a 'pub') usually = *patron* (m).

publicité (f) Publicity. Advertising. Also an advertisement. *Pour insérer une publicité dans ce journal* . . .: to put an advertisement in this paper . . .

pudding (m) Usually used in the sense of steamed pudding, and particularly Christmas pudding (sometimes written *pouding*), though it is sometimes more cake-like.
Pudding (also) = *dessert* (m), *entremets* (m).

puffin (m) Shearwater.
Puffin = *macareux* (m).

pull (m) Pullover (familiar abbreviation for *le pullover*). *Donne-moi un pull*: give me a pullover.
Pull (sometimes) = *attraction* (f).
(colloquial sense) = *piston* (m).
To give a pull = *tirer*.

pulvérisateur (m) Pulverizer, or spray, atomizer.

pulvérisation (f) Pulverization, pulverizing, shattering, also spraying (crops, etc.).

pulvériser To pulverize, crush to bits. May be used literally or figuratively – *record du monde pulvérisé*: world record shattered.
Also means to spray (as of an atomizer). *Vous n'avez qu'à pulvériser cela sur les murs*: you only need to spray that on the walls.

pulvériseur (m) Disc-harrow (farming).
Pulverizer = *pulvérisateur* (m).

pupille (m/f) Ward (of someone), orphan, child in care. *L'oncle Michel pensait à son pupille*: Uncle Michael was thinking of his ward. *Hélas, c'est souvent le cas que ces jeunes 'criminels' sont des pupilles de l'Etat*: alas, it is often the case that these young 'criminals' are children in care.
La pupille is also pupil of the eye.
Pupil = *élève* (m/f).

pur (m) *Pur* means pure, but *les purs* are the out-and-out members of (for example) a political party, the hard-liners.

puzzle (m) This word could be . . . puzzling. It means jigsaw puzzle. *Si vos enfants s'ennuient, donnez-leur un puzzle*: if your children are bored, give them a jigsaw puzzle.
Puzzle = *casse-tête* (m).
(mystery) = *mystère* (m)

quai (m) Three useful meanings. Quay(side) (harbour), (river) embankment, (station) platform. So the context is important.

quarantaine (f) Quarantine, also about forty. *Mettre en quarantaine*: to put in quarantine or to send to Coventry.

quart (m) Quarter (*un quart d'heure*: quarter of an hour, *un quart de rouge*: a quarter (litre) bottle of red wine).
Also watch (at sea), and in the army it is a mug (holding a quarter of a litre).
Note *les trois quarts du temps*: most of the time, and *au quart de tour*: at first go, straight off (of cars starting, or figurative use).
Quart (measurement) = *quarte* (f) (not used).

quartier (m) Quarter, in many senses (fourth part, district, (head)quarters, part of body, mercy). *Les bas quartiers*: slums. Can have the idea of local (*être du quartier*: to be local). *Le quartier réservé*: red light district. *Avoir quartier libre*: to be free, to have some free time (originally a military expression).
Can mean a block of stone. *'Penché à la portière du wagon, Durtal plongeait directement dans l'abîme; sur cette ligne étroite à une seule voie, le train longeait, d'un côté, les quartiers accumulés de pierre et, de l'autre, le vide'* (J. K. Huysmans, *La Cathédrale*, Plon).

quartier-maître (m) Leading seaman.
Quartermaster = *fourrier* (m).

queue (f) Queue. *Il faut faire la queue*: we must queue (up).
Also tail. Tail-end. Other meanings include handle (pan), stalk (fruit, flowers), cue (billiard).
Picturesque idioms are *faire une queue de poisson*: to cut in (cars), *finir en queue de poisson*: to fizzle out, *à la queue leu leu*: single file.

quille (f) Keel (ship).
Also skittle.
Means the equivalent of 'demob' (army slang).
Quill (for writing) = *plume* (f) *d'oie*.
　　　(porcupine) = *piquant* (m).

quitter Occasionally to quit (something), but usually to leave. *Ne quittez pas*: hold the line (telephone).
To quit (usually) = *abandonner*.

race (f) Race. Breeding. *C'est un cheval de race*: it is a thoroughbred horse. *Il chasse de race*: he is a chip off the old block.
Race (running) = *course* (f).
Racehorse = *cheval de course*.

racket (m) Racket (in the criminal sense). *C'est un petit racket mais qui pourrait être embêtant pour les touristes*: it is only a small racket, but it could annoy tourists.
Racket (tennis) = *raquette* (f).
⠀⠀⠀⠀⠀(noise) = *tintamarre* (m).

radiant Radiant (e.g. heat). Really a technical word, though occasionally used in literature.
The normal word for radiant (sun, people) = *radieux*.

radiation (f) Radiation, but also erasure, striking off (a list, etc.).

radio (m) Care is needed, as the word refers to a *person*, the radio operator. *Le radio était déjà là*: the radio operator was already there.
A second meaning is radiogram (message).
Radio (wireless) = *radio* (f) (*à la radio*: on the radio).
⠀⠀⠀⠀(set) = *poste* (m) *de radio*.

radio (f) Radio, wireless.
Another important meaning is X-ray. *Je viens de voir la radio de ma femme*: I have just seen my wife's X-ray.

radiogramme (m) May be either a radiograph, X-ray picture, or a radiogram (radio telegram).
Radiogram (radio plus record-player) = *combiné* (m) (one of its meanings).

rafle (f) Police raid, swoop, round-up, or a raid by thieves.
Raffle = *loterie* (f).

rafler To round-up (police), or to seize, 'swipe' (thieves).
Il a tout raflé: he 'cleared' the lot.
To raffle = *mettre en loterie*.

rafraîchir To refresh, cool.
Also to do up, renovate, and to trim (hair).

rage (f) Rage, in various senses. *Une rage de dents*: severe toothache.
But it is important to know that the word also means rabies.
Rage (also) = *fureur* (f).

raid (m) A raid (into enemy territory), or an air-raid.
Also a long-distance rally (sport).
Raid (police) = *rafle* (f), *descente* (f) *de police*.

raie (f) Line, stroke, streak. Parting (hair).
  Also ray, skate (fish).
  Ray = *rayon* (m) (occasionally *rai* (m)).

rail (m) Rail, track or rail as a means of transport (compare British Rail).
  Rail (handrail) = *rampe* (f), *garde-fou* (m).
       (ship) = *rambarde* (f).

railler To jeer, scoff at.
  To rail (at someone) = *engueuler, déblatérer contre quelqu'un*.

raisin (m) Is not what it seems! Grape(s). *Aimez-vous le raisin?*: Do you like
  grapes?
  (*Raisins de Corinthe*: currants (the English word derives from 'Corinth');
  raisins de Smyrne: sultanas.)
  Raisins = *raisins secs*.

raison (f) Reason, in various senses. *Avoir raison*: to be right.
  Note *raison sociale* which is the imprint, the printed name of a firm.
  Among various expressions – *se faire une raison*: to make the best of something, and *à raison de*: at the rate of (*à raison de trente francs par heure*: at the
  rate of 30 francs an hour).

rallier To rally. Also has the idea of rejoining (e.g. a unit), or (of ships)
  reaching the shore.

rampant Usually means creeping, crawling (literally), also figuratively, i.e.
  grovelling.
  To be rampant (often) = *sévir*.

rampe (f) Has a number of meanings. Ramp, slope, hand-rail, banisters.
  Footlights (theatre). *Rampe lumineuse*: strip-light.

râpe (f) Grater (cheese, etc.).
  Rape = *viol* (m).
       (oil) = *huile* (f) *de colza*.

râper To grate (cheese, etc.), to wear threadbare (clothes).
  To rape = *violer*.

rapport (m) Has various meanings. Report or account (of something, or on
  something).
  Also return, income (financial) – *d'un bon rapport*: with a good return
  (yield). Hence *maison* (f) *de rapport*: block of flats, tenement.
  Can mean relationship, connection, aspects. *J'ai de bons rapports avec lui*: I
  have a good relationship with him.
  Sous d'autres rapports: in other respects. *Par rapport à*: in comparison with,
  with regard to.
  Also ratio.
  Report (school) = *bulletin* (m) (*trimestriel*).
         (weather) = *bulletin météorologique*.
         (gun) = *coup* (m) *de fusil, détonation* (f).
  Of good report = *de bonne réputation*.

rapporter Can mean to report (a fact), and (familiarly) to 'sneak', tell tales. Other meanings are to bring back, to bring in (money). *Ça rapporte beaucoup*: that brings in a lot (of money).

rapporteur (m) Can mean a 'sneak' (school), or an official such as a recorder, chairman.
Also a protractor.
Reporter = *reporter* (m), *journaliste* (m/f).

raquette (f) (Tennis) racket, (table-tennis) bat.
Also means a snow-shoe. *En hiver on peut faire de longues promenades à raquettes*: in winter one can go for long walks in snow-shoes.

rat (m) Rat. But note some other meanings – sneak-thief (*un rat d'hôtel, un rat d'auto*) and *les petits rats* (*de l'opéra*) refer to young ballet girls.
If you come across *rat de cave*, it does not mean a cave rat or even a cellar rat, but either an exciseman or a taper (to light one's way in the cellar).
And where we talk of a bookworm, French has *rat de bibliothèque*.
Pauvre comme un rat: as poor as a church mouse!

rate (f) Spleen. Also female rat.
Rate (birthrate, etc.) = *taux* (m).
        (speed) = *vitesse* (f), *train* (m).
Rates (taxes) = *impôts* (m) (*locaux*).

rater A common familiar word for to miss, fail. *J'ai raté le train*: I missed the train.
To rate (often) = *évaluer, considérer*.
        (scold) = *tancer*.

ravi Although it could mean ravished (from *ravir*), the standard meaning is delighted. *Elle en fut ravie*: she was delighted.
Ravished = *violé(e), enlevé(e)*.

ravine (f) Mountain stream or torrent, or (rare) small gully.
Ravine = *ravin* (m).

ravir Can mean to ravish or rob, but is commonly to delight.

rayon (m) Has a number of useful meanings, but not that of rayon (= *rayonne* (f)).
A ray (of light, etc.), shelf, radius (circle) or range (*un rayon de plusieurs kilomètres*: a range, radius of several kilometres).
Spoke (of a wheel), honeycomb, department (of a store or shop).
And *ce n'est pas mon rayon*: it is not my line (concern).

réaction (f) Reaction. *Un avion à réaction*: a jet plane.

réalisation (f) Realization, carrying out, fulfilment, achievement.
Production (cinema).
Realization (understanding) = *découverte* (f), *constatation* (f).

réaliser To realize, i.e. make real, fulfil, bring about, carry out. *Si je pouvais réaliser cette ambition*: if I could realize this ambition.
To produce films.

Also used to mean to realize, understand, but purists should avoid this usage.
Se réaliser: to be fulfilled (projects, etc.) or (of people) to fulfil one's potential.
To realize = *se rendre compte* (*de*).

réassurance (f) Reinsurance, reassurance (e.g. of a policy).
Reassurance = *réconfort* (m), (*pouvoir rassurer*).

réassurer To reinsure (reassure) (of insurance work).
To reassure = *rassurer*.

rebut (m) The modern sense is of one of waste, rejection. Can refer to the dregs of society, dead letters at a post office, or things that are thrown away. *Je vais les mettre au rebut*: I am going to scrap them.
Rebuttal = *réfutation* (f).

rebuter To rebuff (someone), reject (something), and nowadays commonly to discourage, put off, or to disgust. *Il faut apprendre quand même la grammaire, et ceci rebute quelques-uns*: one must learn grammar none the less, and this puts some people off.
To rebut (something) = *réfuter*.
(someone) = *repousser*.

recette (f) Has the idea of receiving, in various special senses.
But note *la recette* (may be plural also), meaning receipts (not receipt), takings. *Faire recette*: to be a box-office draw, a success (e.g. plays).
Recette is also recipe.
Receipt = *récépissé* (m).

receveur (m) Has a number of meanings, including collector (of taxes) and (bus) conductor, postmaster (*receveur des postes*).
(*La receveuse*: postmistress, conductress and (sometimes) usherette.)
Receveur (*receveuse*) can mean recipient, in its modern sense with regard to transplant operations – the opposite of 'donor'.
Receiver (telephone) = *récepteur* (m).
Recipient (often) = *celui qui reçoit*.

rechercher Basically to look for, search, seek.
A researcher = *chercheur* (m), *chercheuse* (f).
To do research = *faire des recherches* (f).

récipient (m) Receptacle.
Recipient = *destinataire* (m/f) (e.g. letter), *celui qui reçoit*.

récit (m) Recital, account, narrative.
A music recital = *récital* (m).

réclamation (f) Claim (legal), or (more usually) complaint. '*Eh bien, mon brave, vous plaisez-vous au régiment? Avez-vous une réclamation à m'adresser? – Mon Colonel, dit simplement La Guilloumette, j'ai à vous dire que la soupe ne vaut rien*' (Georges Courteline, *Les Gaietés de l'escadron*, Flammarion).
Reclamation (land) = *défrichement* (m).

réclamer To complain, also to ask for, claim, demand.

To reclaim (land) = *défricher*.

To (re)claim (luggage) = *retirer*.

recommandation (f) Recommendation. Also registration (letters, parcels). But *une lettre de recommandation* is a letter of introduction.

recommander To recommend, also to register (letter, etc.). *Je vous recommande de recommander la lettre*: I advise you to register the letter.

récompenser To recompense (i.e. to reward). *Pour récompenser sa victoire*: to reward his victory.

To recompense (often) = *compenser, dédommager*.

réconforter To comfort, but also to restore, give strength, refresh. *Allez! bois ça pour te réconforter*: Here! drink that to buck you up. *Je me réconforte*: I take some refreshment.

I comfort myself = *je me console*.

reconnaissance (f) Reconnaissance, but more likely to be met in the sense of gratitude. *Je voudrais exprimer ma reconnaissance*: I would like to express my gratitude. Also acknowledgment, admission, recognition.

reconnaître To recognize. Also to admit, acknowledge.

Also to reconnoitre.

reconversion (f) (Re)conversion (e.g. of a business, factory), adaptation (to new technology). Also used (of people) to mean taking up a new job.

reconvertir To (re)convert (as of a factory, changing over to some other production), and *se reconvertir* is quite topical with the sense of learning a new job. *A quarante ans il n'est pas trop tard pour se reconvertir*: at forty, one is not too old to learn another job.

record (m) Record (particularly athletic). Thus *un recordman* (an example of two English words being joined to make a *nonsens*) is a record-holder, not a disc-jockey!

Record (music, etc.) = *disque* (m).

recouper To cut again. Also to cross-check. *Votre récit recoupe le mien*: your story cross-checks with mine.

Se recouper: to overlap.

To recoup = *récupérer*.

recouvrir To cover, re-cover or cover over. *Il nous faut recouvrir cette chaise*: we must re-cover this chair.

To recover (something) = *recouvrer, retrouver, récupérer*.

récréer A literary word, meaning to amuse. *Je me récrée en regardant passer le monde*: I divert myself watching the world go by.

(Compare 'recreation' in the sense of amusement.)

Do not confuse with *recréer* (only one accent), meaning to recreate.

récupération (f) Usually means recuperation (strength), or getting back something, recovery; salvage (industrial sense). Rehabilitation.

Recuperation (health) = *rétablissement* (m).

récupérer Although it can mean to recover (as of a sportsman after a strenuous effort) or recuperate (*récupérer ses forces*: to get back one's strength), usually means to retrieve (something), to recover, get back, to recover lost time, to recover or salvage (waste goods), and to re-employ someone in different work (who cannot continue his previous work).
To recuperate (usually) = *se rétablir*.

recyclage (m) Recycling, but also (of people) retraining.

recycler To recycle, but it is also used in the sense of retraining, refresher training, getting up to date. *Je vais me recycler*: I am going to relearn my job, get up to date.

redingote (f) Frock-coat. Or (modern) a woman's (fitted) coat. The word is interesting because it comes from the English 'riding coat'.
Riding coat = *habit* (m) *de cheval*.

reflex (m) A reflex camera (= *un appareil reflex*).
Reflex = *reflexe* (m).

réformer Can mean to reform (something) but the word is deceptive.
It is also to discharge, invalid out (military). *Après deux ans dans l'armée il a été réformé*: after two years in the army, he has been discharged.
Can sometimes mean to scrap (things) – *chemises réformées*: cast-off shirts.
To reform (someone) = *corriger*.

refréner To restrain, curb (compare *freiner*: to brake). English originally had this meaning also. *Il a dû refréner son désir*: he had to curb his desire.
To refrain (now) = *se retenir* (*de*).

refuge (m) Refuge. Mountain hut. Traffic island.

regard (m) Look.
Regard for (someone) = *estime* (f), or in the sense of consideration = *égard* (m).
Kind regards to . . . (in a letter) could = *mes amitiés à* . . .

en regard de Compared with.
With regard to: *au regard de, en ce qui concerne*.

regardant Might be misleading. *Un homme regardant*: a man close (very careful) with his money.
It does not mean with regard for other people, considerate (= *prévenant*).
Regarding = *à propos de*.

régent (m) Could be (prince) Regent, but also used for the director of the Bank of France.

régime (m) Régime, rule, but it may be to do with bananas. *Un régime de bananes*: a hand, bunch of bananas.
Can be the running note of engines.
Also means diet – note the familiar and picturesque *au régime jockey*: on a strict diet. And if one is 'on the wagon', one is *au régime sec*.

regretter Can cause misunderstanding, because it means not only to regret but also to miss. *C'est mon neveu surtout que je regrette*: I especially miss my nephew. *Vous regrettez Paris?*: do you miss Paris? *Notre regretté maire*: our late-lamented mayor.

régulier Regular. Also fair dealing, above-board, straight, in order. *Il m'accuse de ne pas avoir été régulier*: he accuses me of not having been straight.
Regular army officer = *officier d'active* (f).

régulièrement Regularly. But the context is important as there is also the sense of properly, legally, above-board. *Puisque je l'ai acheté régulièrement . . .*: seeing that I bought it quite legally . . .

rein (m) Kidney. Small of the back. *J'ai mal aux reins*: my back hurts.
Rein = *rêne* (f).

relaps (m) **relapse** (f) Relapsed heretic. *Qui ose condamner ce relaps?*: who dares to condemn this relapsed heretic?
Relapse = *rechute* (f).

relation (f) Relation(ship), connection, relations, terms.
Also account (something that has been related, told).
And in particular note the sense of acquaintance, contact, influential connection. *Il a des relations dans la capitale*: he has connections in the capital. *Etre en relations*: to be in touch, contact. *Nous sommes en relations*: we keep in touch.
Relations can also be connection, service (of rail or road). *Quatre relations vers les Pyrénées*: four services in the direction of the Pyrenees.
Relation = *parent* (m), *parente* (f).

relaxer To relax (transitive), but the usual meaning is to release (e.g. a prisoner). *Se relaxer*: to relax (of a person).

relief (m) Relief (sculpture, maps, etc.). *Mettre en relief*: to bring out, bring into relief, to emphasize.
Note the pleasant archaism *les reliefs*: scraps (of food), left-overs.
Relief (feeling) = *soulagement* (m).
         (help)= *secours* (m).

relique (f) Relic (of a saint).
But relic often also = *survivance* (f), *vestige* (m).

remarquer Can mean to remark or say, but it often means to notice, to note. *Je ne l'ai pas remarqué*: I didn't notice (it). *Je n'ai rien remarqué*: I didn't notice anything. *Remarquez que . . .*: note that . . .
To remark (often) = *dire*.

remembrement (m) Consolidation of land (instead of having a number of small plots).
Remembrance = *souvenir* (m).

remembrer A technical agricultural term, meaning to regroup various portions of land into one block (compare the opposite English 'to dis-member').
To remember = *se souvenir, se rappeler*.

remonter The basic sense is to remount – go up again, climb up and similar meanings.
But note its other meaning of replenish (with a new stock), wind up (*j'ai oublié de remonter ma montre*: I forgot to wind my watch) and (familiarly) to cheer up, revive (someone).

rempart(s) (m) Can mean city walls as well as rampart(s).

rentable Profitáble, paying. *Un investissement rentable*: a profitable investment.
Rentable = *louable*.

rente (f) Annuity, pension and often income, private means. *Il possède une grande maison et il vit de ses rentes*: he has a large house and he lives on his income.
Rent (to pay) = *loyer* (m).
    (tear) = *déchirure* (f).

renter An old word meaning to endow. *Renter une école*: to endow a school.
To rent = *louer*.

repaire (m) Den, lair.
Repair = *réparation* (f).
        (clothes) = *raccommodage* (m).

repasser To re-pass. *Il a repassé devant ma maison*: he passed my house again.
Other meanings include to recross (e.g. frontier), to resit (an exam).
Also to sharpen, strop.
Note too that it can mean to iron, and to drop in again, call again. Thus Marcel Aymé is able to pun – '*Il eut besoin de faire une expérience, de s'entendre parler fort et, passant devant une blanchisserie, il poussa la porte de la boutique: – Mesdames, c'est ici qu'on repasse? – Oui, monsieur. – Eh bien, on repassera!*' (*Aller retour*, Gallimard).

répertoire (m) Repertory, in various senses (including theatre).
Also index, hence *un répertoire d'adresses*: address book.

répéter To repeat, and thus to rehearse (plays, etc.).
Cet après-midi on répète: this afternoon we are rehearsing.

répétiteur (m) **répétitrice** (f) Tutor, coach. (The word is now scarcely used.)
Repeater (gun) = *fusil* (m) *à répétition, revolver* (m).

répétition (f) Repetition, also rehearsal. *La répétition générale*: dress rehearsal. Can also be a private lesson.

replacer To replace, put back. *J'ai replacé le livre*: I have put the book back.
Also to find a new job (for someone), to reinvest.
To replace (to take the place of) = *remplacer*. *J'ai remplacé le livre*: I have replaced the book (with another one).

replet Plump. *Un petit homme replet*: a plump little man.
(This sense has disappeared in English.)
Replete = *repu, gorgé de*.

repli (m) Fold, bend.
Often withdrawal (especially military).
Le repli de l'armée: the army's withdrawal.
Reply = *réponse* (f).

réplique (f) Retort. *Cela n'admet aucune réplique*: that brooks no answer.
Also cue (actor). Also replica (art).
Reply = *réponse* (f).

répliquer To answer (back), to retort.
To reply = *répondre*.

reporter To take back, carry back.
Also to postpone, defer.
Thus a headline '*Finale reportée*' might disappoint you, as it would mean 'Final postponed'.
To report (news) = *faire un reportage sur*.
            (someone) = *dénoncer*.

représentation (f) Representation. Performance (theatre). *La représentation commence à huit heures*: the performance begins at eight.
Of officials, etc. *Les frais de représentation*: entertainment allowance (*représentation* refers here to their official life-style).
Faire de la représentation: to be a sales representative for a company, etc.

représenter To represent. Also to perform (theatre). *Une pièce qui a été représentée partout au monde*: a play which has been performed all over the world.

réprouver To condemn, reject (doctrine, also people), to disapprove. (*Les réprouvés*: the outcasts of society.)
To reprove = *réprimander*.

requérir Sometimes to require, often to ask for, request, demand.
To require = *exiger*, *avoir besoin de*.

réservoir (m) Has more general meanings than English reservoir.
Could also be a tank (water), gasometer, petrol tank for cars (*réservoir d'essence*), and a fish-pond.

résidence (f) Residence, in various senses. Also a rather 'in' word for high-class flats. *La nouvelle résidence qui domine la baie*: the new luxury block overlooking the bay.
Often a complex (e.g. for retired people) which includes swimming-pool, restaurant, etc.
May also just mean home. *Résidence secondaire*: second (or holiday) home.
Residence also = *domicile* (m).
To take up residence = *élire domicile*.

résignation (f) Resignation, submission – but not resignation from a job (although the verb *résigner* can have this sense), which = *démission* (f).

respect (m) Respect, but *tenir en respect* is far from holding in respect. It means to keep back, keep at bay. *Le jeune voleur, revolver à la main, tenait les* *assistants en respect*: the young thief, gun in hand, held the bystanders at bay.

To hold someone in respect = *avoir du respect pour quelqu'un*.

respecter To respect, and also with the sense of keeping to (agreements, etc.). *Autant que je sache, le planning est respecté*: as far as I know, the schedule is being kept to.

ressentir To feel (keenly). *Je ressens vivement une telle injure*: I feel such an insult deeply.

To resent (something) = *s'offenser de, en vouloir à quelqu'un de quelque chose*.

ressort (m) Spring (metal, etc.).

Also jurisdiction, competence (e.g. legal). *Ce n'est pas de mon ressort*: that's not my province, concern.

En dernier ressort: as a last resort.

Resort = *recours* (m).

(place) = *station* (f).

restaurateur (m) Restorer (pictures, etc.).

But also restaurant-owner, 'restaurateur'.

restauration (f) Restoration, also catering, running a restaurant.

restaurer To restore, in various senses. Also to refresh, give strength (food). *Se restaurer*: to take refreshment.

reste (m) Rest, i.e. remainder. Left-overs, remains. *Il est parti sans demander son reste*: he left without waiting to hear any more.

Rest (relaxation) = *repos* (m).

rester To remain, stay. *Après ce long voyage je suis resté chez moi*: after this long journey I stayed at home. (As 'rest' may make sense, particular care is needed.)

To rest = *se reposer*.

résumer To sum up. *Je vais résumer l'affaire*: I'll sum the matter up.

En résumé: in short.

To resume = *continuer, reprendre quelque chose*.

être en retard *Des élèves en retard*: backward pupils (retarded).

Could mean pupils who are late (in arriving), as the normal meaning is to be late.

retenir To retain something. Also to detain, keep, or to restrain, keep back. *Je ne veux pas vous retenir*: I don't want to detain you.

Also to book (seat, room, etc.). *J'ai retenu une table*: I have booked a table.

Can be to retain (a servant) (= *engager*).

To retain (often) = *garder*.

retenue (f) A deduction (e.g. from one's salary). It is also (at school) detention – *deux heures de retenue*: two hours' detention.

Can mean reserve. *Malgré ma retenue naturelle*: in spite of my natural reserve.

Retinue = *suite* (f), *cortège* (m).

retiré Secluded, out of the way. *Il vit retiré*: he leads a secluded life. Can sometimes mean retired.
Retired (general term) = *en retraite*.

retirer To pull back, withdraw, remove.
Se retirer: to retire, go off, withdraw. *Se retirer des affaires*: to retire from business.
To retire (old age) = *prendre sa retraite*.
      (go to bed) = (*aller*) *se coucher*.
      (sport) = *abandonner*.

retouche (f) Touching up (art), but the main idea is of alterations (e.g. clothes). *Retouches gratuites*: alterations free of charge.
Touching up (often) = *fignolage* (m).

retoucher To touch up (especially of art), also to alter (clothes).
To touch up (often) = *fignoler, repolir*.

retourner To return, in various senses.
Also to turn inside out, turn over (soil, etc.). *Le policier ma demandé de retourner mon veston*: the policeman asked me to turn my coat inside out.
Note *se retourner*: to turn round. *Il se retourna vite*: he turned round quickly.
But can also be to turn over, overturn. *Mais en quelques minutes la voiture s'est retournée*: but within minutes the car turned over.
To return (give back) (often) = *rendre*.

retracer Should be noted with care. Means to retrace (literally) or to recount, recall (e.g. some event).
To retrace one's steps = *revenir sur ses pas, rebrousser chemin*.

retraite (f) Retreat (military). Tattoo (military). Retreat (place).
Also retirement. *Je vais bientôt prendre ma retraite*: I shall be retiring soon.
Can mean pension – *toucher sa retraite*: to draw one's pension.

rétribution (f) Not a word to be afraid of! It means reward, payment, salary.
Il demande une rétribution: he asks to be paid for it. *Contre une juste rétribution*: for a fair return.
Retribution = *vengeance* (f), *récompense* (f).

réunion (f) Reunion, meeting, (often) party. *La réunion aura lieu ce soir*: the party will be tonight.

revanche (f) Revenge, getting one's own back. Also used in sport for return match, chance for revenge.
Can have a pleasant connotation – *j'accepte ton invitation, à charge de revanche*: I accept your invitation, provided I may return the compliment.
En revanche: on the other hand, to make up for that.
Revenge = *vengeance* (f).

réveil (m) Reveille. *On sonne le réveil*: the reveille is sounded.
Alarm clock. *Le réveil sonne*: the alarm goes off.
Also awakening.

revenu (m) Can mean revenue, but is often income.

réverbérer Usually used of light and heat. *Le mur blanc qui réverbère la chaleur*: the white wall which reflects (throws back) the heat.
To reverberate (sound) = *retentir*.

révérence (f) Reverence. Also bow, and (especially) curtsey.
Also to depart, as in *je vous tire ma révérence*: I must take my leave of you.

revers (m) Could lead to misunderstanding. *Prendre à revers*: to take (the enemy) in the rear.
But *revers* is also lapel. *'Il y avait longtemps qu'Alegria ne portait plus à son tailleur noir l'oeillet rouge, mais elle céda, et épingla la fleur à son revers'* (Joseph Peyré, *Guadalquivir*, Flammarion).
Can also be a trouser turn-up.
Means the reverse side (often figurative), and *le revers de la médaille*: the other side of the picture.
Revers is also a backhand (sport).
Finally, it can be a reverse, setback. *Il a essuyé un revers*: he suffered a setback.
Reverse (car) = *marche* (f) *arrière*.
           (opposite) = *contraire* (m).

reverser Has one or two special senses, but the everyday meaning is to pour out again or pour back.
To reverse (car) = *faire marche arrière*.
           (things) = *renverser, retourner*.
           (legal) = *réformer, révoquer*.

reversible Reversible. Usually of clothes, or figuratively (events, history) or in a technical sense. But reversible (of judgments, etc.) = *révocable*.

réviser (f) To revise. Review (e.g. judgment). Also to service (cars).

révision (f) Revision. Review (e.g. legal). Also servicing (cars, etc.). *Une révision tous les six mois*: a service every six months.
Le conseil de révision: recruiting board (military).

révolter To revolt, but also with the sense of to outrage, as here – *'"Mes papiers!" Norbert jouait bien l'innocence révoltée'* (Cécile Aubry, *Belle et Sébastien: Le Document Secret*, Hachette, Bibliothèque Verte).

révolutionner To revolutionize, also to upset or stir up. *Il y a de quoi vous révolutionner*: it is enough really to upset you. (Familiar usage.)

révoquer To revoke, cancel (something). Also to dismiss (a person). *Les deux fonctionnaires ont été révoqués*: both officials were dismissed.
Révoquer quelque chose en doute: to cast doubt on something, to query (literary usage).
To revoke (cards) = *faire une fausse renonce*.

revue (f) Review (military, etc.), review (magazine) as well as revue (theatre).
Review (book, film, etc.) = *critique* (f).

ride (f) Wrinkle.
Ride usually = *promenade* (f), *chevauchée* (f).

ridelle (f) Rack, slats (at side of a cart).
Riddle = *devinette* (f).

rider To wrinkle.
To ride (horse) = *monter à cheval* (m).

rivière (f) In addition to river, there are other meanings. The water jump at a steeplechase, also openwork stitching and diamond riviere (necklace). *'Mais soudain elle poussa un cri. Elle n'avait plus sa rivière autour du cou'* (Guy de Maupassant, *La Parure*).

robe (f) Robe (for man or woman). Often dress. *Elle porte une belle robe*: she is wearing a beautiful dress.
Can also refer to the coat of an animal (e.g. horse). *'Un peu avant le soir, le cheval commença à se plaindre. Sa robe tout entière frémissait et se ridait comme l'eau sous le vent'* (Gisèle Prassinos, *Le Cavalier* (nouvelles), Plon).
Note *pommes de terre en robe de chambre*: potatoes in their jackets – an even more picturesque image than the English one.

robin (m) An old and pejorative word for lawyer (from *robe*). Compare with old expression *gens* (m) *de robe*: gentlemen of the robe, i.e. lawyers.
Robin = *rouge-gorge* (m).

rocailleux Rocky, and (of style, accent, etc.) harsh, rugged.

rogue Arrogant, scornful. *Il a répondu d'un ton rogue*: he answered in an arrogant tone.
Roguish = *malicieux*.

roman (m) Novel, whereas a romance might be *roman d'amour, histoire* (f) *romanesque, conte* (m) *bleu*.

roman Romanesque.
Roman = *romain*.
Roman nose = *nez* (m) *aquilin*.

romance (f) Sentimental song, ballad. *Pousser une romance*: to sing a sweet song. *'Il la cognait, on entendait des cris affreux, et tout de suite après, il ouvrait la fenêtre et poussait sa romance préférée "Femmes, que vous êtes jolies!"'* (Camus, *La Chute*).
Romance (language) = *langue* (f) *romane*.
    (literature) = *roman* (m).
    (general) = *idylle* (f).
    (novel) = *histoire* (f) *romanesque*.

romanesque Romantic.
Romanesque = *roman*.

romantique Romantic (especially a literary, art term), also used in a more general sense, e.g. countryside.
Romantic (often also) = *romanesque*.

roquet (m) Mongrel, cur, nasty little dog.
Rocket = *roquette* (f), *fusée* (f).

roquette (f) Rocket (weapon).

Rocket (space) = *fusée* (f).
  (slang sense) = *engueulade* (f).

roseraie (f) Rose garden. *La vieille dame regardait sa roseraie*: the old woman was looking at her rose garden.
Rosary = *chapelet* (m).

rot (m) Means belch (familiar).
Rot = *pourriture* (f).
  (nonsense) = *sornettes* (f), *salades* (f).
What rot! = *à d'autres! Balivernes!*

roter To belch (familiar).
To rot = *pourrir*.

roulement (m) Rolling. Also used in many technical senses. *Roulement à billes*: ball bearings.
Rumbling (noise). Taxiing (aircraft).
And note the meaning of taking turns, rotation. *Tu commences à six heures: on travaille par roulement*: you begin at six: we work on a rota system.

rouler Basically to roll. Also much used as a general word for going along (on wheels), travelling. *Nous avons roulé pendant deux jours*: we drove for two days.
Note the familiar sense of to swindle, 'diddle'. *On vous a roulé!*: you've been done!

roulette (f) Small wheel, castor. *Des patins à roulettes*: roller skates. *Ça marche comme sur des roulettes*: It's going like clockwork (familiar usage).
Also the dentist's drill and the game of roulette – so the context is important!

royalties (f) Royalties (commercial), but (for authors) *les droits* (m) *d'auteur* is the proper expression.

rubrique (f) Rubric, but in journalism it is heading, column. To give a picturesque example – *il tient la rubrique des chiens écrasés*: he runs the minor news column (accidents, etc.).

rude Care is needed as 'rude' (in the common sense of impolite) often makes sense, whereas the word normally has the wider sense of harsh, gruff, rough, tough, hard, uncouth. *Il répond d'une voix rude*: he answers gruffly.
(And can have (familiarly) an intensive force – *un rude adversaire*: a doughty opponent.)
L'hiver s'annonce rude: it looks like being a hard winter. *Sous des climats moins rudes*: in less harsh climes.
Rude (impolite) = *impoli, grossier*.

rudement Roughly, harshly, and (familiarly) 'very'. *Il fait rudement froid*: it is jolly cold.
Rudely = *impoliment*.

rudesse (f) Roughness, gruffness, uncouthness, severity. *Il ne faut pas les*

traiter avec rudesse: one must not treat them roughly.
Rudeness = *impolitesse* (f).

ruer To kick (out). *Ruer dans les brancards*: to kick over the traces (familiar).
Se ruer: to rush (at), fling oneself, dash.
Rue (archaic English) = *regretter* (*beaucoup*).

ruffian (m) An old word for procurer or debauched person (also spelt *rufian*).
Ruffian = *apache* (m), *bandit* (m).
Young ruffian = *polisson* (m), *voyou* (m).

ruiner To ruin country, financially, or buildings, reputation, hopes, etc.
Ruin (clothes, books) = *abîmer*.
    (teeth, occasion) = *gâter*.

rumeur (f) Can mean rumour, also a dull noise. *J'ouvre la fenêtre et j'entends la rumeur de la ville*: I open the window and I hear the hum of the city.

rupture (f) Rupture – but in French it has a wide use. Break, breaking, interruption. *Une rupture dans la vie quotidienne*: a break from everyday life.
Rupture (often) = *hernie* (f).

rut (m) Rut, heat (animals).
Rut (ground) = *ornière* (f) (also figurative).

sabbat (m) The Sabbath (of the Jews).
Also witches' sabbath, gathering, and hence sometimes used for noise, din.
Sabbath (often) = *dimanche* (m).

sable (m) Sable (heraldry), but also (commonly) sand.
Sable (animal, fur) = *zibeline* (f).

sac (m) Sack, bag. *Sac à main*: handbag. The word is used in various colloquial expressions, and both languages have the same idea in *l'affaire est dans le sac*: it's in the bag.
Le sac is also sacking (of a place). *Mettre à sac*: to pillage, ransack.
To give (someone) the sack = *congédier, renvoyer*.

sachet (m) Small bag (sachet). *Je mets ça dans un sachet?*: shall I put it in a bag?
Satchel = *sacoche* (f).
    (school) = *cartable* (m).

sacré Sacred. But remember that it may be used before the noun with a defamatory or intensifying effect. *Musique sacrée*: sacred music. *Cette sacrée musique!*: this damned music!

sage Wise (sage). Sensible. Also (of children) well behaved.
Sois sage!: Be good!
Note – *une sage-femme*: a midwife.

sagesse (f) Sageness, wisdom, discretion. Also good behaviour (children), hence *le prix de sagesse*: good conduct prize.

sain Has sometimes the sense of sane, sound (*sain d'esprit*: of sound mind). Usually means healthy, sound. *Une nourriture saine*: healthy food. *Sain et sauf*: safe and sound. (The connection between sanity and health is obvious, and is implicit in the original Latin.)

Saint-Pierre Saint Peter.
But *Saint-Pierre* (m) may also be on a menu, as the equivalent of John Dory (fish).

saisir To seize, grip. Also to understand. *Je ne saisis pas très bien*: I don't quite grasp what you mean.
Also (legal sense) to refer. *La Sûreté a été saisie*: the CID have been brought in (it has been referred to the CID).

salade (f) Lettuce, or salad. Familiarly it can mean mess, muddle, nonsense. And note (also familiar) *le panier à salade*: Black Maria.

salaire (m) Wages (more often than salary).
Salary = *traitement* (m), *appointements* (m).

salon (m) Despite the connection between the words, hardly ever = 'saloon'.
Among its meanings are drawing-room (sitting-room), hairdressers' (*salon de coiffure*), tea-room (*salon de thé*).
Also show – e.g. motor show (*le salon de l'Automobile*).
Saloon (car) = *conduite* (f) *intérieure*.
        (bar) = *bar* (m).

saluer To salute, also to greet, say hullo or good-bye. *Saluer quelqu'un de la main*: to wave to someone.
To salute (military) = *faire un salut*.

salut (m) Salute, but also greeting, bow, wave. *Salut les gars!*: Hi lads! *Bon, je file. Salut!*: Right, I'm off. Cheers!
Can also mean safety, or salvation. *Chercher son salut dans la fuite*: to seek refuge in flight. *L'Armée du Salut*: Salvation Army.

sanguin To do with blood. *Groupe sanguin*: blood group.
Can occasionally be sanguine (complexion), and (of temperament) it may mean irascible.
Sanguine (usually) = *optimiste, confiant, calme*.

sape (f) Sapping, undermining.
Sap (plants) = *sève* (f).
        (slang) = *idiot* (m), *ballot* (m).

satyre (m) Satyr, and now used for sex-maniac. '*Y en a tellement à l'heure actuelle des voyous et des satyres*' (Raymond Queneau, *Un Rude Hiver*, Gallimard).

sauce (f) Sauce or gravy.
Also black crayon (for drawing).
Sauce (slang) = *toupet* (m).

saucier (m) Sauce cook (in large restaurants).
Saucer = *soucoupe* (f).

saucière (f) Sauceboat. *Il a mis la saucière près de l'assiette*: he put the sauce-boat near the plate.
Saucer = *soucoupe* (f).

saucisson (m) Large (cold meat) sausage.
Small sausage (to cook) = *saucisse* (f).

saucissonneur (m) **saucissonneuse** (f) Perhaps worth noting that this is not somebody who makes sausages, but a picnicker (and often a rather untidy one at that). The idea is of someone eating his cold sausage (meat) on the spot. (Familiar usage.)
Sausage-maker = *fabricant* (m) *de saucisses*.

sauvage Has some interesting meanings. Basically savage, but rarely so in practice. Usually wild, untamed, primitive. *Les animaux sauvages*: wild animals. *Un chien sauvage*: a wild dog (not 'a savage dog'). *Un lieu sauvage*: a wild, desolate place.
However can also mean shy, unsociable. *Un garçon sauvage qui ne parlait pas à ses camarades*: a shy boy who did not speak to his friends.
Also has a fairly (perhaps increasingly) common modern sense of free, beyond official control. *L'amour sauvage*: free love. *Le camping sauvage*: unauthorized camping. *Mouillages sauvages*: unofficial moorings.
Une grève sauvage: wild-cat strike.
Savage = *féroce*.

sauvage (m) Savage.
But also a shy person (fleeing the company of others). Hence *vivre en sauvage* is to live a hermit-like life (but not like a savage, which might = *à l'état sauvage*).

sauvagerie (f) Brutality, but also with the near opposite meaning of shy-ness, being unsociable.

sauver To save, rescue.
Note *se sauver* (familiar): to run away, be off. *Allez, je me sauve*: Right, I must be off.
Se sauver can also mean to boil over (liquids).
To save (money) = *épargner*, *économiser*.

scalp(e) (m) Scalping, also scalp – but the latter in a restricted sense (e.g. as a trophy in warfare).
Scalp (normally) = *cuir* (m) *chevelu*.

scandale (m) Scandal, something scandalous or shocking, shameful. *Faire du scandale*: to kick up a fuss.
Scandal (gossip) = *potins* (m), *cancans* (m).

scène (f) Scene (of a play). Scene, happening. *La scène se passe à Rome*: the

scene takes place in Rome. Scenes, episodes. Also stage (theatre). '*De leurs places de balcon, la scène paraissait très éloignée et il fallait se pencher pour voir une partie de la salle, à peu prés déserte encore*' (Gérard Bouttelleau, *La Barre d'appui*, Julliard).
Familiarly one can 'make a scene' in both languages = *faire une scène*.

schème (m) A technical term. Schema (philosophy, etc.). Sometimes design (art).
Scheme = *plan* (m), *idée* (f), *intrigue* (f).

schweppes (m) This trade-name is used for tonic (water). An English person offered 'un schweppes' might choose a specific brand.

science (f) Means science, but it is important to remember that the basic meaning is knowledge (or even skill). *C'est un puits de science*: he is a well of learning. '*Ils savaient d'une science trop sûre que le danger allait venir dans leur direction*' (Henri Queffélec, *Sous un Ciel noir*, Mercure de France).

scientiste (m/f) Christian Scientist (*scientiste chrétien*). Or a scientist who follows scientism (claiming to solve philosophical problems by science).
Scientist = *scientifique* (m/f).

scolaire (m/f) Is somebody who attends school (i.e. a scholar, in the old sense).
Scholar (at school) now = *boursier* (m), *boursière* (f).

scolarité (f) Does not mean scholarship, but being at school. *La prolongation de la scolarité*: the raising of school-leaving age.
Also used to mean (school) fees, or tuition costs for a course. *Scolarité 700 francs*: course fees 700 francs.
Scholarship (knowledge) = *érudition* (f).

scotch (m) A reminder that with this word you could get whisky, or adhesive tape.

script (m) Script-writing, lettering; or script (films) (a similar meaning to *scénario* (m)).
Note *script-girl* (f): continuity girl.
But script (exams, school) = *copie* (f).

scrutiner To poll, ballot.
To scrutinize = *scruter*.

sculpture (f) Sculpture. Carving. Also tread (of a tyre).

secret (m) Secret, also secrecy. *Il m'a juré le secret*: he swore secrecy.
Can have the sense of solitary confinement, and one must distinguish between *on l'a mis dans le secret*: he was let into the secret, and *on l'a mis au secret*: he was put into solitary confinement.

secrétaire (m/f) Secretary. *Un secrétaire* is also a kind of writing-desk (secretaire) with a flap that comes down. *Dans le noir il chercha le secrétaire*: in the dark he looked for the writing desk.

sécréter To secrete, emit.
To secrete (also) = *cacher*.

secteur (m) Sector, area.
Also mains (electricity). *Cq marche sur pile ou secteur*: it works on battery or mains.

sectionner Not always to divide into sections. Also to cut, sever (often accidentally).

séculaire Usually refers to something that takes place once in a hundred years or which is a century old, very ancient. *A l'ombre de ces beaux arbres séculaires*: in the shade of these beautiful ancient trees.
Secular = *séculier, laïque*.

séduction (f) Seduction, also charm, lure.

séduire To seduce, but much used currently in the mild sense of to tempt, attract, delight. *Les prix vont vous séduire*: the prices will tempt you.

séduisant Seductive, also tempting, attractive. *Je la trouve de plus en plus séduisante*: I find her more and more attractive.

sélecteur (m) Selector, in various technical senses (such as for the gears of a motorcycle).
Selector (e.g. sport) = *sélectionneur* (m).

self (m) A familiar abbreviation of *le self-service*. *Il fait froid et je vais dans un self pour manger quelque chose*: it is cold and I go into a self-service restaurant to have something to eat.
Self = *le moi, soi-même*, etc.

seller To saddle (a horse). *J'ai dû seller le cheval ce matin*: I had to saddle the horse this morning.
To sell = *vendre*.

semi (m) A familiar abbreviation for *un camion semi-remorque* (articulated lorry).
In English it is usually a colloquial abbreviation for a semi-detached house (= *une maison jumelée*).

sens (m) Sense. *Le sens commun*: common sense.
Also direction. *Une rue à sens unique*: a one-way street. *Sens dessus dessous*: upside down, or chaotic.

sensible Care is needed! It means sensitive, or appreciable, noticeable. *Des pieds sensibles*: sensitive feet. *Un petit garçon sensible*: a sensitive youngster.
Sensible = *sensé*.

sensiblement Appreciably, considerably. *Il fera sensiblement plus froid demain*: it will be much colder tomorrow.
Also means approximately. *Sensiblement à la même heure*: at about the same time.
Sensibly = *sensément, judicieusement*.

sentence (f) Sentence, in the sense of judgment (to pass sentence), or a maxim (compare English 'sententious'). *'Il y avait là M. Hurder, huguenot à la redingote et au linge sévère, plein de paraboles, de sentences bibliques'* (Marcel Aymé, *Aller retour*, Gallimard).

Sentence = *phrase* (f).
  (legal) also = *condamnation* (f).

séquelle (f) Usually in the plural, meaning after-effects (illness, etc.).
Also has a dated and pejorative meaning of gang, crew, band.
Sequel = *suite* (f), *conséquence* (f).

sergent (m) Sergeant, but note that *sergent de ville*: constable, policeman.
Sergent major is a quartermaster sergeant or sergeant major (*sergent de ville*
is dated).
Police sergeant = *brigadier* (m) *de police*.
Regimental sergeant major = *adjudant* (m) *chef*.

série (f) Series. Note the sense of mass produced – *en* (*grande*) *série, de série*.
And *hors série* consequently means something exceptional, out of the
ordinary. And in shops you may see *fins de série*: remnants, oddments.
And *une Série Noire* is a thriller, crime book.

sérieux Serious, also has subtle nuances. *Un homme sérieux* can be a steady,
reliable, responsible person – without ruling out a sense of humour! *Ce
n'est pas une maison très sérieuse*: it is not a very reliable establishment.

servant (m) Although *servante* is a (maid)servant (though dated), *servant* has
not got a similar sense. Its main meaning is a member of a gun crew. '*Mais
aucun des sept hommes du groupe de protection ne souhaite ouvrir le feu, car les
servants de la batterie de D.C.A. seraient alertés et l'affaire serait manquée*' (Paul
Dreyfus, *Histoires extraordinaires de la Résistance*, Fayard).
Servant = *domestique* (m/f).

service (m) **civil** Is not the Civil Service (which = *l'Administration Centrale*
(f)), but is a form of community service as an alternative to military service
(*service militaire*) for conscientious objectors.

serviette (f) One may be surprised to be asked in one's hotel bedroom if one
has enough *serviettes*. But the word has three useful meanings: towel, as
well as napkin (serviette), and also a briefcase.

(se) shooter To shoot (football), but also belongs to popular French drug
vocabulary: to give oneself a fix. *Encore un garçon qui s'est shooté*: another
boy who took drugs.
To shoot = *tirer, fusiller*.
To shoot oneself = *se tuer* (*d'un coup de fusil*, etc.).

siège (m) Seat, headquarters. *Siège social*: head office (company).
Seat (parliament).
Seat, chair. *Prenez un siège*: take a seat. Also seat of a disease.
A siege (military).

signalement (m) Description (e.g. of wanted person). *D'après ce signalement*:
according to this description.
Signalling = *signalisation* (f).

signaler Sometimes to signal, often to indicate, point out, report. *Signalé
perdu*: reported lost (e.g. ship).
To signal (also) = *faire signe* (*à quelqu'un*).

signer To sign, but *se signer*: to make the sign of the cross, to cross oneself. *Il regarda le livre et se signa*: he looked at the book and crossed himself.

signet (m) Bookmarker. *J'ai perdu mon signet*: I have lost my bookmarker.
Signet = *sceau* (m).
Signet ring = *chevalière* (f).

signifier To mean, signify. Also (legal language) to serve (e.g. a writ).

simple Simple, in various senses, including that of ordinary, natural, unaffected. *Mon fils est resté simple*: my son has remained unaffected.
Un simple soldat: a private.
Note the sense of *les simples* (m): (medicinal) herbs.

singe (m) Monkey. Familiarly, it can also be a mimic (who apes you), the boss, and corned beef.
Singe = *brûlage* (m), *légère brûlure* (f).

singer To ape, imitate (*le singe*: ape).
To singe = *brûler légèrement*.

single (m) Single sleeper (railway carriage). *A 22 heures je suis dans mon single, déjà trés fatigué*: at ten p.m. I am in my single sleeper, already very tired.
Also sometimes used for a single at tennis (instead of *simple* (m)).
Single (room) = *une chambre à un lit*.
    (ticket) = *aller* (m), *billet* (m) *simple*.
    (record) = 45 *tours* (m).

sinistre (m) A word that is (alas) often used. It means disaster, catastrophe.
Les rescapés du sinistre: the survivors of the disaster.
Can also mean the loss through a disaster (insurance term).
Something sinister = *quelque chose de sinistre*.

sinistré(e) (m/f) Not a sinister person, but a victim of a disaster. *Il faut aider les sinistrés*: the victims must be helped. *Une région sinistrée*: a disaster area.
Sinister = *sinistre*.

sirop (m) Syrup. Often medicinal, but may also refer to fruit drinks.
Golden syrup = *mélasse* (f) *raffinée*.

site (m) Sometimes site. Often setting, beauty spot. *Un site enchanteur*: a delightful spot. *Si on veut protéger les sites . . .*: if beauty spots are to be conserved . . .
Site (also) = *emplacement* (m).
    (building) = *chantier* (m).
On site = *à pied d'oeuvre*.

skate (m) It was predictable that the French would use this familiarly for skateboard(ing) (= *le skateboard* = *la planche à roulettes*). *Tous les gosses du quartier font du skate*: all the local kids go skateboarding.
Skate = *patin* (m).
    (fish) = *raie* (f).

sketch (m) Sketch (by actors).
Sketch (drawing) = *croquis* (m).

ski (m) A ski as well as skiing. *Le ski nautique*: water-skiing.

slave Slav, Slavonic.
Slave = *esclave* (m/f).

sleeping (m) Sleeper, sleeping-car (railway). (Familiar and now dated abbreviation of the English word, replaced by *wagon-lit* (m).)
Sleeping (sleep) = *sommeil* (m).

slip (m) Slip, briefs, pants, trunks. *Il met son slip avant de plonger dans l'eau*: he puts on his trunks before diving into the water.
It can also be slipway (ships).
Slip (women's clothes) = *combinaison* (f).
   (mistake) = *erreur* (f), *lapsus* (m).
   (slide) = *glissade* (f).

smok (m) Not a smock (= *blouse* (f)), but a popular abbreviation of *le smoking*: dinner-jacket. *Il portrait un smok*: he was wearing a DJ.

smoking (m) Dinner-jacket. *Des messieurs en smoking*: gentlemen in dinner-jackets.
No smoking = *défense de fumer*.

snack (m) According to the dictionaries, this still means snack-bar (familiar abbreviation of *le snack-bar*). But in practice, doubtless under English influence, it is used also for 'snack', so that one may see advertised *snacks soignés*: tasty snacks.
Snack (more properly) = *casse-croûte* (m).

sobre A deceptive word! It means sober, i.e. abstemious, moderate, temperate. *Un homme sobre*: an abstemious man, *un repas sobre*: a modest meal (in neither case is drink ruled out). A car may well be advertised as *sobre*, i.e. it 'drinks' little petrol.
Sobre also means sober, restrained (colours, etc.).
Sober (not drunk) = *pas ivre*.
Sobered-up = *dessoûlé* (familiar).

sobriété (f) Sobriety, being temperate, restrained. But it is not the opposite of being drunk (which involves a paraphrase or a verb like *désenivrer*). *La sobriété au volant*: limit your drink when you drive.

soc (m) Ploughshare.
Sock = *chaussette* (f).

socialiser To socialize, to put under communal ownership.
To socialize (of people) = *être sociable, aimer rencontrer des gens*.

société (f) Society, in various senses. Company (business). *Société anonyme*: limited company.
Jeux (m) *de société*: parlour games.

socque (m) Clog. Also the light shoes worn by ancient Greek and Roman comic actors.
English 'sock' has the same Latin derivation, and is now specific in its meaning – it originally included clog and light shoe.
Sock = *chaussette* (f).

soda (m) Usually refers to a fizzy drink of some sort.
Soda (chemical sense) (washing-soda etc.) = *soude* (f).
Soda-water usually = *eau* (f) *de seltz* or *eau gazeuse*, though *soda* is sometimes used in this sense, particularly in the popular whisky and soda (*un
whisky soda*).

solde (m) Can mean balance (financial), also stock (shops).
En solde: to clear, going cheap. Unless one understands the latter, one may
miss the chance of a good buy, for the goods have not yet been sold.
Solde (f) means pay (especially military). *Il est à la solde de l'ennemi*: he is in
the enemy's pay.
Sold = *vendu*.

solder To balance (accounts) or to sell off, clear (stock). *Tout doit être soldé*:
everything must be sold off, disposed of.
(*Se solder*: to finish up (of a result) – *cela s'est soldé par . . .*: it ended up
with . . .)
To solder = *souder*.
To sell (sold) = *vendre* (*vendu*).

sole (f) Sole (fish).
Sole (foot) = *plante* (f).
      (shoe) = *semelle* (f).

solliciter To solicit, ask for, earnestly request, apply for, canvass. *Tu es très
sollicité*: you are much in demand.
In literary usage, to urge on.
To solicit someone (pejorative) = *racoler*.

solliciteur (m) Petitioner, suppliant.
Solicitor = *avoué* (m).

soluble Both soluble (dissolvable) or solvable (problems).

solvable (Financially) solvent.
Solvable (problem) = *soluble*.

sombre Sombre, but usually dark. *Un costume sombre*: a dark suit.
Also sad, gloomy.
Note such phrases as *un sombre idiot*: an utter fool (familiar usage).

somme (m) Nap, short sleep. *Dans la classe de maths mon fils fait un petit
somme*: in the maths lesson my son has forty winks.
Sum = *somme* (f), *calcul* (m).

son (m) Sound. *Le mur du son*: sound barrier.
Also means bran. *Les taches* (f) *de son*: freckles.
Son = *fils* (m).

Les (Iles) Sorlingues (f) The Scilly Isles.

sort (m) Lot, destiny, fate. *Assurer le sort de ses enfants*: to provide for one's
children.
(Familiarly) *il a fait un sort aux pâtisseries*: he disposed of, 'wolfed' the cakes.
Tirer au sort: to draw lots. *Jeter un sort*: to cast a spell.

Sort = *sorte* (f).
To be a good sort = *être une bonne pâte* (familiar).

sortie (f) Can mean sortie, but it is commonly exit, going or coming out.
Can also be an outing.
Note that it can have the sense of an outburst of temper.
Une sortie de bain: bath wrap.

sot (m) Fool, ass (literary usage).
Sot = *ivrogne* (m).

souffrance (f) Suffering, but note the technical *en souffrance* for something
which is in abeyance, held up, pending.

souffrant Suffering, but this meaning is often too strong. *Ma fille est souf-
frante*: my daughter is not very well.

souvenir (m) Memory, as well as souvenir.

spasmodique Spasmodic (medical term).
Spasmodic = *intermittent*.

spasmodiquement Spasmodically (medical term).
Spasmodically = *par à-coups, par intermittence*.

speaker (m) **speakerine** (f) Announcer, newscaster (TV, wireless). *Les
speakers doivent avoir un bon accent*: announcers must have a good accent.
Another example of an English word being used in a different way.
Speaker = *parleur* (m), *orateur* (m).
(loud) speaker = *haut-parleur* (m).
     (stereo) = *baffle* (m).

spécialisé You may be misled by the reference to *un ouvrier spécialisé*. It
means a *semi*-skilled worker.
A skilled worker usually = *un ouvrier qualifié*.

spécimen (m) Specimen. Also a sample, inspection copy (book, review,
etc.).

spectacle (m) Spectacle, sight. *Se donner en spectacle*: to make an exhibition of
oneself.
Perhaps more commonly used for play, show (theatre, cinema, etc.).
'. . . *la rue peu à peu est devenue déserte. Les spectacles étaient partout com-
mencés, je crois* (Camus, *L'Étranger*).
Spectacles = *lunettes* (f).

speech (m) Usually a short after-dinner speech (for example in response to a
toast, 'a few words').
Speech (usually) = *discours* (m).
     (ability to speak) = *parole* (f).

spider (m) This dated but delightful word has an equally delightful English
equivalent – dickey (two open seats at the back of a car).
Spider = *araignée* (f).

spirituel May mean spiritual but is often witty. *Comme il est spirituel, ton
mari!*: How witty your husband is!

spirituellement Spiritually or wittily.

spleen (m) Literary word for a feeling of depression (the spleen was sometimes regarded as a seat of melancholy), spleen.
Spleen (literal) = *rate* (f).

spolier To rob (despoil).
To spoil = *gâter*.

spot (m) Normal meanings are spotlight (e.g. theatre), or a commercial on TV.
Spot (often also) = *endroit* (m), *coin* (m).
    (pimple) = *bouton* (m).
    (mark) = *tache* (f).

square (m) Small public square with a garden. *Le square où les enfants jouent*: the garden square where the children play.
(Public) square = *place* (f).
      (shape) = *carré* (m).
      (check) = *carreau* (m).

staff (m) Staff (material for plaster mouldings).
Staff (people) = *personnel* (m).
    (school) = *professeurs* (m).
    (cleaning, etc.) = *domestiques* (m).
    (stick) = *bâton* (m).

stage (m) Period of training, course. *Il va faire un stage en Angleterre*: he is going to England for a period of training.
Stage (theatre) = *scène* (f).
    (journey) = *étape* (f).
    (platform) = *estrade* (f).

stalle (f) Stall (cathedral), stall (horses).
Stall (also) = *stand* (m), *échoppe* (f), *kiosque* (m).
    (theatre) = *fauteuil* (m) *d'orchestre*.

stance (f) Stanza.
Stance = *position* (f) *des pieds*.
    (figuratively) = *position* (f).

stand (m) Stand, stall. Shooting-range, gallery.
Stands de ravitaillement: pits (car-racing).
Stand (grandstand, etc.) = *tribune* (f).

standard (m) Standard (of living).
Also switchboard. *Standard bloqué*: switchboard jammed.
Standard (level) (also) = *niveau* (m).
      (flag) = *étendard* (m).

standing (m) A much used *franglais* word, with the sense of standing, social position, and particularly popular in advertisements – *des appartements de grand standing*: luxury flats.
Standing (often) = *(être) debout*.

starter (m) Choke (car). *Alors d'abord, où est le starter?*: Well, first, where is the choke?
Starter (cars) = *démarreur* (m).

station (f) Small station, station for underground railway, (bus) stop, (cab) rank.
Research establishment, power station.
Resort (winter sports, seaside). *Une station balnéaire bien connue*: a well-known seaside resort. Station (wireless, TV) – *on a toutes les stations au bout du doigt*: you have all the stations at your fingertips.
Halt, pause. *'Après une station au café de la Marine pour son byrrh à l'eau . . .'* (Raymond Queneau, *Un Rude Hiver*, Gallimard).
Also means position – *'. . . Paname, épuisé par cette longue station à genoux, ne pensait qu'à une chose: ne pas s'évanouir . . .'* (Joseph Kessel, *Le Bataillon du ciel*, Gallimard).
Station (railway) = *gare* (f).
      (bus) = *gare routière*.
      (position, rank) = *rang* (m), *situation* (f) *sociale*.

stationner To halt, but mostly used for to park cars. *On ne peut pas stationner ici*: we can't park here.
To station = *poster, aposter*.
To station (oneself) = *se poster*.

statut (m) Statute, also status. *'Les portiers ne sont pas tant chargés d'assurer la protection de votre immeuble que de lui donner le statut qui lui revient'* (Patrice and Leila Blacque-Belair, *New York*, Seuil).

steeple (m) A familiar and quicker way of saying *le steeplechase* (for which there is no single French word, though *la course d'obstacles* is no longer to say).
Steeple = *flèche* (f).

stick (m) Small stick, swagger-stick, hunting-crop.
Stick = *bâton* (m).
      (walking) = *canne* (f).

stop (m) Brake-light (car). Halt sign. Hitch-hiking (familiar abbreviation of *autostop*). *Avez-vous jamais fait du stop?*: Have you ever hitch-hiked?
Stop (bus, etc.) = *arrêt* (m).

stoppage (m) Invisible mending.
Stoppage = *arrêt* (m), (often) *cessation* (f) *de travail*.
      (in a pipe, etc.) = *obstruction* (f).

stopper To stop (both transitively and intransitively).
Also to mend clothes (by invisible mending).
To stop (teeth) = *plomber*.

stoppeur (m) **stoppeuse** (f) Refers to a person – either someone who does invisible mending or a hitch-hiker (abbreviation of *auto-stoppeur*).
Stopper (bottle, etc.) usually = *bouchon* (m).

store (m) Can be misleading. It means a (window) blind. If you are looking

for the stores, an advertisement for *les stores* may not take you there.
Stores (shop) = *grands magasins* (m).
  (stock of food, etc.) = *approvisionnement* (m).

stratège (m) Strategist. *C'est un stratège que j'admire*: he is a strategist whom I admire. An armchair-strategist is *un stratège en chambre*.
Strategy = *stratégie* (f).

strict Strict, in various senses. Plain. *Un homme au strict costume bleu*: a man in a plain blue suit.

striptease (m) Striptease, also the place – strip club. *Allez, on va dans ce striptease?*: Come on, shall we go into this strip club?

studio (m) May be a studio (artist, photographer, etc.), or a film studio.
Also much used for a 'bed-sitter'-type flatlet. *J'ai acheté un studio pour mon fils aîné*: I have bought a flatlet for my eldest son (there is no implication that he is an artist).
Studio (also) = *atelier* (m).

styler To train, school. *Une jeune secrétaire bien stylée*: a well-trained secretary.
To style (often) = *dessiner, créer*.

suave Smooth, suave (people), also pleasant and sweet (e.g. scent).

subalterne Means more than subaltern in English. Usual sense is minor, less important. *Toujours des tâches subalternes*: always inferior jobs (lowly tasks).

subalterne (m/f) Some care is needed, as this noun means an inferior.
Subaltern = *lieutenant* (m), *sous-lieutenant* (m).

substitut (m) Occasionally substitute, deputy, stand-in, understudy.
Quite common (legal term) for deputy public prosecutor.
Substitute (person) (often) = *remplaçant* (m).
  (things) = *succédané* (m).

subtiliser To subtilize. And (familiarly) to pinch, filch. *Il m'a subtilisé mon bic*: he has 'whipped' my biro.

succéder To succeed (not in the sense of to be successful). *Il a succédé à son père*: he succeeded his father.
To give place to, to follow. *Plusieurs attaques se sont succédé*: several attacks followed each other.
To succeed = *réussir*.

succession (f) Succession (series), succession (to the throne).
Also succession (legal sense), therefore often inheritance, estate, rather than the legal word. *Droits* (m) *de succession*: death duties.

Suède (f) Sweden. *Connaissez-vous la Suède?*: Do you know Sweden? Swede = *Suédois(e)* (m/f).
Swede (vegetable) = *rutabaga* (m).
Suede (skin) = *suède* (m).

suer To sweat. And (familiarly) to annoy, bore. *Tu me fais suer!*: You really get on my nerves!
To sue (for libel) = *intenter un procès en diffamation à quelqu'un.*

suffisance (f) Sufficiency, also conceit, being full of oneself (literary usage). *Un jeune homme plein de suffisance*: a conceited young pup.

suffisant Sufficient, also conceited, full of self-importance (literary usage).

suffocant Suffocating (heat, etc.).
Also astounding, shattering (familiar).

suffoquer To suffocate, choke.
Also to knock breathless with surprise, to 'knock backwards' (familiar).

Suisse (m/f) A Swiss.
Remember that *un suisse* is an official (in uniform) such as a porter or beadle (originally they were Swiss).
On the other hand, *un petit suisse* is a make of cheese.

sultane (f) Sultana, sultan's wife.
Sultanas = *raisins* (m) *de Smyrne.*

sunlight (m) If you come across this word, it means an arc-light (a powerful lamp used for film production).
Sunlight = *soleil* (m).

superbe Superb, but may mean proud (old and literary style).

superbe (f) Old literary word for pride, haughtiness. *'Eh bien, je mourrai', répondit-il avec superbe*: 'Well, I shall die,' he replied proudly.
Superbness = *excellence* (f), *magnificence* (f).

superbement Superbly (or in old literary style) haughtily, proudly.

supérieur Superior and (literally) upper. *Sur les rayons supérieurs*: on the top shelves.

supplier To beg, beseech. *Je vous supplie de . . .*: I beg you to . . . *Je vous en supplie*: I beg of you.
To supply = *fournir, approvisionner.*

supporter Normally means to support, bear, tolerate, put up with – even here – *'Est-ce que tu n'auras pas bientôt fini de m'épouser, hein? Crois-tu que je vais te supporter toujours?'* (Marcel Aymé, *Aller retour*, Gallimard).
Care is needed, there is no sense of supporting a wife or family, which needs a phrase like *pourvoir aux besoins, faire vivre.*
However, under English influence, the verb can mean to support (at sport), or in a more general sense.
To support (often) = *soutenir.*

supprimer To suppress (things), to eliminate, deprive; often milder words are needed – to withdraw, discontinue. *Nous avons supprimé les escargots, dit la patronne*: we no longer offer snails, said the restaurant-owner.
Supprimer quelqu'un: to eliminate (kill) someone (familiar).
To suppress (also) = *réprimer, étouffer.*

sûreté (f) Can be a surety, warrant.
More often it means safety or sureness. And *la Sûreté* is similar to Scotland Yard.

surf (m) Surfing (it used to be translated by another *franglais* word – *le planking*). *Si tu veux, on peut faire du surf*: if you like, we can go surfing. Surf = *ressac* (m).

grande surface (f) The large surfaces? In fact they are the supermarkets, large stores. *J'ai couru les grandes surfaces pour trouver cet ouvre-boîte*: I went round all the supermarkets to find this tin-opener.

surgeon (m) Sucker (horticultural sense).
Surgeon = *chirurgien* (m).

surnom (m) Nickname (surname = *nom* (m) *de famille*). So that in the following example the reference is to Bull (and not Bullit).
'– Bull Bullit, hein? dit pesamment le maître du Parc Royal. Son menton s'écrasa davantage sur son poing. Sa figure se ferma. – Bull Bullit, reprit-il. Je n'avais pas entendu ce surnom depuis longtemps' (Joseph Kessel, *Le Lion*, Gallimard).

surnommer To nickname. *Pourquoi l'a-t-on surnommé ainsi?*: why was he given that nickname?
To surname = *donner un nom de famille*.

surpris Surprised, but there is also the sense of being caught (out). *'En sortant du Marigny, Florence fut surprise par la pluie. Elle se réfugia sous un marronnier . . .'* (Gérard Boutelleau, *La Barre d'appui*, Julliard). *Surpris par la nuit*: overtaken by darkness.

susceptible Touchy, susceptible (of a person), also means susceptible, liable to, likely to. *Parmi les livres susceptibles de gagner un prix*: among the books likely to win a prize.
Susceptible (also often) = *sensible*.

suspense (m) Suspense. *Un film de grand suspense*: a nerve-tingling film. Elliptically it can be used for films or books. *Ce suspense n'est pas à manquer*: this cliff-hanger is not to be missed (familiar).
But to keep someone in suspense = *tenir quelqu'un en suspens* (notice the spelling of the proper French word).

suspension (f) Suspension, in various senses (both literal and figurative). Also a (hanging) ceiling-light.
Suspension bridge = *pont* (m) *suspendu*.

sweat (m) You may possibly come across this modern popular abbreviation of *le sweat-shirt. T'as vu son sweat?*: Did you see his sweat-shirt?
Sweat = *sueur* (f).

sycophante (m) Usually means informer, being the basic meaning of the Greek word. (But pedantic and little used.)
Sycophant = *flagorneur* (m), *flagorneuse* (f).

syllabus (m) Syllabus (church term).
Syllabus (school, etc.) = *programme* (m).

sympathie (f) Can mean sympathy.
Also attraction, warmth of feeling and interest, being 'on the same wavelength'.
Sympathy (also) = *compassion* (f), *condoléances* (f).

sympathique An important word. The normal meaning is kind, likeable, pleasant. *Un professeur sympathique*: a nice teacher.
Can mean sympathetic (to someone's ideas, hence the first meaning) or (in a technical sense) as of nerves.
Note the common familiar abbreviation of *sympa* (nice, decent, etc. (of people or things)).
(*Encre* (f) *sympathique*: invisible ink.)
Sympathetic = *compatissant*.

sympathiquement In a friendly, kind way; sympathetically.
Sympathetically (with compassion) = *avec compassion, d'une manière compatissante*.

syndicat (m) Syndicate, also the word for trade union.
The impressive-sounding *syndicat d'initiative* is the local tourist bureau.

T

table (f) Table. *La Sainte Table*: the Communion Table.
Also list of contents, index.
Faire table rase de quelque chose: to make a clean sweep of something.

table (f) **d'hôte** Sometimes used in English for a set meal (which usually = *un menu à prix fixe* in restaurants).
Table d'hôte tends to mean a set meal at a set time, for example for resident guests.

tabler To rely on, count on. *On avait tablé sur un succès beaucoup plus grand*: they had counted on being much more successful.
To table (a bill) = *déposer (un projet de loi)*.

tablette (f) Tablet (to suck). Bar (e.g. chocolate). Shelf.
The phrase *Inscrire quelque chose sur ses tablettes*: to make a note of something comes from the old writing-tablets.

taffetas (m) Taffeta, or sticking-plaster (= *taffetas gommé*).

tailleur (m) Tailor. Also (woman's) tailored suit, coat and skirt. *Une grande femme qui portait un tailleur*: a big woman wearing a tailored suit. Note *s'asseoir en tailleur*: to sit cross-legged.

talon (m) Heel. Counterfoil, stub (cheque, etc.).
Talon (bird of prey) = *serre* (f).

tape (f) Tap, slap.
  Tape = *ruban* (m).
      (recording) = *bande* (f).
  Red tape = *paperasserie* (f) *administrative*.

taper To tap, hit, knock. To type. Also (familiarly) to 'touch' someone (for money).
  To tape (put on tape) = *enregistrer* (*sur bande*).

tapisserie (f) Tapestry. Wallpaper. *Faire tapisserie*: to be a wallflower (at a dance, i.e. a girl not invited to dance).

targette (f) (Flat) door-bolt.
  Target = *cible* (f).

tarte (f) **à la crème** May be something nice to eat, but can (familiarly) mean the same old story with the same old proposed solution.

tartine (f) Slice of bread and butter (or jam). *Sur la table des tartines et un gâteau*: on the table, slices of bread and butter and a cake.
  Tart = *tarte* (f), *tartelette* (f).

tatou (m) Armadillo (tatu).
  Tattoo (on skin) = *tatouage* (m).
      (military = *parade* (f) *militaire*, *retraite* (f) *aux flambeaux*.

teint (m) Dye.
  Bon teint: authentic, staunch. Also complexion. *Une jeune homme au teint jaune*: a young man with a sallow complexion.
  Tint = *teinte* (f).
  Taint = *infection* (f), *trace* (f).

teinter To tint, tinge. '*Quatre ans de guerre, et la même vitalité, teintée, il est vrai, d'une bonne dose d'inconscience: "On ne meurt qu'une fois. Autant vivre dangereusement . . ."*' (Jorg Stocklin, *Le Figaro*, 9 August 1979).
  To taint = *infecter*, *gâter*.

télescope (m) (Reflecting) telescope (for observing stars).
  Telescope (ordinary) = *longue-vue* (f), *lunette* (f) *d'approche*.

tempérament (m) Constitution, temperament.
  Also instalment (buying goods which now usually = *acheter à crédit*). *Comme tout le monde, nous l'achetons à tempérament*: like everyone, we are buying it on instalments (hire purchase).
  Temperament (sometimes) = *humeur* (f).

temple (m) Temple. Church (protestant). *Toute la famille va au temple*: the whole family goes to church.
  Temple (forehead) = *tempe* (f).

temporiser To temporize, play for time.
  To temporize (negotiate) with someone (sometimes) = *transiger*.

tenant (m) Holder (e.g. sport). Supporter (of a point of view).
  Tenant = *locataire* (m/f).

tendance (f) Tendency, but also trend. *Nouvelles tendances*: new trends.

tennis (m) Has two meanings besides the game itself. Tennis-court – *derrière les tennis*: behind the (tennis) courts. *Les tennis* are also tennis- or gym-shoes. (Good examples of ellipsis.)

ténor (m) Not only tenor, but (familiarly) star, champion, 'big noise' (politics, sport, etc.).

tension (f) Tension, also blood-pressure (elliptical for *tension artérielle*). *Si ma tension redevient normale*: if my blood-pressure returns to normal.

terme (m) Term, time, end, limit. Quarter rent. Also term, expression, conditions.
Term (school) = *trimestre* (m).

terrasse (f) Terrace, in various senses, but not that of a street.
A terrace of houses = *une rangée* (*de maisons du même style*).

terrasser Normally means to lay someone low. *Il a terrassé son adversaire*: he floored his opponent. Figuratively, it means to knock back, overwhelm.
To terrace = *disposer en terrasses*.

terrible It may be odd to see someone playing good tennis and to be told that he has *un revers terrible*. Far from being a terrible backhand, it means a terribly good one. This is the familiar meaning of the word – 'terrific'.
Terrible (normally) = *terrible*.

terrier (m) A terrier (dog), also earth, burrow. *Le terrier le fait sortir de son terrier*: the terrier gets him out of his burrow. (Hence the name of this breed.)

tester To test, or to make one's will (compare 'testament').

théâtre (m) Theatre. It is also used for the scene of events (compare 'theatre of war'). *C'est ici même, dit le guide, le théâtre de cet horrible crime*: This is the very scene, the guide said, of this horrible crime.
Sur le théâtre des manifestations: at the scene of the demonstrations.

thème (m) Theme. But also (school, etc.) prose composition. *Tous les élèves trouvent les thèmes difficiles*: all pupils find proses difficult.

théorie (f) Theory. Also a literary word for a procession, file. *Une théorie de jeunes filles*: a 'crocodile' (from its Greek derivation).

tic (m) Tic, twitch.
Tick (mark) = *marque* (f), *coche* (f).
        (clock) = *tic-tac* (m).

ticket (m) A (small) ticket (e.g. for the *Métro*), also coupon (for rationing). (The French use is interesting, because it comes from the English word. But the English word 'ticket' itself comes from old French *estiquet*, being the masculine form of modern French *étiquette*.)

tif(s) (m) Popular word for hair (*les cheveux*). *Toi et tes tifs!*: you and your hair!
Tiff = *prise* (f) *de bec*.

faire tilt Is familiar for to click, hit the mark (figurative). *Soudain quelque chose a fait tilt dans ma tête*: suddenly something clicked inside me.
To tilt = *incliner, renverser*.

timbre (m) Has various senses. Can mean timbre (voice, etc.).
Also a small bell.
Very often a stamp on a document (as well as the stamp that puts it on),
and a postage stamp (abbreviation of *timbre-poste*).
Timber = *bois* (m).

timide Timid, often shy. *Un peu timide, ton ami, mais je l'aime*: a bit shy, your
friend, but I like him.

timidement Timidly or shyly.

timidité (f) Timidity or shyness.

tinter Not to tint = (*teinter*), but to tinkle or ring.

tiquer To twitch, react. *C'est la dépense qui m'a fait tiquer*: it's the expense that
got me (upset me).
To tick (something) = *cocher*.
    (noise) = *faire tic-tac*.

tirer The main meanings are to pull or draw and to shoot or fire.
Sometimes to print.
Tirer à sa fin: to draw to a close. *Se tirer* (*s'en tirer*) is to get out of (a nasty
situation). *Se tirer* (familiar) is to beat it, be off. *Je me tire vite*: I'm off at once
(*je me fatigue vite*: I tire quickly).

toboggan (m) Toboggan. But also slide or chute (playground, swimming-
pool). Also flyover (traffic).

toile (f) Not toil (= *peine* (f), *efforts* (m)), but cloth, linen, canvas (*toile de fond*:
backcloth, backdrop), or sometimes sail. *Toile d'araignée*: cobweb.

toilette (f) Washing, dressing. *Faire sa toilette*: to wash and dress.
Une (*table de*) *toilette*: a dressing-table.
Dress, clothes (women).
Un cabinet de toilette: wash room.
Les toilettes: lavatory.

tolérance (f) Tolerance. Also the word for allowance (e.g. customs). *Voici
une liste des tolérances douanières*: here is a list of what the customs allow.

tonalité (f) Tonality. Also the dialling tone (telephone). *Attendez la tonalité*:
wait for the dialling tone.

tonnelle (f) Arbour, bower. *Elle s'est cachée sous la tonnelle*: she hid under the
arbour.
Tunnel = *tunnel* (m).

top (m) Time pip. *Au troisième top*: at the third pip.
Top = *haut* (m), *sommet* (m).
    (spinning) = *toupie* (f).

toper To agree, 'shake on it'. *Tope là!*: Agreed, then! (familiar).
To tope = *boire*.

topique To the (particular) point (argument, etc.).
Topical = *actuel*.

topique (m) A topical cure (= *un remède topique*) – i.e. applied to one particular part of the body.
Topic = *sujet* (m) *de conversation*.

torpédo (f) Open touring-car. (The word is now dated.) '*Le lendemain matin, un torpédo militaire, gris et énorme, pénétra dans le jardin*' (Vercors, *Le Silence de la mer*, Editions de Minuit) (note that the noun is now feminine).
Torpedo = *torpille* (f).

touche (f) Touch. Also appearance, looks (familiar).
Bite (fishing). Key (piano, etc.).

toucher To touch. To interfere with (*toucher à*).
Toucher quelqu'un: to get in touch with, get hold of, someone.
Note among other uses the common one of drawing, getting money, a salary, cashing a cheque, or drawing rations. *Il a touché de l'argent tout de suite*: he got some pay at once.
To touch someone (for money) = *taper* (familiar).

toupet (m) A tuft of hair over the brow. Also means impertinence, cheek (familiar usage).
Toupet (toupee) = *postiche* (m).

toupie (f) (Toy) top.
Toupee = *postiche* (m).

tour (m) Sometimes tour, but also outing, trip, ride, walk. *Faire un petit tour*: to go for a stroll. Also circuit (*faire le tour de* . . .: to go round).
Among other senses note trick, lathe, turn, size.
Tour (often) = *voyage* (m), *randonnée* (f), *excursion* (f).

tour (f) Tower. Castle, rook (chess).
Tour = *voyage* (m), *excursion* (f).

tourmente (f) Literary word for storm. *Une tourmente de neige*: blizzard. *La tourmente allait le rendre fou*: the storm was going to drive him mad.
Torment = *tourment* (m).

tourner To turn. (Of films) to shoot, or to act, star. *Après avoir tourné toute la matinée*: after 'shooting' all morning.
To turn (round) = *se retourner*.

tourniquet (m) Turnstile, or may be tourniquet (medical – usually = *garrot* (m)).
Tourniquet is also a sprinkler for watering.

tourte (f) Pie (e.g. plum pie).
Tart = *tarte* (f).

tout (m) The whole, the whole lot.
Tout = *aboyeur* (m), *racoleur* (m).

tractable That which can be drawn, towed.
Note that easy to handle = *maniable*.
Tractable (people) = *traitable*.

trafic (m) General word for traffic (road, rail, air). *Trafic ferroviaire*: rail traffic.

Also used for traffic in a pejorative sense (e.g. smuggling). *Le trafic de la drogue*: drug trafficking.
Traffic (e.g. in towns) = *circulation* (f).

trafiquer To traffic, deal in (drugs, etc.). Note the familiar sense of to 'fiddle'. *Un compteur trafiqué*: a milometer that has been 'fiddled'.

train (m) Train. Also among many meanings rate, pace.
Etre en train de faire quelque chose: to be in the middle of doing something.
Un train de pneus: a set of tyres.
Can sometimes mean din, noise, also way of living, style, and (familiarly) backside, rear.
Can stand for undercarriage (*train d'atterrissage*) – '*Je rentre mon train, mais j'oublie de bloquer les freins*' (Pierre Clostermann, *Le Grand Cirque*, Flammarion).
Note *prendre le train en marche*: to jump onto the bandwagon.
Train (dress) = *traîne* (f).

traîner To drag, haul. Loiter. Lie about (clothes, etc.). Drawl.
To train (sport) = *s'entraîner*.
        (someone) = *former*.
        (animals) = *dresser*.

traité (m) Treaty, also treatise. '*Peu de livres sur les casiers de la bibliothèque: quelques ouvrages de mathématiques, une collection de traités d'échecs, dont je fis mon profit*' (Gérard Boutelleau, *La Barre d'appui*, Julliard).

traitement (m) It is important to know that it is not only treatment, but salary.

traiter To treat in various senses, to deal, to handle (business).
Note *il m'a traité en voleur*: he treated me as a thief and *il m'a traité de voleur*: he called me a thief.
Also to entertain. *Il y a une salle spéciale où on peut traiter ses invités*: there is a special room for entertaining one's guests.
To treat (someone to something) = *régaler quelqu'un de quelque chose*.
      (oneself to something) = *se payer quelque chose*.

traiteur (m) Caterer. *Et pendant la guerre? Il était traiteur*: and during the war? He was a caterer.
Traitor = *traître* (m).

tramp (m) Tramp (steamer). *Beaucoup de tramps ce matin dans le port*: a lot of tramp steamers this morning in the harbour.
Tramp (person) = *clochard* (m).

tramway (m) Tramway, but also tram (= *le tram*). *J'attends le tramway*: I am waiting for the tram. '*A cinq heures, des tramways sont arrivés dans le bruit*' (Camus, *L'Étranger*).

transe (f) Trance, but often means (great) fear. *Il était dans les transes*: he was trembling with fear. *Etre* (*entrer*) *en transe* can (as well as the sense of trance) mean to be very agitated, to be 'in a state'.

translation (f) Translation, transfer (bishops, etc.).
Translation (of language) = *traduction* (f).

transpirer To transpire, and also perspire.
Transpire (also) = *arriver, se passer*.

trappe (f) Can be a trap (e.g. for animals), but is usually a trapdoor. *Comment ouvrir la trappe?*: how to get the trapdoor open?
Trap = *piège* (m).
Shut your trap! = *ta gueule!*

travellers (m) Are not, needless to say, what they seem. They refer to travellers' cheques (*le travellers chèque*). *Les travellers en poche, on peut voyager n'importe où*: with travellers' cheques in your pocket, you can travel anywhere. (More properly: *un chèque de voyage*.)
Traveller = *voyageur* (m).

travelling (m) Travelling platform (dolly for camera-shots in film-making).
Travelling = *voyages* (m).

treillis (m) Trellis, lattice. Also means denims, fatigue dress.

trench (m) Trench coat (familiar abbreviation of *le trench-coat*).
Trench = *tranchée* (f).

trépas (m) Death (literary word).
Trespass (sin) = *offense* (f).
            (legal) = *violation* (f), *entrée* (f) *sans permission*.

trépasser To die, pass away (literary word).
To trespass (sin) = *pécher*.
            (legal) = *violer, entrer sans permission*.

trépidation (f) Vibration or (figuratively) bustle, whirl.
'*La* party *a tout du métro: même foule, même vacarme, même trépidation*' (Patrice and Leila Blacque-Belair, *New York*, Seuil).
Trepidation = *grande inquiétude* (f).

trésor (m) Treasure or treasure-house.
Le Trésor: Treasury (ministry).

trial (m) Comedy tenor.
Trial (legal) = *jugement* (m), *procès* (m).
       (test) = *essai* (m).

tribune (f) Grandstand. Gallery (church, etc.). Platform.
Also organ-loft (*tribune d'orgue*).
Tribune (Roman) = *tribun* (m).

tributaire Can mean tributary, but also dependent. *Les vieux surtout sont tributaires du téléphone*: old people above all are dependent on the telephone.

trier To sort out. *Trié sur le volet*: hand-picked.
To sift, arrange (e.g. papers). *Il faut trier cela*: I must go through that.
To try = *essayer*.

trinquer Is deceptive. Can mean (familiar) to drink, but the normal sense is to drink to someone, to clink glasses. *J'ai levé mon verre commes les autres et on a trinqué*: I raised my glass like the others, and we clinked glasses.

Another quite common (and familiar) meaning is 'to catch it'. One might see a headline: *Les flics ont trinqué*: The police had a tough time . . . or the cops copped it.

The *Dictionnaire du Français Contemporain* (*Larousse*) gives a good example which shows how misleading the word can be to English translators – '*Quand les parents boivent, les enfants trinquent*' – i.e. when the parents drink, the children suffer (the consequences).

To drink = *boire*.

trique (f) Cudgel.
Trick = *tour* (m), *supercherie* (f) (among many others).

trivial Formerly trite, ordinary, common.
Now means coarse, vulgar. *Des expressions triviales*: coarse expressions.
Trivial (things) = *insignifiant*.

trivialement Coarsely, in a vulgar way.
Trivially = *banalement*.

trivialité (f) Triteness (old and literary).
Now means coarseness or vulgarity.
Triviality = *insignifiance* (f), *banalité* (f).

trolley (m) Trolleybus (familiar abbreviation of *le trolleybus*).
Trolley (often) = *chariot* (m), *poussette* (f), *table* (f) *roulante*.

trombone (m) It may be surprising to be asked for a trombone. But it means not only a trombone (or trombone-player) but also a paper-clip.

trompe (f) Trump, horn. *Publier quelque chose à son de trompe*: to noise, trumpet something abroad.
Also an elephant's trunk.
Trump = *atout* (m).

tromper To deceive. *Se tromper*: to make a mistake.
Tromper le temps: to while away the time.
To trump (a card) = *couper*.

tromperie (f) Deception.
Trumpery (but with its idea of deception) = the equivalent of *camelote* (f).

trompette (m) A trumpet-player (= *le trompettiste*).
Trumpet = *trompette* (f).

tronc (m) Trunk (of a tree or body).
Also collecting-box in a church.
And in school language *le tronc commun*: common core syllabus.
Trunk (to pack) = *malle* (f).
      (elephant) = *trompe* (f).
      (telephone call) = *communication* (f) *interurbaine*.
Trunks (underwear) = *slip* (m).

trouble Murky, confused. *Eau trouble*: troubled waters.
Voir trouble is to see dimly (literal).

'To see trouble' sometimes = *entrevoir des difficultés*.
Troubled = *en peine, tracassé*.
        (inconvenienced) = *dérangé*.

trouble (m) Occasionally trouble.
Disorder (health), and often agitation, a feeling of unease.
In the plural has a stronger sense of disturbance (e.g. strikes).
Trouble = *peine* (f), *difficulté* (f).

troupier (m) Private (soldier) (archaic).
Trooper = *soldat* (m) *de cavalerie*.

trousse (f) Truss, bundle.
And formerly trunk hose – *être aux trousses de quelqu'un*: to be on someone's heels.
Mostly now used in the sense of kit, case (tools, pencils, or for a doctor's
instruments, etc.).

trousseau (m) Marriage trousseau.
Also used for a bunch of keys – *un trousseau de clefs*.

truand (m) Crook, thief, thug (originally a beggar).
Truant = *quelqu'un(e) qui fait l'école buissonnière*.

truculence (f) Bluntness, forcefulness, colourfulness.
Truculence = *agressivité* (f).

truculent Forceful, down to earth, blunt, colourful.
Truculent = *agressif*.

truster To monopolize (from the idea of being together in a trust).
To trust = *se fier (à), avoir confiance (en)*.

tub (m) Tub, bath (this English sense is dated).
Tub (usually) = *baquet* (m), *bac* (m).

tuba (m) The context is important, as while it may mean tuba, it is also the
word for a snorkel in underwater swimming.

tube (m) Tube.
But note the familiar meaning – a 'hit', or great success (songs), top of the
hit parade. *Il vient de se payer une Rolls, grâce à son dernier tube*: he has just
treated himself to a Rolls, thanks to his latest smash hit.
Tube (also) = *métro* (m).
Tubeless (tyres) = *sans chambre*.

turbulence (f) Turbulence, often unruliness, boisterousness.
Also (usually in plural) turbulence (in flying).

turbulent Turbulent. Often boisterous, unruly. *Il aimait, quand même, ces
enfants turbulents*: he could not help liking these unruly children.
Une classe turbulente: a rowdy class or form.

turf (m) (Horse) racing, the turf.
Turf (often) = *gazon* (m).

tuteur (m) Has two senses. Either a stake or prop (horticultural use) or a

guardian (e.g. of a minor). (It is of the same origin as 'tutor', which used also to have the meaning of guardian.)
Tutor = *précepteur* (m).

type (m) Type. (Familiar) chap, bloke. *Tu vois ce type-là?*: you see that fellow?

typer To mark, classify, stamp.
To type = *taper (à la machine)*.

uni United. Plain (colour, material, etc.). Smooth (surface). '*Vous connaissez le sable uni, le sable droit des interminables plages de l'Océan*' (Guy de Maupassant, *La Peur*).

union (f) Union, in various senses, including association (group of people). *L'union fait la force*: In unity is strength.
Trade union = *syndicat* (m).

unique Is an important word. Can mean unique, but often sole, one and only. *Un fils unique*: an only son. *Une rue à sens unique*: a one-way street. *Mon unique pardessus*: my only overcoat.

uniquement Solely, just, only, rather than uniquely. *Et pour le petit déjeuner? Uniquement des croissants, s'il vous plaît*: For breakfast? Just croissants, please.

unité (f) Occasionally unity, usually unit.
Ce soldat a perdu son unité: this soldier has lost his unit.
Unity (also) = *accord* (m), *union* (f).

universitaire May be university (as an adjective), but may just refer to the teaching profession.

universitaire (m/f) May be misleading. A member of the teaching profession, or an academic. *Une revue pour les universitaires*: a journal for academics.
University (often) = *faculté* (f).
A university professor = *un professeur de faculté*.

université (f) University, also means education, or teaching in general. *Entrer dans l'université*: to go into the teaching profession (in France) (a reference to the sense of *l'Université de France*).

urger Means (familiarly) to be pressing, urgent. *Ça urge!*: It's pressing, or urgent.
To urge = *encourager, exhorter*.

urne (f) Urn. Also a ballot-box, hence *aller aux urnes*: to go to the polls.

usable Likely to wear out.
Usable = *utilisable*.

usage (m) Usage, use, practice. *Hors d'usage*: out of use (e.g. expression), or
out of action.
Les usages: correct behaviour, custom. *C'est l'usage*: it's the done thing.
Can mean manners.
Also has the sense of wearing (e.g. hard-wearing) (clothes, etc.).

usé Is deceptive. Means worn or worn out, and can apply to people or
things. With reference to doors, Pierre Loti writes '*et de lourds frappoirs usés
par les mains*' (*Au Maroc*). *Des vêtements usés*: shabby clothes. *Ce sont des
expression usées*: those are hackneyed expressions.
Used = *employé*.

user Care is needed! *User de* is to use, but *user* (and *s'user*) has the idea of
wearing out, being used up by effort, etc. *Cela s'use vite*: it wears out
quickly.
To use (also) = *employer, se servir de, utiliser*.

usuels (m) It may be worth noting that this word means (familiarly) works
of reference.

usure (f) Usury, charging high interest. *Rendre quelque chose avec usure*: to
pay back something with interest (figurative).
The other meaning is wear, wearing out (not use, but too much use).
And *avoir quelqu'un à l'usure*: to wear someone down. *Une guerre d'usure*: a
war of attrition.

utilitaire Utilitarian. *Les véhicules* (m) *utilitaires* are commercial vehicles –
more commonly just called *les utilitaires*.

utilité (f) Utility, usefulness. *Les utilités* are the small parts (theatre) (played
by a 'utility' actor).

vacation (f) Legal word, meaning sitting, sessions, the attendance of
officials for business, and then the fees for it.
Also (in the plural), vacation, recess.
Vacation may = *les vacances* (f).
            (sense of emptying) = *évacuation* (f).

vaccine (f) Cowpox.
Vaccine = *vaccin* (m).

vaisselle (f) Crockery. *Faire la vaisselle*: to do the washing-up.
Machine (f) *à laver la vaisselle*: dish-washer.
Vessel (in both senses) = *vaisseau* (m) (*vaisselle* comes from *vaisseau*).

valet (m) Valet, servant. *Valet de ferme*: farmhand.
Also the knave (cards).
And a kind of clamp (woodwork). '*Je vis plus tard qu'ils avaient enfoncé le valet de mon établi entre deux pierres, dans un trou du mur, attaché une corde au valet, et les chevaux à la corde*' (Vercors, *Le Silence de la mer*, Editions de Minuit).

valide May mean valid (e.g. objection), but often means fit (Latin *validus*: strong). *On cherche des hommes valides*: able-bodied men sought.
Valid often = *valable* (ticket, etc.).

van (m) A horse-box. *Collision entre un van et deux voitures*: collision between a horse-box and two cars. (The English sense has thus been particularized.)
Also a winnowing-basket (for corn).
Van = *camionnette* (f), *fourgon* (m).

vapeur (m) Steamer (boat). *Tu vois le vapeur blanc à l'horizon?*: Do you see the white steamer on the horizon?
Vapeur (f): vapour or steam.

vaporiser To vaporize, also to spray (e.g. scent).

vase (f) Mud, silt.
Vase = *vase* (m).

végétation (f) Vegetation. In the plural, it can mean adenoids.

véhiculaire Is used of language. *Une langue véhiculaire*: a common language. *Grâce à cette langue véhiculaire, tout le monde ici se comprend*: thanks to this common language, we all here understand each other.
Vehicular refers to tangible vehicles.
No vehicular access = *entrée interdite aux voitures*.

veine (f) Vein.
Also has the common and familiar meaning of (good) luck. *Pas de veine!*: No luck!

vélum (m) Awning (comes from Latin *velum*: a sail). Tony Mayer, describing summer balls at Oxford and Cambridge, writes – '*Les collèges rutilent de lumières, les pelouses se couvrent de vélums . . .*' (*La Vie anglaise*, Presses Universitaires de France, Que sais-je?).
Vellum = *vélin* (m), *parchemin* (m).

vent (m) Wind.
Vent = *fente* (f), *conduit* (m).

venter To be windy.
To vent (anger) = *décharger*.

ventilateur (m) Sometimes ventilator, but is often fan (a mechanical one, as opposed to *éventail* (m)). '*Les officiers du bord ont quitté la vareuse de drap bleu pour la veste de toile, les ventilateurs se sont mis à tourner, le barman a ouvert sa glacière: nous voilà à l'entrée des tropiques*' (Roland Dorgelès, *Partir . . .*, Albin Michel).
Ventilator (car) = *aérateur* (m).

ventiler Normally to ventilate, but has some more specialized meanings – to value separately (as of items in sale), and to analyse, break down (figures, etc.).

venue (f) Is used in English in the sense of (meeting) place (sport, etc.). In French it means arrival or coming.
Meeting-place = *rendez-vous* (m).

verbaliser Common in the sense of a policeman who charges (takes down particulars of) a motorist. To book.
To verbalize (usually) = *être verbeux*.
          (sometimes) = *exprimer*.

verbe (m) Verb. Can also mean speech or way of speaking. *Le verbe rude de ces paysans*: the rough speech of these country folk. *Avoir le verbe haut*: to speak loudly, to dominate, lord it, '*et il se mettait à discourir en maître parmi eux, le verbe haut et assuré*' (Jacques de Lacretelle, *Silbermann*, Gallimard).

verge (f) Rod.
Verge = *bord* (m), *bas-côté* (m).

verger (m) Orchard. *En regardant par la fenêtre, j'ai vu le verger*: on looking out of the window, I saw the orchard.
Verger = *bedeau* (m).

vers (m) Verse (e.g. blank verse), or line (poetry). *Tu connais ce vers de Verlaine?*: Do you know this line of Verlaine's? Or verse (as opposed to prose).
Verse = *strophe* (f).
Verse (Bible) = *verset* (m).

versatile Is deceptive, as it has the old meaning of the word, changeable, fickle. *Un public versatile*: a fickle public.
Versatile (sometimes) = *polyvalent, ayant beaucoup de talents* (m).

versatilité (f) Fickleness, changeability.
Versatility = *variété* (f) *de dons*.

version (f) Version. Also (school, etc.) translation (into one's native language), 'unseen'.

vertigo (m) Staggers (as suffered by horses), so that a doctor may be puzzled if you claim to suffer from *le vertigo*.
Vertigo = *vertige* (m).

veste (f) Should not be confused with vest (*tricot* (m) *de corps*). Means coat or jacket, so *ôte ta veste* means no more than 'take off your jacket'.
Used in one or two expressions such as *ramasser une veste*: to fail, have a setback (familiar).

vêtement (m) Piece of clothing, clothes; only occasionally vestments.

vexant Vexing, tiresome, also hurtful (remark, etc.).

vexation (f) Humiliation, mortification.
Vexation = *ennui* (m).

vexer To upset, offend, hurt. *Il s'est vexé quand je lui ai dit la vérité*: he got upset when I told him the truth.
To vex (annoy) = *fâcher*.

viabilité (f) Viability. Also refers to the (fit) state of a road, and all the pre-construction work (laying of drains, etc.) before building.

vicaire (m) Is the curate, and vicar is *le curé*!

vice (m) Vice. Fault.
Vice squad = *brigade* (f) *des moeurs, brigade mondaine*.
    (implement) = *étau* (m).

vicieusement Nastily or incorrectly.
Viciously = *cruellement, méchamment, violemment*.

vicieux Occasionally vicious. Depraved, corrupt (people). Defective, bad (things). (Of animals) it means restive, ill-tempered. If referring to expressions, they are incorrect or wrongly used.
Vicious = *féroce, cruel, méchant, violent*.

vigile (m) Night-watchman. *Le problème des vigiles en pleine nuit*: the problem for night-watchmen in the middle of the night. A dictionary may perhaps not give this word, as its current use is fairly recent. But in fact it goes back to Latin *vigil*, and in ancient Rome it had virtually the same meaning.
Vigil (usually) = *veille* (f).
    (religious) = *vigile* (f).

vignette (f) Vignette (art). Illustration (in parts of a book).
Official tax-disc (car). Manufacturer's mark (with a motif).

vil May (literary language) be vile, base or infamous, but normally it means low (of prices) – *à vil prix*: very cheap.
Vile (often) = *infect, exécrable, horrible*.

vilain Nasty, unpleasant, ugly, naughty. *Oh! qu'il est vilain! Il a cassé le train*: Oh! the naughty boy! he has broken the train.
Villainous = *scélérat*.

vilain (m) In the middle ages, was a free peasant (villein).
Villain = *scélérat* (m), *bandit* (m), *criminel* (m).

vilenie (f) Low trick, mean behaviour, abuse, low character (literary word).
Villainy = *banditisme* (m), *escroquerie* (f).
Vileness = *bassesse* (f), (*être abominable*).

villa (f) Not always villa, may just be a house. *Il s'est fait construire une petite villa pas loin du centre de la ville*: he has had a little house built not far from the centre of the town. (The implication is of elegance and with a garden.)

villégiateur (m) Not a villager, but a dated word for a holiday-maker in the country or at a resort.
Villager = *villageois(e)* (m/f).

se faire violence This phrase is not as violent as it seems (unlike *faire violence à quelqu'un*). It means to constrain one's feelings. *Chiche! me répète-t-il. Je* *me fais violence et je ne dis rien*: I dare you! he repeats. I control my feelings with an effort and don't say anything.

violer To violate. To rape. To trespass.

virtuel Possible, potential (or used in a technical sense). In phrases such as 'he is the virtual headmaster', it is the equivalent of such words as *de fait, en réalité*.

visible Visible. Obvious, manifest, clear. '*Elle continua de se plaindre en patois en s'adressant au chat, car il n'était que trop visible que plus personne n'écoutait*' (Claude Cénac, *Le Printemps viendra deux fois*, Hachette, Bibliothèque Verte).
Il n'est pas visible ce matin: he is not free to see anyone this morning.
L'appartement est visible à partir de demain: the flat can be seen as from tomorrow.

visiblement Visibly, usually in the sense of clearly, obviously. '*A quelques pas, comme sans la reconnaître, ils obliquèrent cérémonieusement vers les deux sièges qui, visiblement, les attendaient*' (Marcel Béalu, *Contes du demi-sommeil*, Pierre Fanlac).
Visibly (also) = *à vue d'oeil*.

visionneuse (f) Viewer (slides, etc.).
Visionary = *visionnaire* (m/f).

visite (f) Visit, or even visitor.
Also inspection, hence *visite de la douane*: customs examination, and *visite (médicale)*: medical.
Passer la visite: to have a medical.

visiter To visit, but also has the sense of going over, round, inspecting. *Visiter les musées*: to go round the museums. (Of people) it is used usually in a fairly specific sense (*visiter les malades*: to visit the sick), whereas to visit someone socially is usually *rendre visite à quelqu'un*.

vivace Long-living, perennial, continuing.
Vivacious = *animé, plein d'entrain* (m).

vivacité (f) Can be vivaciousness, liveliness, but also means outburst, over-heated feelings. *Et après? répondit-il avec vivacité*: So what? he answered sharply. *Dis, mon chou. Vingt ans et jamais un mot de vivacité entre nous!*: I say, my sweet. Twenty years, and never a sharp word between us!

volatil Volatile (in a technical sense).
Volatile (people) = *volage*.
      (situation) = *inflammable, instable*.

volée (f) Can mean a volley of shots or a volley (tennis).
Also a flight (e.g. of birds), and ringing out, peal (of bells).
Familiarly it means thrashing (i.e. a volley of blows).
Volleyball = *volley-ball* (m).

volontaire Voluntary, but also self-willed, determined. *Un homme de poigne au menton volontaire*: a strong character with a determined chin.

volontairement Voluntarily, and often deliberately. *Je me suis trompé une fois volontairement*: I made one deliberate mistake.

voltige (f) Acrobatic exercises on the flying trapeze, or stunt-riding on horseback (e.g. at a circus). Some of these are called *la haute voltige* – nothing to do with high voltage (= *haute tension* (f)).

vue (f) View, in various senses, also sight. *Il a une belle vue*: he has a beautiful view. *Il a perdu la vue*: he has lost his sight. *A perte de vue* as far as the eye can see, or figuratively, on and on.
In my view = *à mon avis*.

vulgaire Vulgar, also common, ordinary, everyday. *Un vulgaire accident de la rue*: a common or garden street accident. *Un vulgaire escroc*: a common crook.
'*Un soir, Ogygès oublia dans l'île l'un des objets qui ne le quittait jamais: son briquet, un vulgaire briquet*' (Marcel Béalu, *Contes du demi-sommeil*, Pierre Fanlac).
Vulgar (sometimes) = *impoli*.

vulgairement Vulgarly, coarsely, or commonly. *Comme on le nomme vulgairement*: as it is commonly called.

vulgariser To make vulgar or common, also to popularize. *Ce sport se vulgarise de plus en plus*: this game is getting more and more popular.

wagon (m) (Goods) wagon but also (railway) coach. *Wagon-lit*: sleeping-car, *wagon-restaurant*: dining-car.
Wagon (cart) = *charrette* (f), *chariot* (m).

waters (m) Used often for lavatory (from *les water-closets*). *Où sont les waters?*: Where is the WC?
Waters = *eaux* (f).
To take the waters = *faire une cure*.

zèbre (m) Zebra, but you may sometimes look in vain for one, as (familiarly) it means bloke. *Tu vois ce zèbre-là?*: do you see that bloke?

zeste (m) Peel (zest) of orange, lemon, etc.
Zest = *entrain* (m).

zinc (m) Zinc. Also extended to mean the (zinc) counter of a bar (familiar usage). *Il préférait boire un verre sur le zinc*: he preferred to have a drink at the counter (bar).
And (familiarly still) it can mean an aeroplane, 'crate'.

NTC FRENCH TEXTS AND MATERIAL

Cultural History
Tableaux culturels de la France
Le passé vivant de la France
De la Révolution à nos jours

Contemporary Culture
L'Express: Ainsi va la France
L'Express Learning Package (includes text, 3
 audiocassettes, interview transcript)
Le Nouvel Observateur

Text and Audiocassette Learning Packages
How to Pronounce French Correctly
Just Listen 'n Learn French
Just Listen 'n Learn French Plus
Practice & Improve Your French
Practice & Improve Your French Plus
Sans Frontières 1, 2, 3
Parlons français

Handbooks and References
Guide to French Idioms
Guide to Correspondence in French
French Verbs and Essentials of Grammar

Dictionaries
NTC's New College French and English Dictionary
NTC's Dictionary of *Faux Amis*
Plus a large selection of Imported Pocketbook Classics

For further information or a current catalog, write:
National Textbook Company
a division of *NTC Publishing Group*
4255 West Touhy Avenue
Lincolnwood, Illinois 60646-1975 U.S.A.